LEARNING THE LAW

BY

GLANVILLE WILLIAMS, Q.C., LL.D., F.B.A.
*Rouse Ball Professor of English Law in the
University of Cambridge*

" A man has but one youth, and considering the
consequences of employing that well, he has reason
to think himself very rich, for that gone, all the
wealth in the world will not purchase another."
Sir R. North, *On the Study of the Laws.*

NINTH EDITION

LONDON
STEVENS & SONS
1973

First Edition 1945
Second Edition 1945
Second Impression Revised ... 1946
Third Impression 1948
Third Edition 1950
Fourth Edition 1953
Fifth Edition 1954
Sixth Edition 1957
Seventh Edition 1963
Second Impression 1966
Third Impression 1967
Fourth Impression 1968
Eighth Edition 1969
Ninth Edition 1973
Second Impression 1974

Published by
Stevens & Sons Limited of
11 New Fetter Lane, London
and printed in Great Britain
by The Eastern Press Ltd.
of London and Reading

SBN Hardback 420 44110 7
Paperback 420 44120 4

PREFACE TO THE NINTH EDITION

In prefaces to previous editions I have gratefully acknowledged advice and criticism from numerous friends. On this occasion I should particularly like to thank Sir Robert Megarry, who brought his eagle eye and encyclopaedic knowledge to my assistance, Mr. I. J. Stephenson and Mr. J. C. Hall.

G. L. W.

May 1, 1973

CONTENTS

INTRODUCTION

THIS is not a textbook. It is, I hope, a book that the law student will read voluntarily. In several of the chapters there is hardly a word that has not been written as a result of an error committed by some novice; and in most cases the error has been perpetrated not by one but by droves. If my homily can save the youthful reader from even a quarter of these errors, it will surely have been worth while.

The part that looks most like a textbook is the first two chapters, but these are very elementary and are designed to prepare the beginner for reading textbooks, not to be a substitute for textbooks. They embody the type of instruction that I have been accustomed to give my own pupils when their minds are *tabulae rasae* on the subject of law. The account that they give of the judicial system is not intended to be complete, but is thought to be enough to enable the reader to get along more easily with a law report or a textbook on some branch of the law, pending his reading of a larger work on the subject. Chapter 3 takes the reader on a conducted tour of his law library, and Chapter 4 gives him some practical hints on methods of study. Chapter 5 discusses technical terms, pronunciation and abbreviations. Chapter 6 tries to explain case-law technique in simple language, and tells the student how much of a case he should remember. Chapter 7 deals with the corresponding subject of statute interpretation. Chapters 8 to 10 are the fruit of marking many tutorial and examination scripts, which brought to me the conviction that the average examination candidate has little notion of what his examiner wants. These chapters try to tell him. Chapters 6, 7 and 8 are not meant for the absolute beginner, but should be read by the student of case-law subjects (constitutional law, criminal law, contract, etc.) after mastering a portion of his textbooks. Chapter 11 gives some hints on the conduct of moots and mock trials, for the former at least ought to be an important part of the young lawyer's training. Chapter 12 is for the

advanced worker; it tries to give him the sort of mental
equipment that is needed to start any piece of legal research,
whether into a practical problem or into a department of
the law. Chapter 13 outlines the various walks in life for
which a legal training is of use, and Chapter 14 is on wider
reading.

In writing this rather unconventional book I have been
comforted by reflecting that it really carries on, in its own
way, a very old tradition. At one time books for the
guidance of the law student were fairly common. Seven-
teenth-century students could turn for guidance to such
works as Coke's Prefaces to his *Reports* (1600–1616),
Fulbeck's *Preparative to the Study of the Law* (1600),
Doderidge's *English Lawyer* (1631) and Phillips's *Studii
Legalis Ratio* (1675). Roger North's *Discourse on the
Study of the Laws*, which may also have been written in that
century, though not published till 1824, was another work
written specially for law students. The chief aim of these
old works was to give advice on books to read, though some
also concerned themselves with such matters as the number
of hours reading that should be done in a day,[1] legal

---

[1] Some of the advice on this head is amusing. Coke's advice
was expressed in the distich:

> Six hours in sleep, in law's grave study six,
> Four spend in prayer, the rest on Nature fix.

This was amended by Sir Wm. Jones as follows:

> Seven hours to law, to soothing slumber seven,
> Ten to the world allot, and *all* to Heaven.

(See *Memoirs of Sir Wm. Jones* by Lord Teignmouth, ii, XI.)

"As to actual study, it [the law] doth not demand so
much of a day as it need to be esteemed a labour. I have
heard some say, four hours in a morning close application to
books is enough for law. Sir Henry Finch used to say, study
all the morning, and talk all the afternoon."—Sir Roger
North, *On the Study of the Laws.*

Fulbeck devoted six pages to the question whether it was
better to study in the morning or at night. He favoured the
morning, for nine reasons, among them that the three planets
most favourable to study, Sol, Venus and Mercury, are nearest
our hemisphere in the morning; that the air at night is cor-
rupted with contagious exhalations which pierce into the
brain; that it is also thickened, and thus stops the pores; that
the day was made at first for labour, and the night for rest;
that if a man studies soon after supper, the meat putrefies in

abbreviations, amusements suitable for the lawyer (archery, leaping, riding, bowling and fishing were among the recommendations), and the value of keeping a sort of " Where is it? " notebook known as a commonplace book.[2] In the nature of things the advice given in these works is now out of date. The abbreviations listed are abbreviations of law-French words, not of English. We have given up keeping commonplace books; printed works of reference have made them obsolete. Teachers are no longer so disingenuous as to believe that they can regulate their pupils' hours of work or modes of recreation by exhortation; anyway, as much depends upon the intensiveness of study as upon its length. But not only are these ancient admonitory works obsolete in what they say: even their scope is inadequate for the present-day student. They were written in the days before the doctrine of precedent came to bulk so large as a formative influence in the law, and therefore they give no advice on case-law technique. Also, they were written in the days before law examinations, as now understood, and therefore they give no advice on examination technique.

his stomach; and finally the authority of Proverbs viii, 17: " I love them that love me; and those that seek me early shall find me."

[2] The nature of these commonplace books can be seen by looking at the old Abridgements, which Pollock (*Oxford Lectures,* 104) thinks to have been nothing else than the commonplace books of eminent lawyers. *Cf.* Winfield in (1923) 37 H.L.R. at p. 219.

Chapter 1

THE DIVISIONS OF THE LAW

But in these nice sharp quillets of the law,
Good faith, I am no wiser than a daw.
— Shakespeare, *King Henry the Sixth*,
Part 1, II, iv.

CRIMES AND CIVIL WRONGS

ONE of the layman's inveterate errors is to suppose that the lawyer is largely—even exclusively—concerned with criminal law. A venerable legal chestnut that will probably be inflicted upon the reader before he has proceeded far with his studies (so why not by me?) concerns an old lady who was being given a glimpse of the Court of Chancery. She peered round and asked where was the prisoner. (According to a gloss on the tale, someone then explained to her that a Chancery judge did not try anybody except counsel.) In fact the law is divided into two great branches, the criminal and the civil,[1] and of these much the greater is the civil. Since the nature of this division must be grasped at the outset of legal studies, I shall try to give a simple explanation of it.

The distinction between a crime and a civil wrong, though capable of giving rise to some difficult legal problems, is in essence quite simple. The first thing to understand is that the distinction does *not* reside in the nature of the wrongful act itself. This can quite simply be proved by pointing out that the same act may be both a crime and a civil wrong. Occasionally at a bus station there is someone who makes a living by looking after people's impedimenta while they are shopping. If I entrust my bag to such a person, and he runs off with it, he commits the crime of theft and also two

---

[1] " Civil law " is a phrase used in several meanings. It may mean, as in the above context, the law that is not criminal law. It may also mean the law of a State as opposed to other sorts of law like international law; or it may mean Roman law. A " civilian " is a person learned in Roman law.

civil wrongs—the tort of conversion and a breach of his contract with me to keep the bag safe. The result is that two sorts of legal proceedings can be taken against him; a prosecution for the crime, and a civil action for the tort and for the breach of contract. (Of course, the plaintiff in the latter action will not get damages twice over merely because he has two causes of action; he will get only one set of damages.)

To take another illustration, if a railway signalman, to dumb forgetfulness a prey, fails to pull the lever at the right moment, and a fatal accident occurs on the line, his carelessness may be regarded as sufficiently gross to amount to the crime of manslaughter, and it is also the tort of negligence towards the victims of the accident and their dependants, and a breach of his contract with the British Railways Board to take due care in his work. It will be noticed that, this time, the right of action in tort and the right of action in contract are vested in different persons.

These examples show that the distinction between a crime and civil wrong cannot be stated as depending upon *what is done*, because what is done may be the same in each case. The true distinction resides, therefore, <u>not in the nature of the wrongful act but in *the legal consequences that may follow it*</u>.[2] If the wrongful act is capable of being followed by what are called criminal proceedings, that means that it is regarded as a crime (otherwise called an offence). If it is capable of being followed by civil proceedings, that means that it is regarded as a civil wrong.[3] If it is capable of being

---

[2] *Cf. per* Lord Esher M.R. in *Seaman* v. *Burley* [1896] 2 Q.B. 344 at 346.

[3] The astute reader may object that these definitions are " circular "—in other words, that we cannot tell whether an act is a crime unless we know whether it can legally be followed by criminal proceedings, and we cannot tell whether it can legally be followed by criminal proceedings unless we know whether it is a crime; so also with civil wrongs. The difficulty here is more apparent than real. It is true that our definition does not tell us whether a particular act is a crime or a civil wrong; but no definition can. If a definition could be framed to do this, there would be no further law of crime and civil wrongs for the student to learn! All that a definition can do is to explain how lawyers use the terms " crime " and " civil wrong." These terms are in fact shorthand for a

followed by both, it is both a crime and a civil wrong. Criminal and civil proceedings are (in the normal case) easily distinguishable; they are generally brought in different courts, the procedure is different, the outcome is different, and the terminology is different.

CRIMINAL

In criminal proceedings the terminology is as follows. You have a _prosecutor prosecuting a defendant,_[4] and the result of the prosecution if successful is a *conviction*, and the defendant is *punished* by one of a variety of punishments ranging from life imprisonment to a fine, or else is released on probation or discharged without punishment.

Turning to civil proceedings, the terminology is that a *CIVIL.* _plaintiff sues_ (*i.e.* brings an *action* against) a _defendant._ The proceedings if successful result in *judgment for the plaintiff*, and the judgment may order the defendant to pay the plaintiff money, or to transfer property to him, or to do or not to do something (injunction), or to perform a contract (specific performance). In matrimonial cases in the Family Division *FAMILY DIVISION* the parties are called _petitioner_ and _respondent,_ and the relief sought concerns dissolution of the marriage, consequential financial arrangements, and the custody of children.[5] (There are also other kinds of civil relief, but they need not concern us here.)

It is hardly necessary to point out that the terminology of the one type of proceedings should never be transferred to the other. Thus one does not speak of a plaintiff prosecuting

host of legal consequences, which are perfectly well known to every lawyer. Every lawyer knows, for instance, that fine and imprisonment are, in general, included among the legal consequences of crimes, and that a judgment for damages is, in general, included among the legal consequences of civil wrongs. If, therefore, one knows that a particular act gives rise to (say) an action for damages, one knows that that act is a civil wrong, and if one knows that the doer can be prosecuted and (say) be fined or imprisoned for it, one knows that it is a crime.

4 Formerly called " prisoner " in felonies and " defendant " in misdemeanours; felonies have now been abolished as a separate class. The term " prisoner " is invidious for one who has not yet been convicted. Instead of " the defendant " the expression " the accused " is very commonly used.

5 The petitioner *petitions* for a divorce against the respondent; an the proceedings, if successful, result in a *decree* of divorce.

or of the criminal accused being sued. The common
announcement " Trespassers will be prosecuted " has been
called a " wooden lie," for trespass has traditionally been a
civil wrong, not (generally) a crime. (There are some statutory offences of trespass, such as trespass on a railway line ;
and the Court of Appeal has recently made a large exception
from the general proposition by holding that a conspiracy
—an agreement—to trespass is a crime at common law).[6]

Again, the word " guilty " is used primarily of criminals.
The corresponding word in civil cases is " liable " ; but this
word has also crept into criminal contexts.

COURTS WITH CRIMINAL JURISDICTION

It is not only terminology and procedure that differ as
between criminal and civil law, for in addition the courts in
which the two types of wrong are tried are, to a considerable
extent, different. Crimes are tried in the *Crown Court* and
magistrates' courts. Civil cases are tried chiefly in the *High
Court* and *county courts*.

This distinction is sharper in theory than it is in practice.
It does not mean that the judges are altogether distinct, for
the same person may one day try civil cases as a county
court judge and the next day try criminal cases as a circuit
judge of the Crown Court. And a High Court judge on
circuit may one day try civil cases in the exercise of his
High Court jurisdiction and the next day try a murderer as
judge of the Crown Court. Although magistrates are
chiefly concerned with criminal cases, they have important
civil jurisdiction over licensing and family matters. The
Crown Court, too, has some civil jurisdiction, chiefly on
appeal from civil cases in magistrates' courts.

Let us look more closely at the trial of criminal cases.
Crimes are divided into *indictable* (pronounced " indite-
able ") and *summary* offences. Indictable offences are, as the
name implies, triable on indictment (pronounced " indite-
ment "). This means that they are the more serious sort
of crimes, triable by judge and jury (formerly called a petty
jury) in the Crown Court (formerly assizes and quarter

[6] *R. v. Kamara* [1972] 2 W.L.R. 126.

sessions).[7] The Crown Court for the City of London is the Central Criminal Court (the Old Bailey), situated off Ludgate Hill.

The judge in the Crown Court, who controls the trial and directs the jury, is a High Court judge,[8] a circuit judge, or a (part-time) recorder. (The Recorder and Common Sergeant of the City of London, sitting in the Old Bailey, are circuit judges who keep their traditional names.) When you visit a Crown Court you will probably see justices of the peace sitting with the circuit judge or recorder. They vote with him on matters of sentence, but in practice it is the professional judge or recorder who rules on the law and procedure in the course of the trial.

Appeal from the Crown Court lies to the *Court of Appeal (Criminal Division)* [9] and thence (in important cases, with leave) to the House of Lords. It will be understood that by " the House of Lords " in connection with appeals is not meant quite the same body as the House of Lords when sitting as part of the legislature. For when it is sitting to hear appeals, only the Law Lords vote. The Law Lords (more formally called the " Lords of Appeal ") are the Lord Chancellor, the Lords of Appeal in Ordinary (*i.e.* salaried life peers) and peers who hold or have held high judicial office.

Crimes not triable on indictment are known as summary (formerly petty) offences; they are triable without a jury by magistrates' courts (otherwise known as courts of summary jurisdiction or petty sessions—formerly called police courts). Magistrates' courts are usually composed of two or more justices of the peace, who are unpaid; but in some boroughs they are composed of single paid magistrates called stipendiaries (in London, Metropolitan Police Magistrates).

[7] The Crown Court was created by the Courts Act 1971.
[8] A judge of the Court of Appeal may sit as a High Court judge.
[9] Created in 1966 and superseding the Court of Criminal Appeal, which in turn had superseded the Court for Crown Cases Reserved in 1907. The Court of Appeal (Criminal Division) sits in practice in two courts, one composed of the Lord Chief Justice, a Lord Justice of Appeal and a puisne (*i.e.* High Court) judge, and the other composed of one Lord Justice of Appeal and two puisne judges.

Many crimes, though falling within the class of indictable offences, can, with the consent of the accused, be tried in magistrates' courts. Conversely, the more serious types of summary offence must be tried on indictment if the defendant claims to be tried by jury.

Appeal lies from a magistrates' court to the Crown Court. (The court in this case has no jury, but magistrates sit with the judge or recorder.) Magistrates' courts can also be called upon to "state a case" for the determination of a *Divisional Court*, consisting of two or more (generally three) judges of the High Court. By means of the latter procedure the High Court can decide points of law arising in the magistrates' court or (on appeal) in the Crown Court. A further appeal may be taken from the High Court (with leave) to the House of Lords. A peculiarity of this appeal by way of case stated is that it is open not only to the defendant but also to the prosecutor (whereas in trials on indictment there is no appeal from an acquittal).

The scheme of criminal courts can be represented diagramatically as follows:

Summary offences and indictable offences tried summarily	Indictable offences tried on indictment
House of Lords	House of Lords
Divisional Court of High Court (on case stated)	Court of Appeal (Criminal Division) Crown Court
Crown Court	
Magistrates' Courts	

The term "indictment" itself needs explanation. Originally an "indictment" was a "true bill" found by a "grand jury," *i.e.* a jury for presenting suspected offenders. The trial upon it at assizes or quarter sessions was by a "petty jury." Nowadays the grand jury is abolished, but we still retain the word " indictment " for the document commencing criminal proceedings that are to be tried by a petty jury. The present-day indictment may be defined as a document preferred by anyone to the Crown Court, and signed by the clerk of the court. Normally there will have been a preliminary investigation of the charge before magistrates, and they will have committed the accused for trial. A form of indictment for murder is:

> Court of Trial: The Crown Court held at Leeds
> *The Queen* v. *AB*
> charged as follows:
> Statement of Offence.

Murder.

> Particulars of Offence.

AB, on the   day of   , in the county of
, murdered JS.

Date   [Signature of officer of the court]

A person may be said to be charged *with* an offence, or indicted or tried *for* it, or (in the case of summary offences) summoned *for* it.[10] For example, we say that he is tried on indictment *for* conspiring (not *with* conspiring). He may be said to be acquitted or convicted *of* the offence, or (with the same meaning) acquitted or convicted *on* the indictment or *under* a count for the offence.

COURTS WITH CIVIL JURISDICTION

So much for criminal cases. Turning to civil cases, the more important are tried at first instance in the High Court in London or on circuit,[11] with appeal lying to the Court of Appeal (Civil Division) [12] and thence to the House of Lords.

---

[10] Some writers misguidedly use " indicted with," and, even more horribly, a Lord Chief Justice has used the expression " summonsed for." " Summons " is the noun, not the verb.

[11] Trials on the civil side of assizes or with a judge and jury in London were formerly called " *at nisi prius.*" The reason for the phrase was that, when a case arose in the provinces, it was directed to be tried in London " unless before " the trial in London the justice of assize should come into the county to try it.

[12] Consisting in practice of the Master of the Rolls and the Lords Justices of Appeal.

Appeal may also lie from the High Court direct to the House of Lords. The less important civil cases are tried in the county courts, with appeals on questions of law to the Court of Appeal and thence to the House of Lords.

The system of civil judicature explained above may be represented thus:

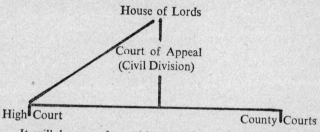

House of Lords

Court of Appeal
(Civil Division)

High Court   County Courts

It will be seen from this that the courts in which civil cases may begin—technically called " courts of first instance " —are the High Court and county courts. As noticed before, magistrates have some civil jurisdiction, chiefly in matrimonial matters, guardianship, adoption, and affiliation (maintenance of illegitimate children). Presumably the reader is vaguely acquainted with the county court of his own district. He may also have seen a civil case tried by a High Court judge on circuit. The High Court in London is divided into three Divisions: the Queen's Bench Division, the Chancery Division, and the Family Division. The first administers primarily the common law, the second primarily equity. More will be said about this particular distinction in the next chapter. The Family Division was created by an Act of 1970 in place of the previous Probate, Divorce and Admiralty Division—a curious miscellany of jurisdictions (over wills, wives and wrecks, as Sir Alan Herbert put it) which were lumped together for no better reason than that they were all founded (to some extent) on Roman and canon law. In 1970, wills went to the Chancery Division and wrecks to the Queen's Bench Division.

A report of a case will sometimes say that it was decided by a Divisional Court. This consists, as already said, of any two or more judges of the High Court. Formerly the chief importance of the Divisional Courts in civil cases was that they heard appeals from county courts. Now that such appeals go direct to the Court of Appeal, the importance of Divisional Courts is much reduced. However, they still hear appeals from magistrates' courts by way of case stated, such appeals in criminal matters going to the Queen's Bench Division and in family matters to the Family Division. Further appeal lies from the Divisional Court to the House of Lords.

Another way in which a civil case may go on appeal direct from the High Court to the House of Lords is under the " leapfrogging " procedure introduced by the Administration of Justice Act 1969. This can happen, with the consent of the parties and on certificate from the judge, if the case turns on the construction of legislation or is governed by a previous decision of the Court of Appeal or House of Lords which one of the parties wishes to overturn.

The present High Court, and the Court of Appeal on its civil side, were set up by the Judicature Act 1873. The High Court superseded the old courts of Queen's Bench, Common Pleas, Exchequer, Chancery, Probate, Divorce and Admiralty, and a few minor courts. The Court of Appeal superseded the old Court of Exchequer Chamber and Court of Appeal in Chancery. Together the High Court and Court of Appeal make up the Supreme Court of Judicature. (The Crown Court is theoretically part of the High Court).

It is an odd fact that the House of Lords, which is the supreme tribunal, is not part of the so-called Supreme Court of Judicature. This was due to a political accident. The Judicature Act 1873, which was passed by a Liberal Government, abolished the House of Lords as a final court of appeal (though not as part of the legislature) ; but the Act was not to come into operation until 1874, later extended to 1875. In 1874 the Conservatives took office, and, fearing (it is said) that the abolition of the Lords as a judicial body might be the thin end of the wedge, leading ultimately to the abolition of the Lords as a legislative body, they restored the appellate jurisdiction of the House of Lords—but forgot to make it a part of the Supreme Court.[13]

---

[13] See Robert Stevens in 80 L.Q.R. 343.

Although, when exercising its appellate jurisdiction, the House of Lords consists exclusively of the Law Lords, it nevertheless sits in the same building as the House of Lords when meeting as a limb of the legislature; but since the last war it has made a practice of sitting in a committee room instead of the House itself (except when the House is in recess).[14] Also, the judgments of the Law Lords are referred to as " speeches." The High Court and Court of Appeal sit in the Law Courts in the Strand.

There are many courts and tribunals of special jurisdiction, chief among which is the National Industrial Relations Court, created by the Industrial Relations Act 1971. Apart from its controversial jurisdiction as a court of first instance, it hears appeals from industrial tribunals on such matters as redundancy payments. The court sits in 5–7 Chancery Lane, London (England and Wales) and in 249–261 West George Street, Glasgow (Scotland).

The House of Lords is no longer our highest court, because the European Court sitting in Luxembourg adjudicates upon the law of the European Economic Community, and its decisions are binding on British courts by reason of the European Communities Act 1972. However, the impact of EEC law is at present somewhat limited, except in certain areas like company law. An English court (in practice the Court of Appeal) can ask the European Court for a ruling on any doubtful question of EEC law.

The Judicial Committee of the Privy Council is the final court of appeal from the colonies (with remnants also of its appellate jurisdiction from the self-governing members of the Commonwealth). Its composition is much the same as that of the House of Lords when exercising appellate jurisdiction, though certain Commonwealth judges may sit in addition. Cases before it are much less frequent than formerly, but if you have the opportunity you should boldly walk in and listen to one of its deliberations. You will find the highest judges in the land sitting unpretentiously, without robes, in a room in Downing Street, and the cases

[14] For an interesting note, see 118 *New Law Journal* 1160.

that they hear are almost always of interest even to a beginner.

The advice to listen to cases in court applies, indeed, to every kind of court. Even when the court-room is somewhat crowded, the police and ushers will generally facilitate the entry of those who announce themselves as law students. The addresses of all courts will be found in the *Law List*.

THE CLASSIFICATION OF CIVIL WRONGS

The more important types of civil wrong may be briefly mentioned. One is the *breach of contract*. This is easy to understand, and all that the student needs to know at the outset of his studies is that a contract need not be in a formal document or indeed in any document at all. You make a contract every time you buy an apple or take a taxi.

Another civil wrong is a *tort*. This word conveys little meaning to the average layman, and its exact definition is a matter of great difficulty even for the lawyer; but the general idea of it will become clear enough if one says that torts include such wrongs as assault, battery, false imprisonment, trespass, conversion, defamation of character, negligence and nuisance. It is a civil wrong independent of contract: that is to say, it gives rise to an action for damages irrespective of any agreement not to do the act complained of. Etymologically the word comes to us from the law-French *tort*, signifying any wrong. This loose and untechnical sense of the word is found as late as Spenser's *Faerie Queene*, and of course it is still so used in France. The law-French word *tort* in turn came from the Latin *tortus*, meaning " twisted " or " wrung." And the very word " wrung " is the same in origin as " wrong." (It is strange how the notion of wrong is wrapped up with that of twisting: the opposite of wrong is right, which is the Latin *rectus*, straight). Nowadays, however, a tort is not any wrong but only a particular kind of wrong, of which examples were given above. The adjective from tort is " tortious ": thus one speaks of a tortious act.

A third civil wrong is a *breach of trust*. A " trust " is not a mere obligation of honour, as the word may seem to suggest; it is an obligation enforced by the courts. Everybody has a rough idea of what a trust is; it occurs where a person, called technically a *settlor*, transfers property (such as land or shares) to another, called a *trustee*, on trust for yet another, called a *beneficiary*. (Actually the same person may combine two or even all three of these capacities; but this complication need not be considered here.) Where the trust is created by will the settlor is also called a *testator* (the name for anyone who makes a will); and an alternative name for the beneficiary is "*cestui que trust*," an elliptical phrase meaning "he [for] whose [benefit the] trust [was created]." In this phrase *cestui* is pronounced "settee" (with the accent on the first syllable),[15] *que* is pronounced "kee," and trust as in English. Grammatically the plural should be *cestuis que trust* (pronounced like the singular); but by an understandable mistake it is sometimes written *cestuis que trustent*, as if trust were a verb.[16] The beginner will perceive by this time that several law-French words survive in our law from the time when French was the language of the upper classes. In the case of a charitable trust there need be no definite beneficiary but the property is held on trust for the public as a whole or for some section of it. Thus the well-known " National Trust " preserves beautiful places for the public enjoyment, and there are many trusts for educational and religious purposes.

The only other type of civil obligation (it is not thought of as a wrong) that the beginner need hear about is the quasi-contractual obligation. Suppose that I pay you £5, mistakenly thinking that I owe it to you: I can generally recover it back [17] in quasi-contract. You have not agreed to pay it back, and so are not liable to me in contract; but in

---

[15] The O.E.D. gives the pronunciation " sestwee," but this is not common among lawyers. Winfield told me that Maitland's pronunciation was the one I have given, and that is good enough authority for anyone.

[16] See Sweet in 26 L.Q.R. 196.

[17] " Recover back " is not, in legal usage, pleonastic; *i.e.* the word " back " is not superfluous. You " recover " damages, a sum of money that you never had before. You " recover back " a certain sum of money corresponding to one that you did have at some time in the past.

justice you ought to pay it back and so the law treats you as if (*quasi*) you had contracted to repay it. There are various other heads of quasi-contract besides the particular example just given, such as the obligation to repay money paid on a consideration that has failed.

THE TITLES OF CASES

There are certain rules for the naming of cases which it is helpful to know. Trials on indictment are in the name of the Queen (as representing the State); thus a criminal case is generally called *Reg.* v. whomever it is—*Reg.* being short for *Regina* (pronounced " Rejyna "), and v. being short for *versus*. When there is a king on the throne, *Rex* is used instead of *Reg. Rex* and *Regina* both conveniently abbreviate to *R.*, which saves having to remember which is which. Thus *Rex* v. *Sikes* or *Reg.* v. *Sikes* may both be written *R.* v. *Sikes*. Some textbooks on criminal law even print simply *Sikes*. This last is a convenient usage for the student of criminal law.

In some types of criminal case the title of the case will not contain *Rex* or *Reg.* before the " v.," but will contain the name of a private person. This happens when the case is tried summarily before magistrates (*i.e.* justices of the peace); here the name of the actual prosecutor (*e.g.* a policeman) appears instead of the nominal prosecutor, the Queen. Again, when an appeal is taken to the House of Lords, the name of an official prosecutor, usually the Director of Public Prosecutions, is substituted for the word *Reg.*[18] (It may be mentioned that the Director of Public Prosecutions acts as a kind of solicitor to the Crown in the more important criminal cases). Conscious of the confusion this causes, the Law Reports now make partial amends by a compromise: the title is given in its official form at the beginning of the case, but is printed at the head of each succeeding page as it was in the court below. For example, *Reg.* v. *Bhagwan* in the Court of Appeal (Criminal Division) is called *Director of Public Prosecutions* v. *Bhagwan* at the

---

[18] Occasionally the prosecutor may be a Government Department, as in *Board of Trade* v. *Owen* [1957] A.C. 602.

beginning of the report in the House of Lords,[19] but then
Reg. v. *Bhagwan* again at the top of each succeeding page.

Civil cases will usually be cited by the names of the
parties, thus: *Rylands* v. *Fletcher*. If the Queen (as representing the Government) is a party she is, in civil cases,
usually called " The Queen," and similarly with the King,
thus: *British Coal Corporation* v. *The King*; but *R.* may
also be used.

The party who appeals is called the *appellant*; the other
is the *respondent*. In order to make life more difficult for
us all, the name of the appellant is put first when an
appeal is taken to the Divisional Court or House of Lords,
even though he was the defendant in the court below; this
means that the names may become reversed. Nattrass, an
inspector of weights and measures, instituted a summary
prosecution entitled *Nattrass* v. *Tesco Supermarkets Ltd.*;
on appeal by the defendant company to the Divisional Court
this became *Tesco Supermarkets Ltd.* v. *Nattrass*, and the
name stayed the same on further appeal by Tesco to the
House of Lords.[20] *Peek* v. *Derry* in the High Court and
(on appeal) in the Court of Appeal became *Derry* v. *Peek*
when it got to the House of Lords,[21] because the defendant
was then the appellant before the House. Here again the
Law Reports now try to simplify by following the traditional
reversal at the head of the report but then going back to
the order of names in the court below at the top of each
succeeding page of the report. For example, *Reg.* v. *Selby*
in the Court of Appeal becomes *Selby* v. *D.P.P.* at the head
of the report in the House of Lords, but then goes back to
Reg. v. *Selby* at the top of each succeeding page of the
report.[22]

There are peculiar conventions in pronouncing the names
of cases. (1) A criminal case, such as *R.* v. *Sikes*, can be
referred to informally as " R. v. Sikes " (pronounced as
written), or " Rex " (or, " Regina ") " v. Sikes " (again pronounced as written). In court, however, the proper method

[19] [1972] A.C. 60.
[20] [1972] A.C. 153.
[21] (1889) 14 App.Cas. 337.
[22] [1972] A.C. 515.

is to call it "The King" (or, "The Queen") "against Sikes." (2) In civil cases the "v." coupling the names of the parties is pronounced "and," both in court and out of it. Thus *Smith* v. *Hughes* is always pronounced (but never written) "Smith and Hughes," and similarly *British Coal Corporation* v. *The King* (which was a civil proceeding against the Crown) is pronounced with an "and." Lawyers thus write one thing and say another.

In some cases, as where a will is being interpreted, the name of the case is "*In re*" (in the matter of) somebody or something; for instance, *In re Smith*. It is permissible to shorten this to *Re Smith*. (*Re* is pronounced "ree"). Certain applications to the courts are labelled "*Ex parte*": *Ex p. Smith* means "on the application of Smith." In probate cases (that is, cases concerned with the proof of a will) the title *In bonis* (*i.e.* in the Goods of) *Smith* may be met with, and in Admiralty cases the name of a ship (*e.g. The Satanita*). Other possible ways of naming cases need not be considered here, but, in order to prevent the student from being puzzled, one oddity may be mentioned. The House of Lords is the final court of appeal for Scotland (and Northern Ireland) as well as England, and a Scots case that goes to the House of Lords may become important in English as well as Scots law. Two such important cases are *McAlister* (or *Donoghue*) v. *Stevenson* [23] and *Hay* (or *Bourhill*) v. *Young*.[24] The oddity is the alternative name in brackets, for which the explanation is as follows. In Scotland a married woman, though she takes her husband's name, does not cease for legal purposes to go also by her maiden name. When she figures in litigation, her maiden name is placed first, and her married name is given as an alternative afterwards. Nevertheless, the correct mode of citation, when brevity is desired, is by the married name.[25] The two cases above may, for brevity, be cited as *Donoghue* v. *Stevenson* and *Bourhill* v. *Young*, but not *McAlister* v. *Stevenson* or *Hay* v. *Young*.

[23] [1932] A.C. 562.
[24] [1943] A.C. 92.
[25] See Lord Macmillan in (1933) 49 L.Q.R. 1; (19..) 61 L.Q.R. 109.

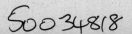

PLEADINGS

This chapter must not be concluded without a word about
pleadings, which are the part of procedure that the student of
substantive law most needs to know. Pleadings are not, as
might be supposed, pathetic speeches before judge and jury ;
they are dry statements on paper of the bare facts on which
each party to a civil case relies. They come after the service
of the writ, which commences the action, and they are
exchanged between the parties before the trial in order to
reveal the apple of discord to the parties themselves and to
the court. In technical language their function is said to be
to settle the " issue " between the parties.

The first pleading [26] is the plaintiff's *Statement of Claim*
(formerly called, in common-law matters, a Declaration [27]).
It may recite, for example, that the plaintiff was on the blank
day of blank proceeding on foot down High Street when the
defendant so negligently drove his car that he ran him down,
thereby causing him personal injury and damage to his
property. There will be particulars of negligence (driving too
fast, on the wrong side of the road, without keeping a

[26] The above statement is concerned with the Queen's Bench and
Chancery Divisions. In divorce cases proceedings are commenced by a petition, and the defence is called an " answer."
[27] Any part of a declaration that in itself, if it stood alone,
would have constituted a ground for action, was called a
count. The word *count* is still used to signify the several
parts of an indictment, each charging a distinct offence.
    Proceedings in Chancery formerly had a terminology of
their own. Underhill's description of them was as follows:
" A suit in Chancery used to be commenced by a document
called ' a Bill in Chancery ' . . . an enormous screed . . .
setting out in great detail the story of the suitor's wrongs. . . .
The next step was to turn this Bill into ' interrogatories ' to
be answered by the defendants on oath. . . . This was called
' scraping the Defendant's conscience,' and he was obliged
to answer on oath in the utmost detail, and if he failed to do
so further interrogatories were administered until sufficient
admissions were obtained to make out a prima facie case. . . .
This practice of interrogatories was usually delegated by
junior counsel (equity draftsmen) to their clerks, and at times
the rough drafts were somewhat comic. [Thus:] ' Did not
the defendant fall down on her knees or on one and which
of them and implore the plaintiff with tears in her eyes or in
one and which of them to advance the said sum of £——
to her husband? ' " Underhill, *Change and Decay*, 77–78.

proper lookout, without giving warning of his approach, and so on—these particulars have become almost common form), and particulars of the injury and damage (the latter called " special damage " to distinguish it from the " general damage " that cannot be precisely specified in terms of money and so does not have to be specially pleaded).

Then comes the defendant's *Defence*. The defence may embody a number of defences, perhaps inconsistent with each other,[28] but they will all be found to belong to one or other of three types:

(1) A *traverse*, that is, a contradiction of some fact stated by the plaintiff. Using the language of Touchstone in *As You Like It*, we may call it the countercheck quarrelsome.

(2) A *confession and avoidance*, that is, an admission (confession) of the facts stated by the plaintiff, but an allegation of other facts that destroy (avoid) their legal effect, in whole or in part. " True, I did agree to buy a tame lion from you, but I was a minor at the time and the lion was not a thing reasonably necessary for my station in life." " True, I negligently ran you down, but you were guilty of contributory negligence." This may be described as the retort courteous.

(3) An *objection in point of law*. This again admits the plaintiff's facts, but objects that in law they disclose no cause of action. " True, I gave you certain advice which was wrong and on which you acted to your detriment; but I am not liable to you because in law I owed you no duty of care." It is not strictly necessary to plead an objection in point of law, for any point of law may be taken at the trial although not pleaded.

For the purpose of reading the older cases it is desirable to know something of the old terminology and practice relating to the defence. The name " defence " for the defendant's

---

[28] Hence the tale in *Punch* of the K.C.'s son who was charged by the Head with having broken the schoolroom window: " In the first place, sir, the schoolroom has no window; in the second place, the schoolroom window is not broken; in the third place, if it is broken, I did not do it; in the fourth place it was an accident." All these defences, except the last, are traverses; the last is a confession and (one hopes) avoidance.

pleading is modern. Formerly, if the defendant pleaded
a traverse or a confession and avoidance, this was called a
plea; and an objection in point of law was called a
demurrer (law-French *demorer*, to wait or stay).[29] The
demurrer was so called because the party who demurred
did not proceed with his pleading but rested his case on the
submission of law and awaited the judgment of the court
thereon. In technical language a demurrer was not a
pleading. When arguing the demurrer the parties were
entitled to imagine any state of facts consistent with the
declaration. Judgment was given by the full court sitting in
banc, so that cases decided on demurrer settled the law in a
peculiarly authoritative way. Nowadays, however, the
decision on an objection in point of law, whether the objection be raised on the pleadings or not, is made by the single
trial judge, usually after the evidence on the issues of fact
has been heard.

After the defence there may sometimes be a *Reply*
(formerly called a *Replication*) from the plaintiff. This reply
may take any of the three forms of the defence, traversing
the facts in defence, confessing and avoiding them, or
objecting in point of law.

The defence may also be accompanied by a *Counterclaim*,
which will result in a *Defence to Counterclaim* from the
plaintiff.

It is necessary to take care in drawing pleadings, because
the judge may refuse to decide matters that have not been
properly pleaded.[30] But the court always has power to allow
an amendment of the pleadings, and, being rightly reluctant
to visit the sins of the pleaders upon their clients, will now
allow amendment wherever this occasions no injustice to the
other side, provided that the party amending pays any costs

---

[29] The " u " in " demurrer " is short, as also in " demurrage "
(the detention of a vessel by the charterer beyond the time
agreed upon, or the payment made in compensation for such
detention). In the verb " demur " (from which " demurrer "
is derived), and in its other derivatives " demurrable " and
" demurrage," the syllable " ur " is pronounced " er."
[30] See *Waghorn* v. *Geo. Wimpey & Co. Ltd.* [1969] 1 W.L.R.
1764.

occasioned by his mistake.[31] This power to allow amendment
diminishes the importance of the pleadings; but it must be
remembered that if counsel does not ask for an amendment
judgment will be given on the pleadings as they stand. Some
judges, even today, when they perceive a defect in the pleadings do not call counsel's attention to it (which they could
do if they were so minded), but keep silence on the point
until delivering judgment, by which time it is too late for
counsel to ask for an amendment. This regrettable attitude,
which may still be heard defended by many lawyers, springs
from the English tradition that a lawsuit is a game of legal
skill in which the judge is neutral. It must also be pointed
out that an appeal court regards itself as hearing an appeal
on the case presented to the lower court; it will generally
refuse to decide a point that was not before the court below
on the pleadings.

FURTHER READING

Dr. R. M. Jackson's *Machinery of Justice in England* is much
the best general description of our courts and their working.
Peter Archer, *The Queen's Courts* (Pelican Books) is shorter.
Historical accounts will be found in any textbook of legal or
constitutional history.

---

[31] The modern attitude towards amendments was wittily explained by Bowen L.J. in *Cropper* v. *Smith* (1884) 26 Ch.D.
at 711: " There is one panacea which heals every sore in
litigation, and that is costs. I have very seldom, if ever, been
unfortunate enough to come across an instance where a
person has made a mistake in his pleadings which has put
the other side to such a disadvantage as that it cannot be
cured by the application of that healing medicine." See, however, *Soar* v. *N.C.B.* [1965] 1 W.L.R. 886, from which it
appears that the court may refuse to allow a plaintiff at a
late stage of the trial to raise a new case after failure of the
pleaded case. Why should not an amendment (with
adjournment) be allowed even then? In the county court, it is
specifically provided (by Order 9, r. 8) that the delivery of a
defence does not prevent the defendant from relying on any
other defence.
   A judge who allows an amendment of a statement of
claim may, at his discretion, allow the defendant costs of the
action up to the date of the amendment, on the ground that
the plaintiff's statement of claim before that time disclosed
no cause of action on which he could have succeeded.

CHAPTER 2

COMMON LAW AND EQUITY

"You are too easily surprised," said Mr. Towkington. "Many words have no legal meaning. Others have a legal meaning very unlike their ordinary meaning. For example, the word 'daffy-down-dilly.' It is a criminal libel to call a lawyer a daffy-down-dilly. Ha! Yes, I advise you never to do such a thing. No, I certainly advise you *never* to do it."

—Dorothy Sayers, *Unnatural Death*, Chap. 14.

Two technical terms of great importance that are likely to puzzle the novice are "common law" and "equity."

The law of England may be said to be composed of three great elements: common law, equity and legislation. The most important kind of legislation is the Act of Parliament (otherwise called a statute), though nowadays what is called delegated legislation, like the many Government orders generally known as Statutory Instruments, has come to be of great importance as well. Even a layman is not likely to experience difficulty in understanding the meaning of legislation. Not so, however, with the other two terms, which need fuller discussion.

THE COMMON LAW

The phrase "the common law" seems at first a little bewildering in use because it is always used to point a contrast, and its precise meaning depends upon the contrast that is being pointed. An analogy may perhaps make this clearer. Take the word "layman." In the foregoing paragraph the word was used to mean a person who is not a lawyer. But when we speak of ecclesiastics and laymen, we mean by "laymen" non-ecclesiastics. When we speak of doctors and laymen, we mean by "laymen" non-doctors. Laymen, in short, are people who do not belong to the particular profession that we are speaking of. Again, take "aliens." In

England if we speak of " aliens " we generally mean by that word people who are not citizens of our own country (" patrials "). But in France the French equivalent of the word would mean people who are not French citizens.

It is somewhat similar with " the common law." (1) Originally this meant the law that was not local law, that is, the law that was common to the whole of England. This may still be its meaning in a particular context, but it is not the usual meaning. More usually the phrase will signify (2) the law that is not the result of legislation, that is, the law created by the custom of the people and decisions of the judges. Within certain narrow limits, popular custom creates law, and so (within much wider limits) do the decisions of the courts, which we call precedents. When the phrase " the common law " is used in this sense it may include even local law (in the form of local custom), which in meaning (1) is not common law. Again (3) the phrase may mean the law that is not equity ; in other words it may mean the law developed by the old courts of common law as distinct from the system (technically called " equity ") developed by the old Court of Chancery. In this sense " the common law " may even include statutory modifications of the common law, though in the previous sense it does not.[1] Finally, (4) it may mean the law that is not foreign law—in other words, the law of England, or of other countries (such as America) that have adopted English law. In this sense it is contrasted with (say) Roman law or French law, and in this sense it includes the whole of English law—even local customs, legislation and equity. It will thus be seen that the precise shade of meaning in which this chameleon phrase is used depends upon the particular context, and upon the contrast that is being made. When I said in the second sentence of this chapter that our law is made up of common law, equity and legislation, I meant it in a mixture of senses (2) and (3), as the context itself showed.

---

[1] Practising lawyers sometimes use the term to mean only the civil-law part of the common law in sense (3), to the exclusion of the criminal law.

EQUITY

The term " equity " is an illustration of Mr. Towkington's proposition that some words have a legal meaning very unlike their ordinary one. In ordinary language " equity " means natural justice; but the beginner must get that idea out of his head when dealing with the system that lawyers call equity. Originally, indeed, this system was inspired by ideas of natural justice, and that is why it acquired its name; but nowadays equity is no more (and no less) natural justice than the common law, and it is in fact nothing else than a particular branch of the law of England. Equity, therefore, is law. The student should not allow himself to be confused by the lawyer's habit of contrasting " law " and " equity," for in this context " law " is simply an abbreviation for the common law. Equity *is* law in the sense that it is part of the law of England; it is not law only in the sense that it is not part of the common law.

The student will learn quite early in his historical studies how equity came into being. He will learn how, in the Middle Ages, the courts of common law failed to give redress in certain types of case where redress was needed, and how the disappointed litigants petitioned the King, who was the " fountain of justice," for extraordinary relief; how the King, through his Chancellor, eventually set up a special court, the Court of Chancery, to deal with these petitions; and how the rules applied by the Court of Chancery hardened into law and became a regular part of the law of the land. The most important branch of equity is the law of trusts, but equitable remedies such as specific performance and injunction are also very much used. The student will learn how, in case of " conflict or variance " between the rules of common law and the rules of equity, equity came to prevail. This was by means of what was called a common injunction. Suppose that A brought an action against B in one of the common-law courts, and in the view of the Court of Chancery the action was inequitable. B's proper course was to apply to the Court of Chancery for an order, called a common injunction, directed to A and ordering him not to continue his action. If A defied the injunction the Court of

Chancery would put him in prison for contempt of court.
Equity thus worked " behind the scenes " of the common-law
action ; the common-law principles were theoretically left
intact, but by means of this intricate mechanism they were
superseded by equitable rules in all cases of " conflict or
variance." [2] The result justified the sarcasm of the critic who
said that in England one court was set up to do injustice and
another to stop it.

This system went on until 1875, when as a result of the
Judicature Act 1873 the old courts of common law and the
Court of Chancery were abolished, and in their place was
established a single Supreme Court of Judicature, each branch
of which had full power to administer both law and equity.
Also, common injunctions were abolished and instead it was
enacted that, in cases of " conflict or variance " between the
rules of equity and the rules of common law, the rules of
equity should prevail.

All this is simple to understand ; what is not so easy to
explain to a beginner is how the two systems, of law (*i.e.* the
common law) and equity, remain distinct at the present day.
Lawyers are familiar with the proposition that the Judicature
Act, although it fused the administration of law and equity,
did not fuse law and equity themselves. As one writer put
it : " the two streams have met and now run in the same
channel, but their waters do not mix." For the beginner this
is a hard saying. " How," he may ask, " can one say that
law and equity are still different, when they are administered
by the same judges? I can understand (he may go on) that
before the Judicature Act one had to know whether a particular rule was a rule of law or a rule of equity, because you
had to be careful to proceed in the right court to get your
rule enforced. But now courts do not matter. Why, then,
should I bother to learn whether a particular rule is part of

---

[2] The common-law courts, after a famous struggle in the
seventeenth century, lay passive under this process ; they did
not help but they did not hinder. In some cases they even
took account positively of equitable doctrines. See *Master* v.
Miller (1791) 4 T.R. 320 at 341, 100 E.R. at 1053 ; *Legh* v.
Legh (1799) 1 Bos. & Pul. 447, 126 E.R. 1002 ; *Bosanquet* v.
Wray (1815) 6 Taunt. 597, 128 E.R. 1166. But such cases
were exceptional.

the system formerly called the common law or part of the
system formerly called equity? Is anyone the worse lawyer
for not knowing it? " The student cannot appreciate the full
answer to this question until he has studied equity, but I
think that a satisfactory preliminary answer can be given him
at once. To start with it may be admitted that very often
the student's impression is right, and it does not now matter
whether a particular rule is law or equity. But sometimes it
does matter. When one says that a particular rule of modern
law (using that term, this time, in its wide sense) is a rule of
" equity," one means that it has to be read in the light of the
whole complex of rules developed by the Chancellors. These
rules do not necessarily apply if the rule in question is a rule
of the common law. To take an illustration of these rules
developed by the Chancellors, one of them was (and is) to
the effect that " he who comes to equity must come with
clean hands." This rule will apply whenever the plaintiff is
relying upon an equitable right, but not necessarily when he
is relying on a common-law right. In other words, to say
that a particular right is an equitable right is shorthand for
saying that all the subsidiary rules of equity apply to it,
including (for instance) the rule that the plaintiff must not
have soiled his hands. On the other hand, to say that a
particular right is a common-law right is shorthand for saying
that it is to be interpreted in a common-law atmosphere,
leaving out of account such equitable rules as apply only to
equitable rights. Thus when a modern textbook draws a
distinction between law and equity, saying that at law the
rule is so-and-so but in equity [3] it is such-and-such, the author
is not indulging in idle verbiage nor yet in mere historical
reminiscence. Although the rule is that when law and equity
conflict, equity prevails, there is always the possibility that a
litigant who relies on an equitable rule may for some reason
find himself outside the limits of that equitable rule; and
when this happens the contradictory common-law rule, which
may generally seem to be a dead letter, becomes very much
alive.

The distinction between law and equity, as I have tried to

[3] Note the prepositions—*at* law, but *in* equity.

explain it, was vividly brought home to me in a case that I listened to in my student days. It was an ejectment action brought by a landlord against his tenant, whom we will call Mr. Isaacson. The latter had what is known as an equitable lease of the premises, that is to say, not a formal lease under seal, but an informal lease valid only in equity. For nearly all practical purposes these equitable leases are just as good as legal leases, and they are habitually relied on, even though they are void at law. This particular tenant, however, had broken the terms of his equitable lease, for shortly after receiving it he had assigned it to a company by the name of Saxon, Ltd., and there was a covenant in the lease not to assign. Mr. Isaacson somewhat disingenuously explained that he did not think this mattered, for the company was his own creation and " Saxon," he said, was none other than the latter part of his name! But Mr. Isaacson's real defence was that, although he might be liable in damages for having broken his covenant not to assign, that was not any reason for his being ejected altogether from the premises. Had the document been a legal lease this defence would have been a good one, for the lease did not contain a proviso for re-entry on breach of covenant. But unfortunately for the tenant it was an equitable lease, and by breaking an important term of it he had soiled his hands *and therefore lost his lease.*[4] Consequently the action succeeded, much, I remember, to my surprise.

The above is not the only answer to the question: What is the present difference between law and equity? But it is, I believe, the only answer that can be given in general terms without having to state exceptions; and it is the answer that is most easily apprehended by the beginner.

FURTHER READING

For a lively account of these and other matters read Fifoot, *English Law and its Background*, Chaps. 1 and 3. The whole book can be read with advantage and pleasure. Further information will be found in the standard legal histories.

[4] *Cf. Coatsworth* v. *Johnson* (1885) 55 L.J.Q.B. 220. But the statutory restrictions on re-entry apply. See Law of Property Act 1925, s. 146 (5) (*a*).

CHAPTER 3

THE MECHANISM OF SCHOLARSHIP

> I hold him not discreet that will *sectari rivulos,* when
> he may *petere fontes.*
>
> —Coke, Preface to 4th part of Reports.

THE man who wants to become a lawyer, and not merely to
pass law examinations (which is not at all the same thing),
must learn to use legal materials. He must get to know the
way about his law library, and must acquire the habit of first-
hand work among what lawyers call the sources. The great
campaigner for this among teachers of law was the man
affectionately known to his own generation as " F.P.," and I
make no apology for repeating his words, since I cannot
better them.

" We no longer make and transcribe notes and extracts, with
infinite manual labour, in a huge ' commonplace book,' as former
generations were compelled to do by the dearth of printed works
of reference. But, since the law is a living science, no facilities
of publishing and printing can ever perfectly keep pace with it.
A student who intends to be a lawyer cannot realise this too
soon. There is no need for him to make voluminous notes
(indeed there is a great deal of vain superstition about lecture
notes); but those he does take and use ought to be made by him
for himself, and always verified with the actual authorities at the
first opportunity. Another man's notes may be better in themselves, but they will be worse for the learner. As for attempts
to dispense with first-hand reading and digesting by printed
summaries and other like devices, they are absolutely to be
rejected. No man ever became a lawyer by putting his trust in
such things; and if men can pass examinations by them so much
the worse for the examinations." [1]

Some may think that put a trifle too exuberantly,[2] but in
essentials the advice is sound. The great disadvantage of

[1] Pollock, *Oxford Lectures,* 104–105.
[2] I am not quite sure what Pollock meant by " printed summaries and other like devices," which are thus absolutely to
be rejected. He could not have meant textbooks, because he

confining oneself to textbooks and lecture notes is that it means taking all one's law at second hand. The law of England is contained in statutes and judicial decisions; what the text writer thinks is not, in itself, law. He may have misinterpreted the authorities, and the reader who goes to them goes to the fountainhead. Besides familiarising himself with the law reports and statute book, the lawyer-to-be should get to know his way about the library as a whole, together with its apparatus of catalogues and books of reference. To quote Pollock again:

" Facility in such things may seem a small matter, but much toil may be wasted and much precious time lost for want of it. To the working lawyer these things are the very tools of his trade. He depends on them for that whole region of potential knowledge which must bear a large proportion to the actual." [3]

But this is preaching; and I do not want to preach, but only to give practical advice to those who wish to hear it. Let us therefore pass at once to:

THE LAY-OUT OF THE LAW LIBRARY

Near the entrance to the library there will probably be either a catalogue of the contents of the library or a card index. In fact there may be two such catalogues or indexes, one arranged alphabetically under authors and another arranged by general subjects. They are both open to the use of readers.

Each entry contains a number of figures or letters or a combination of the two. This is known as the class mark, and it should be accurately noted, for it enables the volume to be traced in the library. You should make a point of discovering the system adopted in your library, by wandering round the shelves—assuming, of course, that it is a library in which you are allowed access to the shelves, and that it is not so large a library as to make this task impracticable. Some classifications use what may be called

himself wrote several. He did not mean case books, because after writing the above passage he went on to approve them. I suppose he was referring to what are commonly called cram books, and, so understood, any teacher would agree with him.
[3] *Ibid.* 106.

a decimal system, even though no decimal point appears. For example, volumes next to each other on the shelf may be marked AF 1, AF 2, AF 22 and AF 7. If you imagine a decimal point before these numbers you will see that they are not out of order. The system enables the library staff to insert new subgroups without altering the main order.

One has to use common sense in consulting a catalogue. Suppose you want a book by a man called Bowen-Rowlands. You should first try " Bowen," but if it is not there try " Rowlands." Libraries vary in their treatment of these hyphenated names. Anonymous books are usually included in the author catalogue under their titles. Thus, *Every Man's Own Lawyer*, by A Barrister, will probably be in the author catalogue under " Every," though it may be under " Barrister " or " A Barrister " or " Anonymous." Periodicals may be in the author catalogue either under their titles or grouped under the general heading of " Periodicals."

Near the catalogues or card indexes there will probably be works of reference, like dictionaries and bibliographies.

The law reports, statutes and periodicals will probably be found in special sections of the library. Usually, too, there will be special sections devoted to such subjects as Roman law, international law, jurisprudence and legal history. Most of the rest of the library will be taken up with English law textbooks. These may be arranged alphabetically under authors, starting (say) with *Abbott on Merchant Ships* and ending with (say) *Zouche on Partnership Accounts*. Or they may be classified by subject, but arranged alphabetically under authors within each subject. Where there is no subject arrangement, and it is desired to find books relating to a particular subject, it will usually be necessary to consult the subject catalogue in the library, or else such a work as *Where to Look for Your Law*.

We shall now look more closely at the law reports, statutes and periodicals.

LAW REPORTS

Law reports are reports of the more important cases decided by the superior courts. Not all cases are reported: only those of legal interest. The reports may be divided very roughly into the old and the new. The old run from the time of Henry VIII to 1865, and the new since that date. Before Henry VIII's time there were the Year Books, which will be described in the next chapter.

Pre-1865 reports were produced chiefly by private reporters under their own names. Altogether there were some hundreds of different series, though many of them ran only for a short time. Most, but not all, have been reprinted in a series known as the English Reports (abbreviated E.R.). A chart supplied with the English Reports indicates the volume of the English Reports in which a particular volume of the old reports is to be found reprinted: the chart will either be found hanging in the library, or be found in a slim volume at the end of the series of English Reports. For instance, if your reference is to 1 B. & Ad. 289 (which means volume one of Barnewall and Adolphus's Reports at page 289), the chart will tell you that the corresponding volume of the English Reports reprint is volume 109. As you take down the volume from the shelf, notice the names in gilt letters at the bottom of the spine. These will tell you the order in which the old reports are reprinted in the particular volume. Volume 109 bears the legend: Barnewall & Cresswell 9–10 ; Barnewall & Adolphus 1–2. This indicates that 1 B. & Ad. will probably be found just beyond the middle of the book. Open the book, and you will find your page reference in heavy (clarendon) type at the top centre of the open pages (top outside corner in the first twenty volumes). If something goes wrong and your case eludes you, try the index at the end of the volume ; failing that, Vols. 177–178 contain a complete index of all cases in the reprint.

A warning may be given that the chart just referred to is not quite complete, because it indexes each of the old reports under one title only, whereas in fact many of the old reports were known under various titles or under various abbreviations of the title. The much fuller chart in *Where to Look for your Law* will, therefore, often be found useful. The latter chart should be turned to if the former fails ; it will indicate definitely whether or not the report that is being sought is to be found reprinted in the English Reports. Alternatively, as said already, the index volumes can be used.

These old reports were of uneven quality, at least in the period before 1757, and need to be handled with some care. Of the worst of them many stories are told. In *Slater* v. *May* (1704) [4] a case was cited from 4 Modern, then a comparatively recent volume of reports. Upon search of the roll (that is, the official record of the case) it was found that the report in 4 Modern had omitted a material fact. Upon this Holt C.J. burst out: " See the inconveniences of these scambling reports, they will make us to appear to posterity for a parcel of blockheads." When another of the early reporters, Barnardiston, was cited before Lord Lyndhurst, the latter exclaimed: " Barnardiston, Mr. Preston! I fear that is a book of no great authority; I recollect, in my younger days, it was said of Barnardiston, that he was accustomed to slumber over his notebook, and wags in the rear took the opportunity of scribbling nonsense in it." [5] Reporters even of the nineteenth century did not always escape judicial condemnation. The one who got most kicks of all was Espinasse who reported Nisi Prius cases between 1793 and 1807. Pollock C.B. said of him that he heard only half of what went on in court and reported *the other half*.[6] And Maule J., when a case in Espinasse was referred to, said with some emphasis that he did not care for Espinasse " or any other ass." [7] Denman C.J.'s response when a case from Espinasse was cited was:

" I am tempted to remark, for the benefit of the profession, that Espinasse's Reports, in days nearer their own time, when their want of accuracy was better known than it is now, were never quoted without doubt and hesitation; and a special reason was often given as an apology for citing that particular case. Now they are often cited as if counsel thought them of equal authority with Lord Coke's Reports." [8]

[4] 2 Ld.Raym. 1071, 92 E.R. 210.
[5] Wallace, *The Reporters*, 424.
[6] Anon., *A Lawyer's Notebook*, 43; (1938) 54 L.Q.R. 368.
[7] Biron, *Without Prejudice*, 88.
[8] *Small* v. *Nairne* (1849) 13 Q.B. 840 at 844, 116 E.R. 1484 at 1486. Some further comments may be added from A. J. Ashton's *As I Went on my Way*, 27–28: " More decorous,

I relate these tales only to put the student on his guard when dealing with some of the old reports, not to discountenance their use altogether. It sometimes happens that even poor maligned Espinasse is the only reporter to give us an important case—*Wilkinson* v. *Coverdale*,[9] which the student may perhaps come across in tort or in contract, is an example —and, as Denman, C.J. indicated, he and others of like stamp

though not more learned, judges than Maule always insisted that the fifth Espinasse must not be cited, and would hardly admit even the earlier volumes. Lowndes, who reported on the Northern Circuit, would barely be tolerated. It is in his rare and amusing volume that the head note is to be found, ' Carlisle. Possession of trousers in Scotland evidence of larceny in England.' It was not desirable to quote the Modern Reports if you could find Lord Mansfield in any other report. Carrington and Payne depended a good deal on the number of the volume. The later it was, the less it was attended to. It would seem that Carrington, like Espinasse, went down the hill, and I have myself heard a judge refuse to hear Carrington and Kirwan cited. These reports follow Carrington and Payne in date; and the judge said he didn't believe the reporter could at that date be trusted. This was a bold commercial judge, now dead. Of Price's Reports in the Exchequer it used to be said that you could find in them anything you wanted, if you looked long enough. He was the Beavan of the common law reporters. I once looked a long time and thought I found something in Price which seemed authority worth citing in a case in which Sir Horace Davey led me. At two or three consultations running, I brought this case forward after the second leader had finished, and Sir Horace always let me read the passage to him and murmured, ' Yes, that seems some authority.' I should point out to my American friends that Sir Horace did not mean what they mean by these words. But I never got him to take the book into his hands until he was arguing in court. He suddenly swerved round and said, ' Give me that case of yours,' and began turning the pages with a listless and indifferent hand—for he was very tired—and glancing at them in a lack-lustre way, said, ' Then there is a case, my Lord, in the fourth Price '—looking at the number on the back of the volume—' which decides a number of interesting matters, including, I see,' pausing at a particular page, ' the ownership of a pond in Hertfordshire, and there is somewhere,' turning a few more pages, ' something that seems to bear on this matter. But, however,' ceasing to turn any more pages from sheer inanition, ' I don't think I'll cite it,' handing the book back to me with a smile." (The author is mistaken as to Lowndes—the report of the case referred to is in 1 Lewin 113, 168 E.R. 980—and it was a horse, not a pair of trousers.)

⁹ (1793) 1 Esp. 75, 170 E.R. 284.

are not altogether unusable, though usable only with caution. Also, this sort of condemnation does not apply by any means to all the old reports, many of which are of outstanding quality.

If the student wishes to know more about these old reporters he may read Pollock's chapter in his *First Book of Jurisprudence*, 6th ed., 292 et *seq.*, or Veeder's article in (1901) 15 *Harvard Law Review* 1, 109, partly reprinted in 2 *Select Essays in Anglo-American Legal History*, 123, or C. G. Moran's *The Heralds of the Law* (1948). Detailed monographs are Wallace, *The Reporters*, and Fox, *Handbook of English Law Reports*.

In 1865 there commenced the semi-official "Law Reports," published by the Incorporated Council of Law Reporting. These were divided into eleven series—roughly speaking, one for each of the superior courts. After the Law Reports had been running for ten years, the Judicature Act 1873 came into force, and this (since it altered the superior courts) brought about changes in the names of the series and reduced the eleven series to six. Another change occurred in 1881, when the Exchequer and Common Pleas Divisions of the High Court were incorporated in the Queen's Bench Division, with the result that the corresponding reports were likewise incorporated, reducing the series to four. A change in the mode of citation was made in 1890, when instead of quoting the volumes by number the practice was started of referring to them exclusively by the year. In 1972 the series called Probate (containing cases in the Probate, Divorce and Admiralty Division) was replaced by a series called Family (containing cases in the new Family division). All these changes are shown in the table on p. 37. The net result is that the series now running are called the Appeal Cases, Queen's Bench, Chancery and Family. A case in these series is referred to by the year of the report in square brackets, followed by the abbreviations, A.C., Q.B., Ch. or Fam. (formerly P.), and the number of the page. Thus "[1944] P. 1" means the Law Reports, Probate series (covering the Probate, Divorce and Admiralty Division of the High Court) for the year 1944, page 1. If there are two or

TABLE OF THE LAW REPORTS

The mode of citation is given in brackets. In the first, second and third columns, dots (...) are put where the number of the volume would appear in the citation. In the fourth column square brackets ([ ]) are put where the year would appear in the citation.

1866–1875	1875–1880	1881–1890	1891–present
House of Lords, English and Irish Appeals (L.R. ... H.L.) House of Lords, Scotch and Divorce Appeals (L.R. ... H.L.Sc. or L.R. ... H.L.Sc. and Div.) Privy Council Appeals (L.R. ... P.C.)	Appeal Cases (...App.Cas.)	Appeal Cases (...App.Cas.)	Appeal Cases ([ ] A.C.)
Chancery Appeal Cases (L.R. ... Ch. or Ch. App.) Equity Cases (L.R. ... Eq.)	Chancery Division (...Ch.D.)	Chancery Division (...Ch.D.)	Chancery Division ([ ] Ch.)
Crown Cases Reserved (L.R. ... C.C., or, ... C.C.R.) Queen's Bench Cases * (L.R. ... Q.B.)	Queen's Bench Division (...Q.B.D.)	Queen's Bench Division (...Q.B.D.)	Queen's (or King's Bench Division ([ ] Q.B. or K.B.) †
Common Pleas Cases (L.R. ... C.P.)	Common Pleas Division (...C.P.D.)		
Exchequer Cases ‡ (L.R. ... Ex.)	Exchequer Division (...Ex.D.)		
Admiralty and Ecclesiastical Cases (L.R. ... A. & E.) Probate and Divorce Cases (L.R. ... P. & D.)	Probate Division (...P.D.)	Probate Division (...P.D.)	Probate Division ([ ] P.) Since 1972 Family Division ([ ] Fam.)

* Note that there is also a series called Queen's Bench Reports in the old reports (113–118 E.R.).
† After 1907 this includes cases in the Court of Criminal Appeal, later the Court of Appeal, in place of the previous Court for Crown Cases Reserved.
‡ Note that there is also a series called Exchequer Reports in the old reports (154–156 E.R.).

three volumes of the series for the year, the number of the particular volume will be put after the date, thus: [1894] 3 Ch. 260. The Appeal Cases include only cases in the House of Lords and Privy Council; cases in the Court of Appeal are printed in the three other series according to the Division in which the case started. The Incorporated Council of Law Reporting also publishes a weekly series known as the Weekly Law Reports (W.L.R.). This is bound in three volumes, the first containing cases that are not afterwards included in the Law Reports, and the second and third those cases that are expected to be superseded by the version in the Law Reports. The Weekly Law Reports replace the earlier Weekly Notes (W.N.).

In addition to the Law Reports there are various privately owned series still current. The most important is the All England Law Reports (All E.R.). The Times Law Reports (T.L.R.) ceased at the end of 1952. The Law Times Reports (L.T.) became merged with the All England Law Reports at the beginning of 1948, and the Law Journal Reports (before 1947 cited as L.J.Ch., L.J.K.B., etc.) likewise became merged with the All England Law Reports in 1950. Note that many volumes of the Law Journal Reports have different page-runs for the different courts. Thus (1865) 34 L.J.C.P. 1 is not the first page of the bound volume but is in the middle of the volume.

The student of criminal law should seek out in his library two series of reports of particular interest to him: Cox's Criminal Cases (Cox), and the *Criminal Appeal Reports* (C.A.R. or Cr.App.R.). He may also have to use the *Justice of the Peace Reports* (J.P.). Before volume 96, these are usually bound at the end of the *Justice of the Peace* newspaper (note the independent pagination after volume 67); from that volume onwards they are separate. Brief reports of cases are also given in the *Criminal Law Review* (Crim.L.R.).

In the past the collateral reports have published many cases not to be found in the Law Reports. Now, however, the Weekly Law Reports contain virtually all reportable cases. A second advantage of having the collateral reports in the library is that if the reader wants a volume of the Law Reports and finds that it is being used by someone else, it is often more convenient to turn up the case in one of the collateral series than to wait for the Law Reports version. For citation in court the Law Reports are preferred, because the judgments they print have been revised by the judges. The Law Reports have the further advantage that counsel's argument is summarised.

Indexes of legal abbreviations used in references to cases and lists of reports will be found in the *Manual of Legal Citations* published by the Institute of Advanced Legal Studies (1959); *Where to Look for your Law,* reprinted in Osborn's *Concise Law Dictionary* and *The Pocket Law Lexicon*; Sweet and Maxwell's *Law Finder* and *Guide to Law Reports and Statutes*; Jelf, *Where to Find Your Law*; Mozley and Whiteley's *Law Dictionary*; any volume of Halsbury's *Laws of England*; any volume of the *English and Empire Digest*; the *Encyclopaedia of the Laws of England*, 3rd ed., 1: xii; Mews' *Digest*, 2nd ed., 1: xix; Stroud's *Judicial Dictionary*, 3rd ed., 1: cxcvii; and Hicks, *Materials and Methods of Legal Research*.

There is a useful note on Scottish reports in [1958] *Criminal Law Review* 368.

If the name of a case is roughly known but not its date or reference, it can be traced through the index volumes of the *English and Empire Digest*, the current edition of which deals with all cases up to 1952. Cases between 1952 and 1966 are covered in Continuation Volumes A and B and cases after that date are covered in Annual Supplements. The most useful work of reference for recent cases is the *Current Law Consolidation*, 1947–1951, and the *Current Law Year Books* for 1952 and subsequent years. Every five years there is a Master Volume with added references to the previous four volumes. (The *Scottish Current Law Year Book* is the same as the English with the addition of Scottish cases). A separate volume called *Current Law Citator* covers all the cases reported from 1947 to a recent date and all the cases, of whatever date, which have been judicially considered or affected by statute since 1947. A reference to the Case

Citator shows immediately if a case has been digested, overruled, applied, considered, followed, referred to, or made the subject of an article. The Consolidated Index to the All England Reports covers cases reported in that series since 1936. A Consolidated Index to the Law Reports and Weekly Law Reports has been published each year since 1953. If the case is before 1865 and is included in the English Reports, it can be found through the index volumes of the English Reports.

If the date of a modern case is known but not its name, the best place to look for it is in *Current Law*. It appears in monthly parts with cumulative Year Books and consolidation volumes, as explained above.

In consulting the indexes at the beginning of a volume of Law Reports, distinguish between the " Table of Cases Reported " and the " Cases Judicially Considered." The former alone indexes the cases reported in the volume. Between 1940 and 1949 the latter table was omitted.

Sometimes the reader's reference will contain two page references, thus " [1892] 1 Q.B. 273, 291 " or " [1892] 1 Q.B. 273 at 291." Here the first page contains the beginning of the case and the second page the dictum to which the real reference is being made. I have known beginners spend many hours reading a case to which they were referred only for a single dictum in the middle of it. Generally speaking, if a case is quoted for a dictum there is no need to read the whole of the case.

The use of square and round brackets surrounding the dates of cases requires a word of explanation. Compare the two following references:

> *Stanley* v. *Powell* (1890) 60 L.J.Q.B. 52.
> *Stanley* v. *Powell* [1891] 1 Q.B. 86.

Why are the dates different, and why the two different sorts of brackets? To answer the second question first, the custom is to use square brackets where the date is an indispensable part of the reference to the case, round brackets where it is not. As to the first question, the judgment in the case was pronounced in 1890, which is therefore its true date. But some time elapses before the cases are reported in the Law

Reports, and this case did not get in till 1891, which is the date in the second reference. Where cases are reported in the Law Reports it is customary to adopt the date of publication of the Law Reports version as the date of the case. The reader need not trouble to learn any of this; it is explained here simply to save bewilderment.

In referring to a report the student should not allow himself to fall into the lax habit of reading merely the headnote. The headnote is only a summary of the case prepared by the reporter; it may be positively wrong, and anyway it does not state the reasons for the decision. At the very least, therefore, the student should read one of the (majority) judgments, in whole or in part, in addition to the headnote. It is also a good plan to read the argument for the side that lost, or a dissenting judgment if there is one, in order to appreciate that there were two sides to the question, as there always are in cases that get into the law reports. The only legitimate use of the headnote is (1) (where there is more than one judge) to indicate whether the court was unanimous, or if not who dissented; (2) to give the short facts. If the facts are adequately stated in the headnote it is to my mind quite permissible in ordinary cases to skip the facts as stated in detail by the judge, and to come forthwith to the part of his judgment that deals with the law.

STATUTES

Statutes are cited in three ways: by the short title, which includes the calendar year (*e.g.* the Fatal Accidents Act 1846 [10]), or by the regnal year or years and the chapter (*e.g.* 9 & 10 Vict. c. 93 [11]), or by a compromise of the two (*e.g.* the Fatal Accidents Act 1846 (c. 93)). Two regnal years are given (as in the foregoing example) when the session of Parliament in which the statute was passed did not fall within a single regnal year. The chapter indicates the number of the

[10] Acts passed before 1963 had a comma in the short title before the date; in 1962 a change was made and the comma was omitted. It seems sensible now to drop the comma in pre-1963 Acts as well.

[11] Pronounced as " the statute nine and ten Victoria, chapter 93," or " the ninth and tenth Victoria, chapter 93."

statute—formerly, the number in the session. It will be seen that " 9 & 10 Vict. c. 93 " means an Act that received the royal assent in the session of Parliament beginning in the ninth year of Queen Victoria and concluding in her tenth year, being the ninety-third statute passed in that session. Since 1962, chapter numbers have referred to the calendar year.[12]

The most convenient place in which to turn up a statute that is still in force is in Halsbury's *Statutes of England.* A particularly useful feature is the " Table of Repeals and Replacements," which will be found at the end of consolidating Acts and which enables the effect of the Act upon earlier legislation to be quickly ascertained. At the beginning of the index volume is an alphabetical table of statutes according to their short titles; from this table the position of the statute in the whole work can be quickly traced. If only the regnal year and chapter are known, it will be necessary to consult the consolidated table in the same volume. If the statute is later than 1968 it will be found in the Continuation Volumes, which are all indexed in the latest Cumulative Supplement.

The official publication *Statutes in Force* will be even more convenient when the series is completed. It is arranged in encyclopaedic form, in loose-leaf binders, some statutes being reprinted with amendments from time to time. There is to be an annual Cumulative Supplement which follows the order of the main work.

There is also an edition of the statutes in yearly volumes (called either *Public General Statutes* or *Law Reports— Statutes*). Note that the alphabetical index is at the end of the volume. Until 1940 these volumes contained the statutes passed during a particular session. This has one tiresome consequence, that if one knows only the short title and calendar year, the statute may sometimes be in either of two volumes, and nothing but a process of trial and error

---

[12] They do things better in some other parts of the Commonwealth like the provinces of Canada, which issue current statutes without a number. At the end of the year the statutes are arranged alphabetically and only then given a number. United Kingdom Statute Law Committee, please copy.

can ascertain which. Since 1939 a very sensible change has
been made ; each volume contains the statutes passed during
a single calendar year, and so the difficulty arises only for
statutes passed before 1940.[13] Another useful publication of
statutes is *Current Law Statutes Annotated*.[14]

The student should buy or note the principal statutes
relating to his subject, particularly those that have been
passed since his textbook was published. These he can find
by consulting the volumes of *Current Law Year Book* and the
numbers of *Current Law* published since his textbook, or by
consulting the latest Cumulative Supplement to the *Statutes
in Force* or to Halsbury's *Statutes of England*, under the
title of his subject. Statutes can be ordered through any
bookseller.

The student is not likely to have much to do with Statutory

[13] " Before leaving the topic of regnal-year citation, it may be
worth while to repeat a warning of one of its seldom
explained mysteries. There is risk of confusion where one
Parliamentary session is completed within a single year and
another is begun in that year. We may then have to distinguish two citations which look somewhat similar—*e.g.* ' 22
Vict. c. 20 ' and ' 22 & 23 Vict. c. 20 '; these are two different
statutes, the Evidence by Commissions Act 1859 and the
Military Savings Bank Act 1859. On the other hand, where
one session runs into two regnal years, one may discover
duplicate forms of citation for one and the same statute.
Take, for example, the Law of Property (Amendment) Act
1924. It received the royal assent long before the end of the
first regnal year of the session and was then correctly cited
as ' 15 Geo. 5, c. 5.' King George V had come to the
throne on May 6, 1910. When this Act was passed in
December 1924, the King's Printer could not gamble on the
probability of the session surviving the Accession Day on the
following May and thus running into its second regnal year.
Actually, as we know now, the session did so survive and
thus became the session 15 & 16 Geo. 5. The result is that
we find the same Act referred to as ' 15 Geo. 5, c. 5 ' and
' 15 & 16 Geo. 5, c. 5.' The latter citation, containing the
two regnal years, should supersede the former; the incomplete
and early part of the session becomes merged in the final
whole; Mr. Gladstone was ' Master William ' once, but
nobody so referred to him when the boy had become a man.
It cannot be helped that official copies of the Act where it is
described as ' 15 Geo. 5, c. 5 ' will be in existence." Sir C. T.
Carr in (1940) 56 L.Q.R. at 460–461.
[14] These collections do not include Local and Personal Acts
which are published separately.

Instruments (" S.I."—formerly known as Statutory Rules and Orders—" S.R. & O."), though exceptionally he may have to consult them.[15] When referring to Statutory Instruments, instead of calling the particular provisions of the Instrument " section " and " subsection " as with statutes, one calls them " articles " or " rules " and " paragraphs " respectively.[16]

PERIODICALS

Legal periodicals contain articles of great importance for the lawyer and student.

Special mention must be made of the *Law Quarterly Review* (L.Q.R.), which is published quarterly, the *Modern Law Review* (M.L.R.), published every two months, and the *Cambridge Law Journal* (C.L.J.), published twice yearly; students may obtain them at half subscription rates. *Current Legal Problems* appears annually.

The legal weeklies (*New Law Journal, Law Times, Solicitors' Journal, Justice of the Peace Newspaper*) are published chiefly for practitioners and are not of great value to the student; he will derive much more benefit from the monthly *Law Notes*. This costs £2·15 per annum, post free,

---

[15] Those in force at the end of 1948 are published in an official collection, supplemented by annual volumes. There is an *Index of Government Orders*, published in alternate years, and a cumulative annual *Table of Government Orders*, which is in turn supplemented by Annual, Monthly and Daily *Lists of Statutory Instruments*. Statutory Instruments made under particular sections of statutes are listed under the section in the front of the *Index of Government Orders*, and in the *Index to the Statutes in Force*. All these are official publications. For the lawyer, the most convenient source is often Halsbury's *Statutory Instruments*, with Service volume, which is arranged like an encyclopedia.

[16] The following is the complete table of citation drawn up by Parliamentary Counsel and approved by the Editor of the *Revised Statutes*. It is inserted here for reference only.

Instrument	First division	Second division	Third division
Statute	Section	Subsection	Paragraph
Bill	Clause	Subsection	Paragraph
Order in Council, or Order	Article	Paragraph	Sub-paragraph
Regulations	Regulation	Paragraph	Sub-paragraph
Rules	Rule	Paragraph	Sub-paragraph
Schedules	Paragraph	Sub-paragraph	(None)

from " *Law Notes*," 25 Chancery Lane, London WC2A 1NB,
and can be strongly recommended to beginner and advanced
student alike for its entertaining and instructive articles.
Specialist publications include *Public Law*, the *Criminal Law
Review*, the *Conveyancer*, the *Journal of Planning and
Environment Law*, *Family Law* and the *International and
Comparative Law Quarterly*. Space does not allow mention
of the numerous periodicals published overseas.

The Times newspaper is available to students at a reduced
price. Particulars can be obtained from a newsagent, or
from the Circulation manager, *The Times*, Printing House
Square, London EC4P 4DE. The Weekly Law Reports, the
Law Reports and the All England Reports also offer
considerable reduction to student subscribers.

I should not need to remind my readers not to deface
library books, however urgently the text may seem to need
correction, emphasis or comment. It is distracting to have
to endure the handiwork of other readers.

CHAPTER 4

METHODS OF STUDY

Learning by study must be won;
'Twas ne'er entailed from son to son.

—Gay, *Fables*, ii, II.

TEXTBOOKS

How is my time better spent: sitting in the library reading
cases in the reports, or stewing over a textbook in my own
room? This is a question often put by beginners, and it is
a hard one to answer. One can, of course, answer it dis-
creetly by saying: do both. But then the question is: in
what proportion? What is the relative importance of the
two modes of study?

Before answering this question let me remind the reader
that when studying law he has not one aim but two. His
primary and most important aim is to make himself a lawyer.
His secondary (but also very important) aim is to pass his
law examinations with credit.

Now to a large extent these two aims can be pursued by
the same means. For both purposes one must study cases,
either in the original law reports or in case books. It is
through applying oneself to cases that one gets to understand
how legal problems present themselves and how legal argument is conducted. That understanding is important whether
one's object is to solve examination problems or to give
sound opinions on points of legal practice.

But there is one difference between preparation for practice and preparation for examinations. For the practising
lawyer, having a large field of what Pollock calls potential
knowledge is more important than having a small amount of
actual knowledge. What the practitioner needs is a grasp of
general legal principles, a sound knowledge of practice and
procedure, an ability to argue, and a general knowledge of

where to find the law he wants. But it is not essential for him—though, of course, it is a great help—to carry much law in the mind.[1] To shine at examinations, on the other hand, one must not only know how to argue, and be able to display a first-hand knowledge of the sources; one must also be able to parrot a considerable number of rules and authorities. From the examination point of view there is a danger in discursive reading that is not accompanied by a considerable amount of learning by rote.

Teachers of law regret this, but they have not agreed upon effective counter-measures. It is true that the introduction of problems into examination papers has done something to redress the balance between intelligence and memory; but too much memorising is still required. Often it seems to smother constructive thought. Some examination scripts are positively shocking for the amount of word-perfect memorising that they display, coupled with lack of individuality. Copies of statutes are now allowed to be used in some law examinations. The result is not to lower the standard of the examination but to raise it, for it means that the examination can be made more starkly a test of intelligence and lawyerly ability. There is no reason why case books should not be permitted, or at least lists of names of cases. Some American teachers allow their pupils to take in to the examination all material that they have prepared themselves.

But I must not vex my present readers with problems of educational reform. My reason for writing the above was merely to underline the importance, as matters now stand, of

---

[1] There is an old tale of a solicitor who won great renown for his deep knowledge of the law. His secret was this. He had had three copies of *Every Man's Own Lawyer* bound to resemble law reports and lettered respectively " 3 Meeson and Welsby," " 1 Term Reports " and " 7 Manning and Granger." When a client propounded a legal question, the solicitor would ring for his clerk and say: " Bring me 3 Meeson and Welsby," or " 1 Term Reports," or " 7 Manning and Granger." When the volume came he would gravely look up the point and then say triumphantly: " Ah! here it is. I thought so. The very authority we wanted." The solicitor was not such a fraud as a layman hearing this story might think. At least he knew his way about that particular book better than his clients did.

memory work. It is distressing when a man who has worked industriously and read widely fails to achieve his due place in the examination merely because he has not committed a due proportion of his reading to memory.

There is another observation to be made about the learning of law through the medium of textbooks. It is an observation that everyone inured to learning has already made for himself, but it is, perhaps, worth putting on paper for the sake of those whose acquaintance with this discipline has hitherto been slight. It is this. The more often a book is read, the easier and quicker it is to read (which is obvious), and the more it repays the reading (which is, perhaps, not quite so obvious). When a book on an unfamiliar subject is read for the first time it is rather heavy going, and one seems not to remember very much of it. The second reading is both easier and more interesting, and more (but still not much) is remembered. Many men take their examination at this point. Had they had the perseverance to read through the book a third, fourth and fifth time, they would have found that each sucessive reading came more easily and that the residue left in the mind each time went up in geometrical progression.

While on the subject of memory work it is worth pointing out that learning by heart is best performed in short periods distributed over as long a time as possible. For instance, it is better to devote one hour a day to revision than six hours at a stretch once a week. By the same token, you can learn the same amount in less learning time by distributing your learning evenly over term and vacation than by crowding your learning into the term and leaving the vacations an academic blank. The greater the gaps you leave between your periods of learning, the less learning you have to do.[2]

" It has been found," says a psychologist, " that when acts of reading and acts of recall alternate, *i.e.* when every reading is followed by an attempt to recall the items, the efficiency

[2] See the experiment described by Ian M. L. Hunter, *Memory* (Penguin Books, 1957), 58.

of learning and retention is enormously enhanced." [3] This means that learning is best done by reading a paragraph or page or similar convenient amount, and immediately reciting the gist of it: it has been found better to recite aloud than to perform the recall in the head. If you find that you cannot remember the passage properly, read it again and then try another recall. The longer the passage that you set yourself for recall the better; in other words, read as much at a time as you will be able to reproduce at the next recall. Tests have shown that when time is thus distributed between reading and recall, fifty per cent. more is remembered than when the same time is spent merely in reading the passage over and over.[4]

Heavy footnotes to a book are sometimes distracting, and it is then a good plan to read the book through a first time without looking at the footnotes.

It is a mistake to spend valuable time in digesting a text-book on paper, unless the digest consists of little more than subject-headings and names of cases. Mere transcription from a book that one owns oneself is certainly folly. " Many readers I have found unalterably persuaded," wrote Dr. Johnson, " that nothing is certainly remembered but what is transcribed; and they have therefore passed weeks and months in transferring large quotations to a commonplace book. Yet, why any part of a book, which can be consulted at pleasure, should be copied I was never able to discover. The hand has no closer correspondence with the Memory than the eye. The act of writing itself distracts the thoughts, and what is twice read is commonly better remembered than what is transcribed." [5]

---

[3] C. A. Mace, *The Psychology of Study*, 2nd ed., 38. Those who find it difficult to settle down to University studies may find further help in T. H. Pear, *The Art of Study* (1930), Chaps. 6–8.

[4] Ian M. L. Hunter, *op. cit.* 54. Sir Cyril Burt, who also gave the above advice, added: " Exploit your strongest form of imagery; if you are a visualiser, invent mental pictures; if you hear things easily in your mind's ear, use rhythms, rhymes, and alliterations " (*The Listener*, December 7, 1950).

[5] *The Idler*, No. 74.

CASE BOOKS

Some teachers of law do not recommend the use of case books. In their view, the only way to become a proficient lawyer is to sit down in the library and read cases, not contenting oneself with the headnote or any other bowdlerised version of the case, but reading through the whole of the statement of facts and the whole of the judgments. Faced with such a counsel of perfection the student may well echo from the heart the words of Doderidge J., written when legal literature was but a fraction of its present bulk: " *Vita brevis est, ars longa*, our life is short and full of calamities, and learning is a long time in getting." [6] A teacher must consider, before he gives advice like the above, the amount of time actually available to a law student for his studies. Taking first those at the universities, their period of residence is only about six months in the year, and few work for more than eight months in the year altogether. In that time they have to cover from four to six subjects. This means an average of between six and eight weeks for each subject. Into this alarmingly short space they must fit attendance at lectures, the reading of the textbook, wider reading in the library, and revision, as well as the manifold activities that very properly occupy the undergraduate outside his work. Those attending technical colleges or studying for professional examinations, particularly those engaged in office work during the day, will probably have less rather than more time than undergraduates.

It becomes obvious, then, that time must be husbanded. Granting that the student must read cases, it is to my mind a permissible economy of time to buy a good case book for each department of law that is being studied. Using a case book has two advantages for the learner. First, the case book saves him some of the trouble (beneficial, but time-consuming) of making his own notebook of cases. Secondly, it does something to eliminate immaterial facts, thus helping in the search (again beneficial, but again time-consuming) for the facts that are legally material.

---

[6] *The English Lawyer* (1631), 38.

It should be added that the use of case books by no means dispenses with the need for reading the original reports. For one thing, many of the more important cases in the case book can profitably be read in full in the law reports, using the case book version only for revision. Also, there are bound to be many cases that the keen student will come across and want to read that are not in his case book: among them, cases decided since the case book went to print.

To the man of modest means the high price of law books is intimidating, but it is false economy to do without basic works. Many are now available at reasonable prices in paperback. Money can sometimes be saved by buying secondhand books, but the beginner who does this should be careful never to buy anything but a latest edition, except on his teacher's advice.

The following is a London firm specialising in second-hand and new law books. A postcard will bring a quotation.

> Wildy & Sons, Ltd., Lincoln's Inn Archway, Carey Street, W.C.2.

LECTURES AND CLASSES

In the Middle Ages lectures were necessary because of the shortage of books. Now that printing has been with us for some hundreds of years, is there any need to continue the lecture system?

This is a vexed question, and perhaps the only comprehensive answer is that it depends upon the particular lecturer and the particular lectures. But, speaking generally, lectures may be said to possess several merits as a means of instruction. They can quicken interest. To listen to a competent lecturer makes a welcome change from the reading of books. The lecturer, too, can help his audience by giving the " basis and essentials " of the subject, elucidating the broad principles and indicating what is matter of detail. He can dwell on the parts of the subject that in his experience cause special difficulties. Another point in his favour is that by varying his emphasis he can make himself more readily understood than can the toneless words of a book. Finally, the lecturer can bring textbooks up to date, and in a smallish class he can solve individual difficulties.

Some lecturers regard it as their sole function to stimulate and inspire ; they do not particularly want notes to be taken. Certainly there is no greater waste of time than to sit through the average lecture making notes mechanically without thinking what they are about. Either concentrate on the lecture and rely upon your books for acquisition of facts, or form the habit of taking notes and at the same time of following the line of argument. It may set an edge upon your attention if you imagine that you are due to be tested in the subject immediately after the lecture. Another inestimable habit (though few cultivate it) is that of spending a part of each evening reading through all the notes taken in the day.

Some lecturers are blamed for saying too many valuable things in too short a time, making it difficult for the pens of their audiences to keep pace with them. To meet this, use abbreviations. The following are particularly useful:

H	husband	W	wife
L	landlord	T	tenant
M	master	S	servant
P	principal	A	agent
V	vendor	P	purchaser

In land law it is customary to refer to imaginary pieces of land as Blackacre, Whiteacre, etc. The conventional abbreviations for these are Bacre, Wacre, etc.

Some traditional abbreviations make use of the stroke, /. Apart from a/c, account, they all represent two words, the stroke being placed between the initial letters of each:

b/e	bill of exchange
b/l	bill of lading
b/n	bank note
b/s	bill of sale
h/p	hire purchase
p/n	promissory note

This method can, of course, be extended to other common legal phrases:

a/b	act of bankruptcy
a/t	abstract of title
A/P	Act of Parliament
b/f	bona fide
e/r	equity of redemption
l/a	letters of administration
n/i	negotiable instrument
n/k	next of kin
p/a	power of appointment
p/p	personal property, part performance
p/r	personal representative
r/p	real property
r/c	restrictive covenant
s/g	sale of goods
s/p	specific performance

Alternatively the initial letters may be separated by periods:

b.f.(p)	bona fide (purchaser)
c.q.t.	*cestui que trust* (c.q.tt., *cestuis que trust*)
p.f.	prima facie

Or they may even be joined up:

DHSS	Department of Health and Social Security

Another traditional method of abbreviation is to write the first pronounceable part of the word and then write the ending. Common examples of this method are *assn.* for *association*, *dept.* for *department* and *insce.* for *insurance*.

If you fail to catch or understand a particular sentence, no lecturer minds being asked to repeat or amplify it. Some lecturers invite questions and argument; in that case see that you play your part.

It need hardly be added, after what has already been said about transcription, that the making of a fair copy of one's own lecture notes is a dismal waste of time.

Considerably more important than the average lecture is the discussion class, generally called a class, supervision or tutorial. And of discussion classes, the most beneficial are those in which the discussion is centred on legal problems.

With regard to these classes my injunctions are limited
to two: first, attend them, and secondly, prepare for them
by attempting to work out the problems for yourself before
the class. Half the value of the class is missed if you sit
supinely back and let the instructor or the other members
of the class do the problems for you. The larger the class,
the less likely it is that you will be pressed to speak, and the
more important it is that you should speak—in order to
cultivate self-possession and to get used to the sound of your
own voice in public.

Talking about your work, whether in class or with a
friend, has the further very important advantage of helping
the memory. To quote our psychologist again: " Some form
of action or of expression would seem to be essential to
unimpaired retention. It seems that good conversationalists
and great talkers generally have good memories. It is over-
simple to suppose that this is due to the fact that, having
good memories, they are well supplied with topics of
conversation. The reverse connection would seem to be
involved. What is talked about is more firmly impressed
upon the mind. Such men when they read a book immediately discuss it with a friend, thus unconsciously employing
the potent principle of active repetition." [7]

Apart from this necessary conversation, form the habit
of working a full morning, because this is the part of the
day when you are freshest. Do not do minor chores in
the morning. As for the rest of the day, you will wish to
make your own choice between the afternoon and evening,
but at either time you will find that alcohol is totally
inconsistent with study.

In conclusion, a few words on a comparatively humble
matter, that of materials. The use of bound lecture notebooks is not to be recommended, because they are cumbrous
and inelastic. If you use such notebooks and have three or
four lectures to attend in a morning, this means a considerable weight and bulk to be carried about. Also, if you want
to expand the lecturer's remarks with notes of your own you
will find it difficult to do so within the confines of the

[7] C. A. Mace, *op. cit.*, 40–41.

notebook. On both counts the loose-leaf system is greatly preferable. The man who adopts this system needs to take with him to lectures only a single loose-leaf notebook, the day's work being transferred to larger specialised files in the evening. Notes taken down in this form can be rearranged and expanded at pleasure.

THE STUDY OF HISTORY

In my experience, there is not one student in a hundred who approaches the historical side of law in the best way. The usual course is simply to study a textbook. Textbooks are, of course, necessary; but they need to be supplemented by reference to the original sources. For instance, when you read about the Assize of Clarendon or the Bill of Rights, the sensible thing to do is to find these historical monuments and read them for yourself, just as you would read an important case or statute bearing on modern law. In this way the interest of history is vastly increased, and it becomes much more easily remembered.

Where, then, are the sources to be found? A good source book on constitutional history, which can also be used for the subject known as the history of the legal system, is Stephenson and Marcham's *Sources of English Constitutional History*. The major part of private law is excellently covered by C. H. S. Fifoot's *History and Sources of the Common Law—Tort and Contract*.

But the student who has access to a good library should not confine himself to source books. For example, having read about Glanvil, Bracton, Littleton, Coke and the rest, you should seek out copies of their works in the library (those originally written in law-French or Latin are available in translations) and browse among them. In doing so, look for the characteristics that your textbook has led you to expect. See, for example, how " Glanvil " is written round the forms of writs, and how Bracton builds up his treatise not only from writs but also from decided cases and Roman law.

When you have a nodding acquaintance with the text writers, try your hand at the Year Books. Start with the

Selden Society edition, which gives both the original law-French text and a translation on the opposite page. The easiest cases to understand are, usually, the actions of trespass. At the end of some cases is a " Note from the Record." Study it, and see how the version of the case in the record (*i.e.* the plea roll) differs from the Year Book version. (Better still, for this purpose, look at the full transcription from the record in an Ames Foundation edition of the Year Books of Richard II.) Then glance at the two other editions of the Year Books: (1) the black-letter editions, published chiefly during the sixteenth and seventeenth centuries, and (2) the Rolls Series edition, published chiefly during the second half of the nineteenth century. Note how the Selden Society and Ames Foundation editions, which both belong to the present century, have improved on the Rolls Series edition. Finally, look at one of the early reporters, like Dyer (73 E.R.) and compare him with the Year Books.

A well-stocked library will contain much more of the raw material of history to interest you. Examine a printed copy of the Register of Writs, an Abridgement, a Book of Entries. Several volumes in the Selden Society series, besides the Year Books, make good discursive reading, and often they have useful introductions. (Maitland's introduction to the *Mirror of Justices* is acknowledged to be better than *Punch*). On the history of the legal profession, turn to the entertaining account in Fortescue's *De Laudibus Legum Angliæ*, Chapters 47–51. (There are several translations of this work.) Again, in reading the history of some part of common law or equity, make a point of reading in the old reports the more important cases referred to in the textbook, such as for instance, *Slade's Case* (1601) 4 Co.Rep. 92b ; the *Case de Libellis Famosis* (1605) 5 Co.Rep. 125a, and the *Earl of Oxford's Case* (1615) 1 Chan.Rep. 1. Legal history at second hand is often a dull thing: go back to the sources, and it springs to life.

Before the student comes to the study of constitutional and legal history it is very desirable for him to have some knowledge of English history in general. The ordinary Englishman is supposed to acquire this at school, but for the overseas student, and for everyone who wants to brush up his school learning, Trevelyan's *History of England* may be strongly recommended.

I suppose that most English students know the order and the dates of the kings and queens of England. They will find such knowledge necessary in the study not only of constitutional but purely legal history, for regnal years are the foundation of legal chronology. Overseas students, and others whose historical knowledge is shaky, may possibly be glad of the following mnemonic rhyme, which was once learnt by little Victorian boys and girls; I set it out with the corresponding regnal years at the side:

First William the Norman,	1066–1087.
Then William his son;	1087–1100.
Henry, Stephen, and Henry,	1100–1135, 1135–1154, 1154–1189.
Then Richard and John;	1189–1199, 1199–1216.
Next Henry the third,	1216–1272.
Edwards, one, two and three,	1272–1307, 1307–1327, 1327–1377.
And again after Richard	1377–1399.
Three Henrys we see.	1399–1413, 1413–1422, 1422–1461.
Two Edwards, third Richard,	1461–1483, 1483, 1483–1485.
If rightly I guess;	
Two Henrys, sixth Edward,	1485–1509, 1509–1547, 1547–1553.
Queen Mary, Queen Bess,	1553–1558, 1558–1603.
Then Jamie the Scotchman,	1603–1625.
Then Charles whom they slew,	1625–1649.
Yet received after Cromwell	[1649–1660].
Another Charles too.	1649 [8] (1660)–1685.
Next James the second	
Ascended the throne;	1685–1688.
Then Good William and Mary	
Together came on.	1689–1702.
Till, Anne, Georges four,	1702–1714, 1714–1727, 1727–1760, 1760–1820, 1820–1830.
And fourth William all past,	1830–1837.
God sent Queen Victoria:	1837–1901.
May she long be the last!	

[8] Although Charles did not become king *de facto* until 1660, his regnal years were computed from the death of his father in 1649.

A racier version, and I think one easier to remember is:

> Willy, Willy, Harry, Ste,
> Harry, Dick, John, Harry 3;
> One, two, three Neds, Richard 2,
> Henry, 4, 5, 6. Then who?
> Edward 4, 5, Dick the Bad,
> Harrys twain and Ned the Lad;
> Mary, Bessie, James the Vain,
> Charlie, Charlie, James again;
> Will and Mary, Anna Gloria,
> Georges four, Will, Victoria.

If the regnal years are not already known, and the task of learning them all seems too great, the student should at least notice the sovereigns whose reigns commenced at or shortly after the turn of each century. Knowledge of this, combined with a knowledge of the order of the sovereigns, will place every sovereign in his proper century. The sovereigns just referred to are:

Henry I	...	...	...	...	1100
Henry III	...	...	...	...	1216
Edward II	...	...	...	...	1307
Henry V	...	...	...	...	1413
Henry VIII	...	...	...	...	1509
James I	...	...	...	...	1603
Anne	...	...	...	...	1702
George IV	...	...	...	...	1820

Not only regnal years, but dates in general are often a bugbear to students of history. The intelligent way to remember dates is to memorise a few key dates, and then to remember others by working backwards and forwards from these. For instance, Lord Mansfield became Chief Justice of the King's Bench in 1756, an easy date to remember and an important one. Suppose that it is desired to remember also that Blackstone delivered his first course of lectures on English law in 1753. By relating this in the mind to 1756, and noticing the difference in years (3), the one will become linked to the other, and both can be recalled together. In time the same date can be related to several other dates, so that all important dates become interlocked in the mind. This method of memorising helps to build up the sense of historical perspective, which is the only rational justification for remembering dates.

There is a useful *Dictionary of British History* edited by S. H. Steinberg. *The Dictionary of English History* by Low and Pulling is out of print.

CHAPTER 5

TECHNICAL TERMS

'Zounds! I was never so bethump'd with words.
—Shakespeare, *King John*, II, i.

DICTIONARIES

AT first the beginner will find himself rather lost among the many technical terms used in a report, and will find some difficulty with Latin and law-French phrases and maxims.[1] Many are the tales that are recounted of these difficulties. There was the youth who innocently asked whether the phrase *en ventre sa mère* meant the same thing as *in loco parentis*. There was the examination candidate who expressed the opinion that the whole of Lord Atkin's speech in *Donoghue* v. *Stevenson* was *per incuriam*. To two other candidates belongs the credit of suggesting that *fructus naturales* means illegitimate children, and that *animus revertendi* means the transmigration of souls. Weak latinity may also result in ungrammatical constructions. Thus the word " *obiter* " in " *obiter dictum* " (a judge's " saying by the way " or " passing remark ") is not a noun: one should

---

[1] The law-French phrases survive from the time when French, or rather Anglo-Norman, was the language of the courts. See Pollock, *First Book of Jurisprudence* (6th ed., 1929), 297–302; Holdsworth, *History of English Law*, ii, 477–484; Theo. Mathew in (1938) 54 L.Q.R. 358.

Latin was formerly the language for official documents, like writs; and sometimes survives in the names of writs. Also, maxims are usually in Latin because they are derived from Roman law or because they were invented by medieval jurists.

In 1730 Parliament passed an Act abolishing law-Latin in legal proceedings. But it was found that technical terms like *nisi prius, quare impedit, fieri facias* and *habeas corpus* were (as Blackstone put it) " not capable of an English dress with any degree of seriousness," and so two years later another Act was passed to allow such words to be continued " in the same language as hath been commonly used."

not write, as another examinee once did, that a lawyer in reading cases needs to " hack his way through the *obiter* to reach the actual decisions."

In all such troubles a good law dictionary can be a great help. The cheapest paperback suitable for students is Mozley and Whiteley's *Law Dictionary* (£1·20); the cheapest hardback is Osborn's *Concise Law Dictionary* (£1·50). Earl Jowitt's *Dictionary of English Law* (£15·00) is founded upon earlier works by Wharton and Byrne. Jowitt is expensive, but it is the biggest and the best of those mentioned ; and speaking for myself I would rather have a secondhand copy of Jowitt, or of an old edition of Wharton or Byrne, than a new copy of one of its slenderer brethren, good as they are in their own way.

Alternatively, a good English dictionary, like the *Concise Oxford Dictionary* (a miracle of exactitude, compression and cheapness), can afford considerable assistance on the meaning of individual English words, though not, of course, on Latin maxims.

PRONUNCIATION

A few words may be said about pronunciation. Latin words and phrases are generally pronounced by lawyers in the same old barbaric way as they were in the Middle Ages,[2] that is to say, as if they were English. To the man who has been taught the new style of pronunciation at school this occasions some difficulty. Generally speaking in the old style the Latin " *a* " is pronounced " ay," " *e* " is pronounced " ee," and " *i* " like " y " in " by." Thus *mens rea* is pronounced " reeah," and the writ of *fi. fa.* is pronounced " fy fay." This mode of pronunciation lends point to Mr. Punch's translation of *pendente lite*[3] as " a chandelier." " *C* " and " *g* " are soft

[2] There is a medieval tale of some nuns who needed extra help about the convent and who accordingly sent down to the village by word of mouth for *servitia*. The request was understood by the villagers as a request for *cervicia*, an alefeast, and they acted accordingly. The anecdote shows that the " c " in *cervicia*, and probably also the " t " in *servitia*, were pronounced like " s."

[3] " While the suit is pending."

where they would be in English,[4] and the pronunciation of such syllables as *atio* in *ratio decidendi* is also anglicised.[5] The first word of *vice versa* is pronounced " visee " (not " vice "). Where the first syllable of a Latin dissyllable is short it is customarily lengthened in English; thus *nisī* is pronounced " nysy " and *căpias* " caypias." The same is done for some polysyllables, such as *ŏbiter* (frequently pronounced " ōbiter "). For Latin phrases and maxims the student can retain the pronunciation that he was taught at school if he wishes, but with single words like *elegit* it is simpler to anglicise them (" ĭleejĭt ").

Law-French words are pronounced much as they were in the Middle Ages; it is a solecism to utter them as if they were modern French. The pronunciation is, indeed, much nearer to modern English than it is to French. Thus the town crier quite correctly said " Oy-ez," not Oy-ay." The following are pronunciations of legal terms deriving from medieval French.

attorn ⎫
attorney ⎭ (-er)

autrefois acquit ⎫ (oterfoyz, with " acquit " and " convict "
autrefois convict ⎭ pronounced as usual in English)

detinue (det-)
distress damage feasant (feezant)
emblements (embliments)
formedon (" e " pronounced indeterminately, as in " added ")
feme sole [6] (femm)
feme covert (cuvert)
feoffment (feff-)
laches (laytshiz)

[4] Hence R. H. Barham's lines in allusion to Sir C. Wren's epitaph in St. Paul's Cathedral:
   And, talking of epitaphs, much I admire his,
   " Circumspice, si monumentum requiris,"
   Which an erudite verger translated to me,
   " If you ask for his monument, Sir—come—spy—see! "
[5] But there are no immutable rules, any more than there are in the pronunciation of English. Thus *si* is pronounced " see " by old and new school alike, though to be consistent the old school should pronounce it " sy," as indeed it does in the word *nisi*.
[6] Another tale concerns counsel who departed from usage by pronouncing this phrase " femmee sole." The judge pricked up his ears and said, " What is that? I have heard of a camisole, but not of a femme sole."

lien (lee-en)
mesne (meen)
misfeasance
nonfeasance $\Big\}$ (-feez-)
pur autre vie (pur ōter vee)
que (in the phrase " in the *que* estate " and in *cestui que
    trust*; pronounced kee)
seisin (-eez-)
semble—anglicised as written
Statutes of Jeofails (jefailz) [7]
venue (vĕnue, with accent on first syllable)
villein (villen)

In some instances lawyers still jealously retain the archaic
pronunciations of English words. " Patent " has a short
" a," and the noun " record " is pronounced like the verb,
with the stress on the second syllable.[8] The term for an
insured person, " assured," has the last syllable pronounced
like " red " and stressed. In " cognisance," " recognisance "
and " cognisable " we refuse to " take cognisance of " the
intrusive " g " in speaking, though we do in writing. (The
" g " comes through latinising the law-French word conu-
sance). In these words the lawyer's pronunciation is different
from the layman's. Lastly, the " committee " of a person
of unsound mind was a single person to whom the care of
such person was entrusted by the court, the stress being on
the last syllable. Committees are no longer appointed.

LEGAL ABBREVIATIONS

Legal abbreviations are another frequent source of vexation
to a beginner. The possession of a law dictionary is again

---

[7] So the O.E.D. Sutton, *Personal Actions*, 119, gives " jeefailz."
  [8] Condemn the fault, and not the actor of it?
    Why, every fault's condemn'd ere it be done.
    Mine were the very cipher of a function,
    To fine the faults whose fine stands in record,
    And let go by the actor.
        —Shakespeare, *Measure for Measure*, II, ii.
    Then turning to the Judge, he cry's, My Lord,
    (And thus runs o'er their Crimes upon record).
        —Edward Ward, *A Journey to H———, or a visit
        paid to the D———* (or, *The Infernal Vision*), Part
        I, Canto II (A.D. 1700–1705).

a great help, but something may be said here of the more common abbreviations and short-cut terms seen in print.

First, as to the titles of judges. " Smith J." means " Mr. Justice Smith," [9] and when speaking of him in public he will be given that full title. Never say " Justice Smith " or (except for a circuit or county court judge) " Judge Smith " ; these are Americanisms, to be shunned and avoided on this side of the Atlantic. The plural abbreviation is JJ.: " Smith and Byles JJ.," which is read out as " Mr. Justice Smith and Mr. Justice Byles." Similarly, the following letters placed after the names of the judges have the following meanings:

B.	=	Baron [of the Exchequer]. A member of the former Court of Exchequer—not to be confused with Barons who are peers. Plural BB. Title now obsolete.
C.B.	=	Chief Baron: the head of the former Court of Exchequer. Title now obsolete.
C.J. (or L.C.J.)	=	(Lord) Chief Justice. Head of the Q.B.D.
J.A.	=	Justice of Appeal. Title found between 1875 and 1877, and now obsolete.[10]
L.C.	=	Lord Chancellor. Head of the judicial system.
L.J.	=	Lord Justice. Member of the C.A. Plural L.JJ.: Lords Justices.
M.R.	=	Master of the Rolls. Member (and virtually head) of the C.A.
P.	=	President. Head of the Family Division (formerly Probate, Divorce and Admiralty Division).
V.-C.	=	Vice-Chancellor. Subordinate judge in the old Court of Chancery. Title now obsolete, except in the Chancery Court of Lancaster.

Do not omit or abbreviate " Lord " before the name of a judge who is a Law Lord or other peer. Thus you will write " Lord Hailsham L.C." not " Hailsham L.C."; and similarly " Lord Widgery C.J." (or " Lord Widgery L.C.J."). These are read out as " Lord Hailsham, Lord Chancellor " and " Lord Widgery, Chief Justice " (or " Lord Chief Justice "). In the

---

[9] Sometimes called a puisne (pronounced " pewny "—ew as in few) judge, meaning any judge of the High Court (or the older courts that it replaced) other than the chiefs.
[10] See (1945) 61 L.Q.R. 231.

case of Chief Justices who were not peers, like Rufus Isaacs, the written designation is " Isaacs C.J." (or " L.C.J."), which is read out as " [Lord] Chief Justice Isaacs." Lords Justices are not peers as such, so that, for example, " Buckley L.J." is read out as " Lord Justice Buckley." " Buckley and Roskill L.JJ." are " Lords Justices Buckley and Roskill." Lord Denning M.R. is " Lord Denning, Master of the Rolls." Where this last office is not held by a peer the former usage was that one had to remember the holder's Christian name when speaking of him, so " Pollock M.R." was " Sir Ernest Pollock, Master of the Rolls," and " Brett M.R." was " Sir Baliol Brett, Master of the Rolls" (79 L.Q.R. 190). But at the present day it would be acceptable to say " Pollock, Master of the Rolls," and so on.

Certain abbreviations and shorthand expressions supply a convenient mechanism for referring to authorities. A librarian once showed me a request form filled in by a reader asking for a supposed book called " *Ibid.*" Evidently the reader had seen this referred to many times in footnotes, and thought that it must be an extremely important book, written perhaps by an eminent Persian. Of course, " *ibid.*" is short for *ibidem*, meaning " in the same place "; it is simply a way of repeating a reference previously given. Similarly, *op. cit.* means the book previously cited, and *loc. cit.* means the page previously cited in the book previously cited. *Passim* means " everywhere in the book." S.C. means " same case " (*i.e. ibid.* as applied to a reported case), and S.P. " same principle." Other compendious expressions are *per*, *semble*, *aliter* (or *secus*) and *contra*. *Per* generally means " statement by ": thus "*per* Lord Dunedin " following a quotation means that the remark quoted is that of Lord Dunedin. *Per curiam* and *per incuriam* are not opposites. *Per curiam* means that the statement is by the whole court. *Per incuriam* means that a judge's remark was made by mistake. *Semble* is law-French for " it seems " or " it seems that " (when the authority for a proposition is weak or not completely satisfactory ; usually it indicates an *obiter dictum*). *Aliter* and *secus* mean " otherwise " and *contra* refers to an authority contradicting what one has first said.

Thus one can write " *Semble* the phrase ' carcase or portion of a carcase ' in this statute does not include a sausage—see *per* Tripe L.J., *obiter*, in *Sage* v. *Onions* (C.A.); *contra*, *Ham* v. *Eggs* (Div.Ct.) ; *aliter* if the sausage meat is not yet minced." This may not be an elegant style but it does represent an economy of effort, which to some minds has a beauty of its own.

CHAPTER 6

CASE LAW TECHNIQUE

Mastering the lawless science of our law,
That codeless myriad of precedent,
That wilderness of single instances,
Through which a few, by wit or fortune led,
May beat a pathway out to wealth and fame.

—Tennyson, *Aylmer's Field.*

RATIO DECIDENDI AND OBITER DICTUM

ENGLISH courts make a habit of following their previous decisions within more or less well-defined limits. This is called the doctrine of precedent. The part of a case that is said to possess authority is the *ratio decidendi*, that is to say, the rule of law upon which the decision is founded. Finding the *ratio decidendi* of a case is an important part of the training of a lawyer. It is not a mechanical process but is an art that one gradually acquires through practice and study. One can, however, give a general description of the technique involved.

What the doctrine of precedent declares is that cases must be decided the same way when their material facts are the same. Obviously it does not require that *all* the facts should be the same. We know that in the flux of life all the facts of a case will never recur; but the legally material facts may recur and it is with these that the doctrine is concerned.

The *ratio decidendi* of a case can be defined as the material facts of the case plus the decision thereon.[1] The same learned writer who advanced this definition went on to suggest a helpful formula. Suppose that in a certain case facts A, B and C exist; and suppose that the court finds that facts B and C are material and fact A immaterial, and then reaches conclusion X (*e.g.* judgment for the plaintiff, or

---

[1] Goodhart, " Determining the *Ratio Decidendi* of a Case," *Essays in Jurisprudence and the Common Law* (1931) 1.

judgment for the defendant). Then the doctrine of precedent
enables us to say that in any future case in which facts B
and C exist, or in which facts A and B and C exist, the
conclusion must be X. If in a future case facts A, B, C
and D exist, and fact D is held to be material, the first case
will not be a direct authority, though it may be of value as
an analogy.

What facts are legally material? That depends on the
particular case, but take as an illustration a " running down "
action, that is to say, an action for injuries sustained through
the defendant's negligent driving of a vehicle. The fact that
the plaintiff had red hair and freckles, that his name was
Smith, and that the accident happened on a Friday are
immaterial, for the rule of law upon which the decision
proceeds will apply equally to persons who do not possess
these characteristics and to accidents that happen on other
days. On the other hand, the fact that the defendant drove
negligently, and the fact that in consequence he injured the
plaintiff, are material, and a decision in the plaintiff's favour
on such facts will be an authority for the proposition that
a person is liable for causing damage through the negligent
driving of a vehicle.

The foregoing is a general explanation of the phrase " the
ratio decidendi of a case." To get a clearer idea of the way
in which a *ratio decidendi* is extracted, let us take a decided
case and study it in detail. I set out below the case of
Wilkinson v. *Downton*,[2] where the plaintiff was awarded
damages by a jury for nervous shock, and the trial judge
then heard argument on the question whether the verdict
could be upheld in law. The first part of the judgment,
which is all that need be considered here, runs as follows.

WRIGHT J. In this case the defendant, in the execution of
what he seems to have regarded as a practical joke, represented
to the plaintiff that he was charged by her husband with a
message to her to the effect that her husband was smashed up in
an accident, and was lying at The Elms at Leytonstone with
both legs broken, and that she was to go at once in a cab with
two pillows to fetch him home. All this was false. The effect

2 [1897] 2 Q.B. 57.

of the statement on the plaintiff was a violent shock to her nervous system, producing vomiting and other more serious and permanent physical consequences at one time threatening her reason, and entailing weeks of suffering and incapacity to her as well as expense to her husband for medical attendance. These consequences were not in any way the result of previous ill-health or weakness of constitution; nor was there any evidence of predisposition to nervous shock or any other idiosyncrasy.

In addition to these matters of substance there is a small claim for 1s. 10½d. for the cost of railway fares of persons sent by the plaintiff to Leytonstone in obedience to the pretended message. As to this 1s. 10½d. expended in railway fares on the faith of the defendant's statement, I think the case is clearly within the decision in *Pasley* v. *Freeman* (1798) 3 T.R. 51. The statement was a misrepresentation intended to be acted on to the damage of the plaintiff.

The real question is as to the £100, the greatest part of which is given as compensation for the female plaintiff's illness and suffering. It was argued for her that she is entitled to recover this as being damages caused by fraud, and therefore within the doctrine established by *Pasley* v. *Freeman* and *Langridge* v. *Levy* (1837) 2 M. & W. 519. I am not sure that this would not be an extension of that doctrine, the real ground of which appears to be that a person who makes a false statement intended to be acted on must make good the damage naturally resulting from its being acted on. Here there is no *injuria* of that kind. I think, however, that the verdict may be supported upon another ground. The defendant has, as I assume for the moment, wilfully done an act calculated to cause physical harm to the plaintiff—that is to say, to infringe her legal right to personal safety, and has in fact thereby caused physical harm to her. That proposition without more appears to me to state a good cause of action, there being no justification alleged for the act. This wilful *injuria* is in law malicious, although no malicious purpose to cause the harm which was caused nor any motive of spite is imputed to the defendant.

It remains to consider whether the assumptions involved in the proposition are made out. One question is whether the defendant's act was so plainly calculated to produce some effect of the kind which was produced that an intention to produce it ought to be imputed to the defendant, regard being had to the fact that the effect was produced on a person proved to be in an ordinary state of health and mind. I think that it was. It is difficult to imagine that such a statement, made suddenly and with apparent seriousness, could fail to produce grave effects under the circumstances upon any but an exceptionally indifferent person, and therefore an intention to produce such an effect must be imputed, and it is no answer in law to say that more harm was done than was anticipated, for that is commonly the case with all wrongs.

The reader will notice that the judge does not cite any authority for his decision that the £100 is recoverable. The only authorities he cites are authorities on which he says he prefers not to rely. The reason is that at the date when the case was decided there was no English authority on the general question whether it was a tort intentionally to inflict bodily harm on another. There was, indeed, the very ancient tort of battery, which is committed when D hits or stabs or shoots P. But Downton committed no battery upon Mrs. Wilkinson; nor did he assault her by threatening a battery. Consequently, the case was one " of first impression," and the judge decided it merely on common-sense principles. It would be a grave reproach to a civilised system of law if it did not give a remedy on such facts.

Let us now see how the *ratio decidendi* is to be extracted. This is done by finding the material facts. The judge has already done much of the work for us, because he has omitted from his judgment many of the facts given in evidence which were obviously irrelevant to the legal issue—*e.g.* the address at which the plaintiff lived. But the judgment mentions the address at which the husband was supposed to be lying, which also is clearly irrelevant. As a first step in boiling it down we may say that the essential facts, and the pith of the judgment, were as follows:

The defendant by way of what was meant to be a joke told the plaintiff that the latter's husband had been smashed up in an accident. The plaintiff, who had previously been of normal health, suffered a shock and serious illness. Wright J. held that the defendant was liable, not perhaps for the tort of deceit but because the defendant had wilfully done an act calculated to cause physical harm to the plaintiff, and had in fact caused such harm.

The above would represent the sort of note that an intelligent student would make of the case. How are we to frame the *ratio decidendi*? There are two main possibilities.

The first would be to take such of the detailed facts as may be deemed to be material, plus the decision on the

facts. This would result in the following rule: that where
the defendant has wilfully told the plaintiff a lie of a
character that is likely to frighten and so cause physical
harm to the plaintiff, and it has in fact caused such harm,
the defendant is liable, in the absence of some ground of
justification.

This *ratio* omits to specify the particular lie told by the
defendant, because this was immaterial. What mattered was
not the particular lie as to the plaintiff's husband's alleged
injury, but the more general fact of lying. The particular
lie told by the defendant was material only in the sense that
it was the sort of lie that was calculated to frighten and
cause physical harm to the plaintiff.

But, it may be objected, such a *ratio* would be too
narrow, because the learned judge evidently intended to lay
down a wider rule. He did not confine his judgment to lies,
but spoke only of wilfully doing an *act* which is calculated
to and does cause physical harm; and this gives us the true
ratio. It was immaterial that the particular form of mischief
perpetrated by the defendant took the form of a verbal lie;
it might have been some other act calculated to cause harm,
and the legal outcome would have been the same. This,
indeed, is common sense. A person with Downton's juvenile
sense of humour who dresses up as a ghost, or who puts a
squib under somebody else's chair, would doubtless find himself in the same legal category as Downton.

Again, the learned judge did not speak of fright when he
formulated the principle of his decision. He spoke of
causing physical harm, which is much wider. On this principle, an outrageous *threat* causing suffering is a tort. In a
subsequent case [3] which approved *Wilkinson* v. *Downton*, the
defendant threatened to arrest and prosecute the plaintiff, a
foreign servant-girl, if she did not give certain information;
the defendant knew that any charge he brought against the
girl would be quite unfounded, and the girl became ill with
distress. It was held that she had a good cause of action.
Another application of the principle occurs where the harm
operates directly on the plaintiff's body, not indirectly

[3] *Janvier* v. *Sweeney* [1919] 2 K.B. 316.

through the mind—as where the defendant blackens a towel with which the plaintiff is about to wipe his face, or secretly adds poison to the plaintiff's drink. Although these situations have not come before the English courts, there is no doubt that they would fall under the principle of the decision.

The reader may now be feeling rather puzzled as to the meaning of *ratio decidendi*. We started off with a possible narrow *ratio decidendi* of the case, incorporating the fact of lying and the fact of fright. Then we passed to a wider *ratio*, which evidently accords with common sense as well as with the language of the judgment, in which the facts of lying and fright have disappeared. How can this be reconciled with our definition of *ratio decidendi* as the material facts plus the decision thereon? Were not the lie and the fright material facts in *Wilkinson* v. *Downton*? If there had been no lie and no fright, and no equivalent facts in their place, the plaintiff would not have won. What exactly do we mean by a " material fact "?

The answer is that we have not been using this expression in a consistent way, and it is necessary to restate the position in more exact language. What is really involved in finding the *ratio decidendi* of a case is a process of abstraction. Abstraction is the mental operation of picking out certain qualities and relations from the facts of experience. Imagine a baby in whose household there is a terrier called Caesar. The baby will be taught to call this dog " bow-wow," because " bow-wow " is easier to say than " Caesar." If he sees another dog he will guess or be told that this other dog is to be called " bow-wow " as well. This is an example of one of the baby's earliest feats of abstraction. Abstraction comes through the perception of similarities between individual facts, and all language and all thinking depend upon it.

The next point to be noticed is that this process of abstraction may be carried to progressively higher flights. The individual dog Ceasar is, at a low level of abstraction, a terrier ; at a higher level he is a dog ; higher still, a mammal ; and then an animal and a living thing. In the same way a man might say that he was born at the Piccaninny

Nursing Home; in London; in England; in Europe. All
these are " facts," but they are facts belonging to different
levels of abstraction.

We are now in a better position to state the *ratio decidendi* of a case. The ascertainment of the *ratio decidendi* of
a case depends upon a process of abstraction from the totality
of facts that occurred in it. The higher the abstraction, the
wider the *ratio decidendi*. Thus a rule that " it is a tort to
tell a lie that is calculated to and does cause fright and
consequent physical harm " is a narrow rule, belonging to a
low level of abstraction from the facts of the particular case
in which it was laid down; leave out the reference to fright,
and it becomes wider; replace " tell a lie " by " do any
intentional act " and it becomes wider still. It is the last rule
that is the *ratio decidendi* of *Wilkinson* v. *Downton*. We
carry on the process of abstraction until all the particular
facts have been eliminated except the fact of the intentional
doing of an act which is likely to cause physical harm,
and the fact of the occurrence of such harm.

How do we know when to stop with our abstraction?
The answer is: primarily by reading what the judge says in
his judgment, but partly also by our knowledge of the law
in general, and by our common sense and our feeling for
what the law ought to be. It so happens that in the case we
have been considering the learned judge formulates the rule
fairly clearly, but sometimes the rule stated in the judgment
incorporates facts which as a matter of common sense are
not essential, and sometimes it goes to the opposite extreme
of being too sweeping—as can be demonstrated either by the
use of common sense or by referring to other decided cases.
The finding of the *ratio decidendi* is not an automatic
process; it calls for lawyerly skill and knowledge.

DISTINGUISHING

Certain general truths implicit in the foregoing discussion
may now be stated more explicitly.

In the first place, a case may have not one but several
rationes decidendi, of ascending degrees of generality. We
have seen two or three possible *rationes* in *Wilkinson* v.

Downton. The third was accepted not only because it was stated by the judge but also because it accorded with common sense and with other authorities. Sometimes a judge will lay down a rule that is narrower than is required by common sense, and a later court may then say that the rule ought to be read more widely, by abandoning some limitation unnecessarily expressed in it. Indeed, one such unnecessary limitation can be found in the judgment in *Wilkinson* v. *Downton.* The rule stated by Wright J. refers to a person who has " wilfully " done an act calculated to cause physical harm, and the primary meaning of a " wilful " act is one that is done with the intention of bringing about a particular consequence.[4] Downton did not, perhaps, intend to cause Mrs. Wilkinson a serious illness, but he did intend to frighten her, and that was sufficient. But, as a matter of common sense, the rule should extend also to one who is merely *reckless* as to the harm in question. If Downton had made the lying statement to Mrs. Wilkinson in order to persuade her to accompany him for some secret end of his own, realising that the statement would be likely to frighten her but not desiring (and therefore not intending) the fright itself, his liability should be just the same as for a tort of intention. This was, indeed, the essential position in the case of the foreign servant-girl referred to before: what the defendant intended in that case was to put pressure upon the girl to make her talk ; he must have foreseen the possibility of causing her great distress, but his mind was directed towards making her do what he wanted, not towards causing distress. In analysis, the case is one of recklessness as to the plaintiff's fright, not one of wilfulness or intention as to the fright ; but the legal liability should be, and is, the same.[5]

---

[4] " Wilful act," or " doing an act wilfully," is a telescoped expression. In a sense, every act is wilful, or it is not an act but merely a spasm. In legal discussions, the notion of wilfulness or intention usually refers to the *consequences* of conduct; it is the consequence that is intended, or wilfully brought about, not the movement of the defendant's body which constitutes the act.

[5] A word may here be added upon the meaning of the word " calculated," which Wright J. used in his judgment. Judges are fond of this word, but it is an unfortunate expression

One may argue that there is another unnecessary limitation contained in the judgment in *Wilkinson* v. *Downton*. The judge referred to the fact that the plaintiff had been in normal health, yet it is not only possible but probable that the decision would have been just the same even if her health had previously been poor—for the fact that the plaintiff is in poor health can be no excuse to a defendant who tells such a cruel lie as would distress even a woman who is in good health. The fact that the particular plaintiff had been in good health removed a complication that the judge might otherwise have had to consider, and for that reason he referred to it; but all the same a later court may, on mature consideration and when the question arises, decide that the limitation is unnecessary. Conversely, it sometimes happens that a judge will lay down a rule that is unneccessarily wide for the decision of the case before him; a later court may say that it is too wide, and needs to be cut down.

This point leads on to the second. The phrase "the *ratio decidendi* of a case" is slightly ambiguous. It may mean either (1) <u>the rule that the judge who decided the case intended to lay down and apply to the facts</u>, or (2) <u>the rule that a later court concedes him to have had the power to lay</u> down. The last sentence is rather clumsy, but what I mean is this. Courts do not accord to their predecessors an unlimited power of laying down wide rules. They are sometimes apt to say, in effect: "Oh yes, we know that in that case the learned judge purported to lay down such and such

because it suggests a meaning which it is not intended to convey. Originally, "calculated to" bore its literal meaning of "intended to," but in time it came to mean merely "likely to," and it is in this sense that Wright J. uses it. What the learned judge means is that the defendant intended to give the plaintiff a fright (this was the "wilful act"), and what he did was likely ("calculated") to cause the injury it did, even though the defendant did not intend to cause the full degree of the injury that occurred. The judge's decision would not apply (1) if the defendant merely acted carelessly in passing on information which was not true (for then there would be no "wilful act"), or (2) if, although the defendant intentionally told a lie and intended to cause the plaintiff some slight perturbation, a reasonable man would not have foreseen that the plaintiff would be seriously upset (for then the lie would not be "calculated" to cause physical harm).

a rule; but that rule was unnecessarily wide for the decision of the case before him, because, you see, the rule makes no reference to fact A, which existed in the case, and which we regard as a material fact, and as a fact that ought to have been introduced into the *ratio decidendi*." [6] One circumstance that may induce a court to adopt this niggling attitude towards an earlier decision is the necessity of reconciling that decision with others. Or again, the court in the earlier case may have enunciated an unduly wide rule without considering all its possible consequences, some of which are unjust or inconvenient or otherwise objectionable. Yet another possibility is that the earlier decision is altogether unpalatable to the court in the later case, so that the latter court wishes to interpret it as narrowly as possible.

This process of cutting down the expressed *ratio decidendi* of a case is one kind of " distinguishing." It may be called " restrictive " distinguishing, to differentiate it from the other kind, genuine or non-restrictive distinguishing. Non-restrictive distinguishing occurs where a court accepts the expressed *ratio decidendi* of the earlier case, and does not seek to curtail it, but finds that the case before it does not fall within this *ratio decidendi* because of some material difference of fact. Restrictive distinguishing cuts down the expressed *ratio decidendi* of the earlier case by treating as material to the earlier decision some fact, present in the earlier case, which the earlier court regarded as immaterial.[7]

[6] A common form of statement is to say that the earlier judges " were speaking of, and their language must be understood by reference to, the particular facts which were brought before them in that case": 62 L.J.Ch. 126.

[7] Dr. Goodhart in the article cited above, p. 67, n. 1, says that (1) it is for the judge who decides the case, and for him alone, to determine what facts are material, and the judge may express his decision that facts are immaterial merely by leaving them out of the rule of law that he propounds. But on the other hand (2) the *ratio decidendi* of a case is not necessarily the rule of law stated by the judge, because that may be too wide. It seems to me that these two statements are contradictory and the truth I take to be that the second is right and the first wrong. The rule stated by the judge may be " too wide " in the view of the later court, and that means that the judge has not an unlimited discretion to jettison facts as being immaterial. For Dr. Goodhart's reply to a controversy on this question, see 22 M.L.R. 117.

Wilkinson v. *Downton* has not been cut down, because the wide principle has commended itself to later judges.[8] If, however, a case ever arises in which Wright J.'s wide rule is thought to carry the law too far, the decision can be restrictively distinguished.

I have stressed this matter of distinguishing because it plays a most important part in legal argument. Suppose that you are conducting a case in court, and that the other side cites a case against you. You then have only two alternatives (that is, if you are not prepared to throw your hand in altogether). One is to submit that the case cited is wrongly decided, and so should not be followed. This is possible only if the case is not binding on the court. The other is to " distinguish " it, by suggesting that it contains or lacks some vital fact that is absent or present in your client's case. Sometimes you may have the sympathy of the judge in your effort to distinguish it, even though the distinction you suggest involves tampering with the expressed *ratio decidendi* of the precedent case and even though you have no authority for the suggested distinction. Your judge may be gravely dissatisfied with the case and yet, owing to our excessively strict doctrine of precedent, it may be impossible for him to overrule it. In such circumstances it is simply human nature that he will distinguish it if he can. He may, in extreme and unusual circumstances, be apt to seize on almost any factual difference between this previous case and the case before him in order to arrive at a different decision.[9] Some precedents are continually left on the shelf in this way, as a wag observed, they become very " distinguished." The limit of the process is reached when a judge says that the precedent

---

8 The only English case in which *Wilkinson* v. *Downton* was directly relevant was *Janvier* v. *Sweeney*, p. 71, n. 3. But the validity of principle is amply supported by American decisions.

9 Perhaps Pollock C.B. had restrictive distinguishing in mind when, in a letter to his grandson, " F.P.," in 1868, he made the following remark: " Even Parke, Lord Wensleydale (the greatest legal pedant that I believe ever existed) did not always follow even the House of Lords; he did not overrule—oh no! μὴ γένοιτο but he did not *act upon* cases which were *nonsense* (as many are)." Hanworth's *Lord Chief Baron Pollock* (1929), 198.

is an authority only " on its actual facts." For most practical purposes this is equivalent to announcing that it will
never be followed. It is not suggested that this extreme form
of distinguishing is a common occurrence, for generally judges
defer to the decisions of their predecessors both in the letter
and in the spirit, even though they dislike them. But restrictive distinguishing does happen, and the possibility of its
happening makes it of great importance to the lawyer.

OBITER DICTA

In contrast with the *ratio decidendi* is the *obiter dictum*. The
latter is a mere saying by the way, a chance remark, which is
not binding upon future courts, though it may be respected
according to the reputation of the judge, the eminence of the
court, and the circumstances in which it came to be pronounced. An example would be a rule of law stated merely
by way of analogy or illustration, or a suggested rule upon
which the decision is not finally rested. The reason for not
regarding an *obiter dictum* as binding is that it was probably
made without a full consideration of the cases on the point,
and that, if very broad in its terms, it was probably made
without a full consideration of all the consequences that may
follow from it ; or the judge may not have expressed a
concluded opinion.

   An example of an *obiter dictum* occurs in *Wilkinson* v.
Downton when the learned judge is considering the argument
that the plaintiff is entitled to recover damages for the tort
of deceit. At first sight this may seem a good argument,
because the defendant could certainly be said in a popular
sense to have deceived the plaintiff. But it is generally taken
to be essential for the tort of deceit that the defendant should
have intended the plaintiff to have acted on the statement,
and that the plaintiff should have so acted to his detriment,
for which detriment he now claims damages. Mrs. Wilkinson
recovered 1s. 10½d. as damages for deceit, because this was a
sum of money that she had spent in reliance on the defendant's deceitful statement. But the fact that she became ill
was not an act of reliance upon the statement. It was a
spontaneous reaction to the statement. Consequently, the

learned judge preferred not to rest his judgment upon this ground. He did not positively pronounce against it, but his words seem to indicate that he thought that as the law now stands the claim could not properly be based on the tort of deceit. One may say, therefore, that there is a very tentative dictum against the plaintiff on this particular issue. But the point was not finally decided, and in any case was not made the ground of the decision, and so the observations made upon it were *obiter*.

There is another kind of *obiter dictum*, which perhaps is not, properly speaking, an *obiter dictum* at all, namely a *ratio decidendi* that in the view of a subsequent court is unnecessarily wide. It is not an *obiter dictum* in the primary meaning of that phrase, because it is constructed out of the facts of the case and the decision is rested upon it. But, as we have seen, later courts reserve the right to narrow it down, and in doing so they frequently attempt to justify themselves by declaring that the unnecessarily wide statement was *obiter*. The real justification for the practice of regarding what is really *ratio decidendi* as *obiter dictum* is the undesirability of hampering the growth of English law through the too extensive application of the doctrine of precedent.

It is frequently said that a ruling based upon hypothetical facts is *obiter*. This is often true. Thus if the judge says: " I decide for the defendant; but if the facts had been properly pleaded I should have found for the plaintiff," the latter part of the statement is *obiter*. But there is at least one exception. In the past, when the defendant pleaded an " objection in point of law " (the former " demurrer "), legal argument might take place on this before the trial, and for the purpose of the argument and the decision it was assumed that all the facts stated in the plaintiff's pleadings were true. A decision pronounced on such assumed facts is not an *obiter dictum*. However, the practice of arguing the law before adducing evidence is now virtually obsolete.

HOW MUCH OF A CASE TO REMEMBER

A question that frequently vexes the beginner is: how many of the facts of a case should he remember, for the purpose of

learning the law and for the purpose of making a good showing in the examination? Ought he to try to remember (1) all
the facts stated in the report, or (2) a selection of those facts,
or (3) only those facts that are incorporated in the statement
of the *ratio decidendi*? Take again as an illustration the
case of *Wilkinson* v. *Downton*. The three possibilities just
referred to are exemplified by (1) the passage from the judgment on pp. 68–70, above, (2) the first attempt at condensa-
tion on p. 70, and (3) the statement of the *ratio decidendi* on
p. 73.

The answer to the question is that both (2) and (3) should
be remembered. (1) is obviously ruled out; it would be a
waste of effort to remember every minor circumstance that
may be stated in the report, such as the fact that Mr.
Wilkinson was stated to be lying at The Elms at Leytonstone.
On the other hand, (3) is as obviously included, for it is the
pith and marrow of the law. About the necessity for
remembering (2) the reader may be inclined to be argumenta-
tive. He may contend that he is learning to be a lawyer, not
a chronicler of tragedies, and that if he learns the rules of
law there is no need for him to burden his memory with the
facts of cases that as a matter of history gave rise to those
rules.

There are two answers to this objection, the first of
interest to examination candidates only, and the second of
wider interest.

The first answer is that examiners are suspicious creatures,
and in particular they are suspicious of " footnote " knowledge. Suppose that in the examination your only reference
to *Wilkinson* v. *Downton* is as follows: " A person is liable
in tort if he causes physical injury by an intentional act
likely to cause such injury: *Wilkinson* v. *Downton*."
The rule is correct and the name of the case is correct; and
you may in fact have satisfied yourself that the rule is
deducible from the case; but the examiner will not know it.
For all he knows, you saw the rule in your textbook and the
name of the case in a footnote. To dispel his suspicion, you
must give some statement of the concrete facts.

The second answer is more important, but we need spend

no further time over it because enough has really been said
on it already. It is a mistake to suppose that every case has
one and only one fixed and incontrovertible *ratio decidendi*.
What exactly is the *ratio decidendi* of a case is often a matter
for much argument. Also, the pick-lock art of distinguishing
depends upon a critical examination of all the facts of the
case that might by any possibility be regarded as material.
If, therefore, there is any sort of doubt about the correctness
of a decision, or about its limits, as many of the facts as can
conceivably be looked upon as material should be
remembered.

There are some cases, however, where nothing more than
the simple *ratio decidendi* need be remembered, because
apart from the facts stated in the *ratio decidendi* the case
contains no facts except the trivialities of date, amount, etc.
An illustration is *Byrne* v. *Van Tienhoven*.[10] The facts of
this case were as follows:

October 1.—The defendants in Cardiff by letter offered to
sell to the plaintiff 1,000 boxes of Hensol Tinplates.
October 11.—The plaintiffs received this letter. The plaintiffs
wired to defendants. " Accept thousand Hensols." But
October 8.—The defendants posted a letter revoking their
offer, ending " and we must consider our offer to be cancelled
from this date."
October 20.—The plaintiffs received second letter.

It was held that there was a good contract and that the
defendant's revocation of their offer was ineffective.

The reason why the above facts are set out in a case book
is to show the student how the legal question as to revocation
of offers is likely to arise in practice. By digesting the facts
in his own mind, and seeing how the problem arises out of
them, the student is preparing himself to answer examination
problems and to deal with cases in his legal practice. But
this does not mean that he is expected to memorise any of
the particular facts of *Byrne* v. *Van Tienhoven*. All the facts
of this case are immaterial except the fact that the offerors
attempted to revoke their offer by a letter that did not arrive
until after the offerees had accepted ; and the *ratio decidendi*

[10] (1880) 5 C.P.D. 344.

is that such a revocation is ineffective. If this is grasped, all the rest of the facts can be forgotten.

THE NAMES OF CASES

Another question frequently asked by law students is as to remembering names of cases. The questioner realises, of course, that he is expected to read cases and to quote them, where relevant, in his answers; but must he behave as though he were learning the telephone directory?

The first and most important reply to the question is this: *Never* refrain from referring to a case in the examination merely because you have forgotten its name. The name is the least important part of the case. Most important is the rule of law contained in the case; next important are the facts; even the name of the court that decided the case is of more legal value than the proper names of the parties. If the name of the case is imperfectly remembered the approximate name can be given, with a question mark in brackets; thus, *Derry* v. *Peek* [11] might be rendered as " *Perry* v. *Deek* (?)." Or the case can be referred to by the name of the plaintiff if that only is remembered: *e.g.* " *Derry's* case." Or the name of only the defendant may be given—though in this case it is desirable to make it plain that the name is that of the defendant: *e.g.* " in an action against one *Peek*," or " in . . . v. *Peek*." Or the case can be identified by reference to some salient fact: *e.g.* " in the case concerning the tramway company's power to use steam." Even if both name and facts are forgotten, the student can at least indicate that there is authority for his proposition by saying: " In one case it was held that . . ."

But although the name is the least important part of the case, it is not altogether without importance. For the immediate purpose of the examination a script in which cases are referred to by name has naturally a more " finished " appearance than one that merely refers to " cases " in the air. Moreover, in your professional life (if, indeed, you intend to make the law your profession), you will find that a memory of the names of leading cases will be of help. If you are

[11] (1889) 14 App.Cas. 337.

turning up a point of law in a practitioner's book, and happen
to remember a case bearing upon it, you will usually find that
by tracing the case through the case index you will come
upon that portion of law in the book more quickly than by
any other method.

In order, then, to lay the foundation of a sound legal
knowledge, it behoves the student to make some effort to
remember the names of the outstanding cases. Many of
these, the most important, will be acquired simply through
pondering over and discussing the cases themselves. For the
rest, the amount of energy that he puts into the memorising
of their names must be left to the individual. Certainly no
more than a very small part of his time should be devoted to
this task, and too much should not be attempted. Some men
find it useful to compile a wall chart of cases (with an
identificatory tag in brackets following the name), which they
ruminate upon over their breakfast marmalade. Or a short
recital of the cases can be recorded on tape and played back
while you shave, etc. Another suggestion is to tabulate the
cases on postcards, carrying a selection of them in the pocket
and revising them from time to time at odd moments.[12]

The precise date of a case need never be committed to
memory, but if it is a very old case the century to which it
belongs may be mentioned, for extreme old age sometimes
weakens its authority. And it may be important to say that
a case was decided before the passing of a particular statute.

THE HIERARCHY OF AUTHORITY

For my part I consider, as I have said already, that more
important than the name of the case is the rank of the court
in which it was decided. To mention the court that decided
a case is a mark of awareness of the doctrine of precedent,
with its hierarchy of authority. The rule is that every court
binds lower courts [13] and that some courts bind even themselves. In 1966 the House of Lords declared (reversing its
previous practice) that it would not be bound by its own

---

[12] The suggestion is made for memory work in general by C. A.
Mace, *The Psychology of Study*, 2nd ed., 37.
[13] *Broome* v. *Cassell & Co. Ltd.* [1972] A.C. 1027.

decisions.[14] The day after the declaration, Osbert Lancaster's cartoon in the *Daily Express* portrayed one Law Lord saying to another: " I say, Uptort, I can't get used to the fact that we can ever have been wrong." Their Lordships still haven't got used to it, and are singularly disinclined to exercise their new-found freedom.[15]

The Court of Appeal generally binds itself in civil cases,[16] but in criminal cases it is not bound by a previous decision which would work against the accused, if it is now satisfied that the previous decision was clearly wrong.[17]

When one of these appeal courts reverses or overrules a case in a court below, the case so reversed or overruled loses all authority. *Reversal* is when the same case is decided the other way on appeal; *overruling* is when a case in a lower court is considered in a different case taken on appeal, and held to be wrongly decided.

Turning to decisions of the High Court, they are binding upon inferior courts (county courts and magistrates' courts), but they do not absolutely bind the High Court itself. One High Court judge may, if he feels strongly enough, refuse to follow another High Court judge, and the result will be a conflict of authority that will one day have to be settled by the Court of Appeal. In other words, a High Court judge cannot overrule one of his brethren, he can only " disapprove " his decision and " not follow " him. Refusal to follow is, however, rare.

When two or more High Court judges sit as a Divisional Court, they regard themselves as bound by previous decisions

---

[14] *Practice Statement* [1966] 1 W.L.R. 1234.
[15] See Julius Stone in 35 M.L.R. 449; *R.* v. *Knuller (Publishing etc.) Ltd.* [1972] 3 W.L.R. 143. In *Jones* v. *Secretary of State for Social Services* [1972] 2 W.L.R. 210 their Lordships announced that they would not normally reconsider their own decisions on the construction of a statute. A Procedure Direction in [1971] 1 W.L.R. 534 requires advance warning to be given by a party to an appeal who wishes to ask the House to depart from its own precedent, presumably in order to enable the House to sit in extra strength. See M. D. A. Freeman in 121 *New Law Journal* 551.
[16] *Young* v. *Bristol Aeroplane Co.* [1944] K.B. 718.
[17] *R.* v. *Gould* [1968] 2 Q.B. 65.

of a Divisional Court [18]; but this is doubtless subject to the same exception in criminal cases as is recognised in the Court of Appeal. Presumably, the Divisional Court binds the Crown Court in its appellate jurisdiction.

Decisions of courts inferior to the High Court do not bind anybody, not even themselves.

In legal theory decisions of the Judicial Committee of the Privy Council do not bind English courts, nor even the Judicial Committee itself. But, of course, they have great persuasive authority.

My suggestion is that the student should try to remember when a case belongs to the House of Lords, the Court of Appeal (or its predecessors the Court of Exchequer Chamber, the Court of Appeal in Chancery, the Court for Crown Cases Reserved, and the Court of Criminal Appeal), or the Privy Council. Since he cannot remember everything, he can usually permit himself to forget the exact court that decided cases of authority inferior to these. Nothing is gained by trying to distinguish between the three common-law courts (King's Bench, Common Pleas, Exchequer) before 1875, or the various branches of the High Court today. He should, however, remember whether a particular rule was established by the common-law courts or by the Court of Chancery, *i.e.* whether it is a rule of common law or one of equity, for on that, important questions sometimes depend (see Chap. 2). Also, he should remember if a particular decision was simply that of a judge given by way of direction to a jury. Such decisions are of inferior authority, largely because in a jury trial questions of law are unlikely to have been fully debated. It is no longer usual to report these directions to a jury, though, as Pollock says, "many of the older ones have become good authority by subsequent approval, and some of them are the only definite reported authority for points of law now received as not only settled but elementary." [19] It may be added that directions to a jury have been more important in criminal than

---

[18] *Huddersfield Police Authority* v. *Watson* [1947] K.B. 842.
[19] *First Book of Jurisprudence*, 6th ed., 348. The old *nisi prius* cases are reprinted in Vols. 170–176 of the English Reports.

in civil law, because there used to be no appeal from a jury verdict of not guilty, and thus if on a particular point of law judges were in the habit of directing the jury in the defendant's favour the appeal court may have had no opportunity to pronounce upon it. Since 1972 the Attorney-General may refer an acquittal for the opinion of the appellate courts, but this does not affect the particular defendant.[19a]

American and overseas Commonwealth cases will sometimes be found cited in English legal treatises. Though not binding upon English courts, they have what is called " persuasive authority," particularly when English authority is lacking or unsatisfactory. Scottish decisions are generally in the same category, but they are accorded binding force on ponts common to Scots and English law.[20]

A word may also be said about international law. In studying this subject the student will be expected to know the more important decisions of international and municipal (*i.e.* national) tribunals. Always distinguish between the two, for the pronouncement of an international court is generally more authoritative for other international tribunals on a matter of international law than that of a merely national body. (But the decision of a municipal court may be more authoritative for other courts of the same State).

CIRCUMSTANCES AFFECTING THE WEIGHT OF A DECISION

The good lawyer will often make a mental note of some circumstances that go to increase or diminish the authority of a case. Among the circumstances adding to its authority are: the eminence of the particular judge or judges who decided it; the large number of judges who took part in it; and the fact that the judgment was a " reserved " one, *i.e.* not delivered on the spur of the moment. (This last is indicated in the report, at the end of the arguments of counsel, by the words *C. A. V., Curia advisari vult.*) Among the circumstances that detract from the authority of a case are: the presence of strong dissenting judgments; the fact

[19a] Criminal Justice Act 1972. s. 36.
[20] See Bentil in 35 M.L.R. 537.

that the majority do not agree in their reasoning but only in their result ; the failure of counsel to cite an inconsistent case in argument; (in old cases) the low repute of the reporter ; the disapproval of the profession ; and the fact that the case was taken on appeal and that the appeal went off on another point.[21]

These circumstances have no importance if the case is absolutely binding on the court before which it is cited and if it is incapable of being distinguished. But they are of great importance if the case is not absolutely binding, or if on the facts of the later case it is capable of being distinguished or extended at the pleasure of the court.

INTRODUCING CASES INTO AN ANSWER

Some textbooks state a proposition of law and follow it by a case in small type in a separate paragraph. Do not adopt this practice. It may be a good teaching method, but you are not teaching the examiner the law: you are showing him that you can use authorities like a lawyer. Therefore, introduce cases into your answer in literary form.

Remember that the citation of cases is not an end in itself ; it is a means to the establishing of legal principle. For this reason you should try to avoid making your written work look like a mere bundle of cases. As a matter of style, an essay that sets out the principle involved in the case before mentioning the case is preferable to one that merely blurts out one case after another without introduction. Here are two answers to the same examination question in constitutional law: both are made out of the same raw material, but observe how much more intelligible the second is than the first.

---

[21] This last-mentioned event happened with Phillimore J.'s decision on the treaty point in *The Parlement Belge* (1879) 4 P.D. 429, which is know to students of constitutional and international law. It was reversed in the C.A. on a different ground : (1880) 5 P.D. 197. Nevertheless, Phillimore J.'s decision on the treaty point is universally approved—which shows that affirmation or reversal on a different ground, though it may prevent a decision from having binding authority, will not affect the usefulness of a decision that obviously accords with principle.

Q.—To what extent is Act of State a defence in respect of acts done on behalf of the British Government which would otherwise be torts?

Answer 1.—" In *Buron* v. *Denman* [22] the defendant, a British naval commander, had set fire to Spanish slave barracoons [23] on the coast of Africa (not British soil), and his act was ratified by the Crown. It was held that the aggrieved Spaniard, being a foreigner, had no action in England, Act of State being a defence.

" In *Walker* v. *Baird* [24] the defendant, again a British naval officer, had trespassed upon the plaintiff's lobster fishery in New-foundland. In doing so he acted under the orders of the Crown. The Privy Council held that Act of State was no defence, the reason evidently being that the plaintiff was a British subject and that the act was done on British soil. A similar conclusion was reached in *Nissan* v. *Attorney-General*,[25] where the plaintiff was a British subject and the act was done in the Republic of Cyprus.

" In *Johnstone* v. *Pedlar* [26] the plaintiff was an alien resident in England. His property was seized by the police with the ratification of the Crown. The House of Lords held that Act of State was no defence."

The foregoing answer sets out the authorities but it does not clearly extract the principles from them.

Answer 2.—" Act of State is a good defence where the tort was committed by a State servant against a foreigner outside British soil, and the act was authorised or ratified [27] by the Crown. In *Buron* v. *Denman* all these conditions were satisfied. The facts were that a British naval commander fired Spanish slave baracoons on the coast of Africa (not British soil), and his act was ratified by the Crown. The defence availed.

" The law has, however, been thrown into some doubt by the decision of the House of Lords in *Nissan* v. *Attorney-General*. According to Lord Wilberforce, Acts of State are confined to ' acts committed abroad in the conduct, under the prerogative, of foreign relations with other states.' It seems that not every act authorised by the Crown will fall under this definition. Could it even be applied to the act done in *Buron* v. *Denman*?

" Discordant views were expressed in *Nissan's* case on whether the defence availed in respect of a tort committed to a British subject on foreign soil. It seems that British subjects are fully

[22] (1848) 2 Ex. 167, 154 E.R. 450.
[23] Sheds.
[24] [1892] A.C. 491.
[25] [1970] A.C. 179.
[26] [1921] 2 A.C. 262.
[27] The difference between authorisation and ratification is that the first comes before the act, and the second after it.

protected where the act is done on British soil: see *Walker* v. *Baird*, where the Privy Council held that Act of State did not excuse a trespass committed on a British subject's lobster fishery in Newfoundland.

"Equally the defence cannot be set up in respect of a tort committed against a person resident on British soil, even though that person is an alien: *Johnstone* v. *Pedlar*, H.L. (property of alien in England seized by the police with ratification of Crown; Act of State no defence)."

In writing down the name of a case it is a good habit to underline the proper names of the parties. It is because lawyers do this that the names of cases come out in italics in print. For the student the practice has two advantages. It helps him in revising, because it makes the names of the cases stand out to the eye; and it makes his examination-script easier for the examiner to read.

THE SUCCINT WAY OF STATING CASES

A difficulty that is likely to press upon the better student in dealing with cases in the examination room is that of lack of time. If a single question demands the citation of (say) a dozen cases, how can these be adequately dealt with in the time allowed? The answer is as follows: If at all possible, each case should be dealt with fully, giving in due order the principle involved in the case, its name, its facts, (possibly) the argument of counsel, or the losing argument, (possibly) the court before which the case came, the decision, (possibly) the reasons for the decision, and the *obiter dicta* (if any). If time does not allow of this there is another method. This is to state the rule of law contained in the case, and then to put a full colon, followed by the name of the case, (possibly) the court that decided it, and (in brackets) some outstanding fact or facts. This method was used for *Johnstone* v. *Pedlar* in Answer 2 above. As another instance, the case of *R.* v. *Coney*,[28] an important decision on participation in crime, could be stated as follows: " Mere presence as an onlooker at a crime does not involve a person as a party to it: *Coney*, C.C.R. (spectator at a prize fight not

[28] (1882) 8 Q.B.D. 534.

an abettor; *aliter*, perhaps, where encouragement given)."
An example from contract would be: " Where it is reasonable to accept by letter, acceptance dates from the posting:
Household Fire Insurance Co. v. *Grant*,[29] C.A. (lost letter of
allotment; held, contract to take shares was complete)."
This shows in a minimum of words that the student knows
the rule of law contained in the case and also could state the
facts more fully if he had the time. But the method should
not be used if time permits a more orthodox presentation of
the case. Stating the facts and decision in the ordinary way
occupies little more time and looks much better.

" MAY I CRITICISE? "

Some lawyers assert that no case in an appellate court can
be said to be " wrongly decided." It is the law, until
reversed or departed from. This is a mere matter of words.
Obviously one can say that the case was badly decided, or
poorly reasoned, or unfortunate in its outcome, or inconsistent with other cases. And why not say that it was
wrongly decided, thereby expressing the hope that it will be
overruled? Anyway, in university examinations you may
always criticise decided cases, and statutes as well if you
think it profitable. In professional examinations the primary
object is to test your knowledge of the present law. But
criticism is often relevant to deciding whether a case will be
followed or not. An objectionable precedent may be distinguished, or not followed, or overruled.

Lawyers are much too prone to assume that what has
been decided cannot be upset. It often happens that a plainly
wrong decision is given at first instance or even by the Court
of Appeal, which is followed unquestioningly for many years
because counsel do not advise their clients to take the point
further on appeal. When, eventually, some counsel is found
who has the courage and acumen to take the point, the
precedent is reversed.[30] Now that the House of Lords has

---

[29] (1879) 4 Ex.D. 216.
[30] *e.g. R.* v. *Gould* [1968] 2 Q.B. 65. In *R.* v. *Taylor* [1950]
2 K.B. 368 counsel had allowed his client to plead guilty on
the strength of a decision in an earlier case notwithstanding

decided that it can question its own previous decisions, there is hardly any decided point that cannot be reopened if the arguments against it are strong enough.

FURTHER READING

On the doctrine of precedent, see Rupert Cross, *Precedent in English Law* (2nd ed., 1969); Dias, *Jurisprudence*, Chap. 3.

that it was plainly erroneous. An appeal was taken against the sentence only, but, on being informed of the facts and of the earlier decision, the Court of Criminal Appeal was so surprised that it allowed the appeal to be converted into an appeal against conviction; it then allowed the appeal and overruled the precedent.

CHAPTER 7

THE INTERPRETATION OF STATUTES

The golden rule is that there are no golden rules.
—G. B. Shaw, *Man and Superman.*

FINDING THE MEANING OF WORDS

IN ordinary life, if someone says something that you do not understand, you ask him to explain his meaning more fully. This is impossible with the interpretation of statutes, because when Parliament has passed an Act the words of the Act are authoritative as words. It is only these words that have passed through the legal machinery of law-making, and individual Members of Parliament cannot be put into the witness-box to supplement or interpret what has been formally enacted. Hence the words of an Act carry a sort of disembodied or dehumanised meaning: not necessarily the meaning intended by any actual person in particular, but the meaning that is conventionally attached to such words.

The most important rules for the interpretation (otherwise called construction) of statutes are those suggested by common sense. The judge may look up the meaning of a word in a dictionary or technical work; but this ordinary meaning may be controlled by the particular context. As everyone knows who has translated from a foreign language, it is no excuse for a bad translation that the meaning chosen was found in the dictionary; for the document may be its own dictionary, showing an intention to use words in some special shade of meaning. This rule, requiring regard to be had to the context, is sometimes expressed in the Latin maxim *Noscitur a sociis*, which Henry Fielding translated: a word may be known by the company it keeps. One may look not only at the rest of the section in which the word appears, but at the statute as a whole, and even at earlier legislation dealing with the same subject-matter—for it is assumed that when

Parliament passes an Act, it probably had the earlier legislation in mind, and probably intended to use words with the
same meaning as before. Somewhat anomalously, reference
may even be made to later statutes, provided that they are
close in point of time.

A statute will often contain an interpretation section which
assigns a special meaning to some of the words used in it.
In addition, the Interpretation Act 1889 operates as a standing
legal dictionary of some of the most important words used in
Acts of Parliament. This Act declares, among other things,
that the plural includes the singular, and the singular the
plural, unless a contrary intention appears. Also, since 1889,
if not before, " man " has embraced " woman."

INTERPRETATION IN THE LIGHT OF POLICY :
" FRINGE MEANING "

When interpreting statutes the courts often announce that
they are trying to discover " the intention of the legislature."
In actual fact, if a court finds it hard to know whether a
particular situation comes within the words of a statute or
not, the probability is that the situation was not foreseen by
the legislature, so that Members of Parliament would be
just as puzzled by it as the judges are. Here, the " intention
of the legislature " is a fiction. What the court is really
doing is guessing what the legislature *would* have said on
the point *if* it had thought of it. The intention is not actual
but hypothetical. There is, of course, a limit to what a
court can do by way of filling out a statute, but to some
extent this is possible.

An illustration is the familiar legal problem of " fringe
meaning." The words we use, though they have a central
core of meaning which is relatively fixed, have a fringe of
uncertainty when applied to the infinitely variable facts of
experience. For example, the general notion of a " building " is clear, but a judge may not find it easy to decide
whether a temporary wooden hut, or a wall, or a tent, is a
" building." In problems like this, the process of interpretation is indistinguishable from legislation : the judge is,

whether he likes it or not, a legislator. For, if he decides that the wooden hut is a building, he is in effect adding an interpretation clause to the statute which gives " building " an extended application ; whereas if he decides that the hut is not a building, he adds a clause to the statute which gives it a narrower meaning. The words of the statute, as they stand, do not give an answer to the question before the judge ; and the question is therefore legislative rather than interpretative. This simple truth is rarely perceived or admitted: almost always the judge pretends to get his solution out of the words of the Act, though he may confess in so doing to be guided by its general policy. The rational approach would be to say candidly that the question, being legislative, must be settled with the help of the policy implicit in the Act.

This kind of " interpretation " may be legally and socially sound although it reaches results that would surprise the lexicographer. Thus it has actually been held that murder can be an " accident." [1] The word " accident " was being interpreted in the context of the Workmen's Compensation Act, and the result of the decision was that the widow of the deceased workman was entitled to compensation from the employer,[2] because the murder in question arose out of and in the course of the employment. The court admitted that it was giving an unusual meaning to the word, for a historian who described the end of Rizzio by saying that he met with a fatal accident in Holyrood Palace would fairly be charged with a misleading statement of fact. Similarly, Farwell L.J. remarked that one would not in ordinary parlance say that Desdemona died by accident, because " the horror of the crime dominates the imagination and compels the expression of the situation in terms related to the crime and the criminal alone." Yet, if one looks at the situation from the point of view of the victim, it is an accident, in the sense that it was not expected or intended by the victim himself. In preferring this wider meaning of the term " accident," which could

[1] *Nisbet* v. *Rayne & Burn* [1910] 2 K.B. 689.
[2] Now turned into an industrial injury benefit as part of the national insurance scheme (National Insurance (Industrial Injuries) Act 1965).

not have been found in any dictionary, the court looked to the general purpose of the Act.

IMPLYING QUALIFICATIONS UPON STATUTES: THE " GOLDEN RULE "

Judges vary in the extent to which they are prepared to modify the words of an Act to arrive at a just and sensible result. Some judges insist that statutes are to be applied literally, however absurd the consequences; it will be for Parliament to put the absurdity right. This is called the " literal rule " of interpretation. Others, more liberal in their approach, will modify the words to prevent absurdity; this is sometimes called the " golden rule." [3] The literal rule and the golden rule are not really two rules of law, for they are in flat opposition to each other. The one disregards absurdity, the other does not. They are, therefore, not fixed rules binding on the court, but rather modes of approach; and it depends on the temperament of the judge which is adopted in any particular case.

At the present time the most forceful exponent of the liberal approach to statutory interpretation is Lord Denning. He said on one occasion:

" Whenever a statute comes up for consideration it must be remembered that it is not within human powers to foresee the manifold sets of facts which may arise, and, even if it were, it is not possible to provide for them in terms free from all ambiguity. The English language is not an instrument of mathematical precision. Our literature would be much the poorer if it were. This is where the draftsmen of Acts of Parliament have often been unfairly criticised. A judge, believing himself to be fettered by the supposed rule that he must look to the language and nothing else, laments that the draftsmen have not provided for this or that, or have been guilty of some or other ambiguity. It would certainly save the judges trouble if Acts of Parliament were drafted with divine prescience and perfect clarity. In the absence of it, when a defect appears a judge cannot simply fold his hands and blame the draftsman. He must set to work on the constructive task of finding the intention of Parliament. . . . Put into homely metaphor it is this: A judge should ask himself the question: If the makers of the Act had themselves come

[3] *Mattison* v. *Hart* (1854) 14 C.B. at 385, 139 E.R. at 159.

across this ruck in the texture of it, how would they have straightened it out? He must then do as they would have done. A judge must not alter the material of which it is woven, but he can and should iron out the creases." [4]

This opinion was expressed by Denning L.J., as he then was, in the Court of Appeal. The House of Lords, however, took occasion to disapprove his views on interpretation, preferring what their lordships regarded as a more literal approach.[5] At bottom the question is how one conceives the role of the judges and of Parliament. Are the judges mere automata to give effect to the literal words of statutes at their face value, leaving an active and all-wise legislature to rectify any injustices? Or have the judges a more creative part to play in securing the just result? Whatever the theory, the hard truth is that Parliament pays little attention to the working of the law, so that if injustice occurs, decades or centuries may pass before the position is remedied by statute. Also, the literal rule has the disadvantage of making statute law an arbitrary body of rules without underlying reason. When the judges develop the common law they do so in the light of certain general principles of justice, and it seems obviously desirable that these principles should apply also to statutes, unless Parliament clearly intended to exclude them.

A good example of the golden rule in operation is *Re Sigsworth*.[6] Under legislation now contained in the Intestates' Estates Act 1952, a child has certain rights of succession on the death of the parent intestate. For the purpose of his decision in *Re Sigsworth*, the trial judge assumed it to have been proved that the deceased, Mary Ann Sigsworth, had been murdered by her son; and the question was whether the son was entitled to her estate as " issue " under the Act. The learned judge held not, for the reason that no one is entitled to profit from his own wrong. The decision was rendered somewhat easier by the fact that a similar conclusion had

---

[4] *Seaford Court Estates Ltd.* v. *Asher* [1949] 2 K.B. at 498–499.
[5] *Magor and St. Mellons* v. *Newport Corporation* [1952] A.C. 189. For a corrective, see *per* Lord Reid in *Coutts & Co.* v. *I.R.C.* [1953] A.C. at 281.
[6] [1935] Ch. 89.

already been arrived at in the law of wills: a murderer cannot take under his victim's will. In *Re Sigsworth*, the judge extended this rule to the interpretation of the intestacy statute which made no mention of it. Even statutes may be read as subject to certain fundamental principles of justice which are to be discovered in the common law.

Incidentally, *Re Sigsworth* is enough to disprove the oft-repeated assertion that " where the words of an Act of Parliament are clear, there is no room for applying any principles of interpretation." [7] This proposition may have a useful application in limiting some of the more pedantic rules of interpretation. But it does not exclude the golden rule, which, as *Re Sigsworth* shows, may be used even where the words taken by themselves are clear.

THE " MISCHIEF " RULE

The liberal approach to the construction of statutes is fortified by the " mischief " rule, otherwise known as the rule in *Heydon's* case.[8] This bids the judges to look at the common law before the Act, and the mischief in the common law which the statute was intended to remedy; the Act is then to be construed in such a way as to suppress the mischief and advance the remedy.

The practical utility of this rule depends to some extent upon the means that the courts are entitled to employ in order to ascertain what mischief the Act was intended to remedy. A true historical investigation would take account of Press agitation, party conferences, Government pronouncements, debates in Parliament, and so on; but all these are ruled out by a rule excluding evidence of the political history of a statute. In practice, therefore, the judge generally divines the object of a statute merely from perusal of its language, in the light of his knowledge of the previous law and general knowledge of social conditions.[9]

---

[7] *Per* Scott L.J. in *Croxford* v. *Universal Insce. Co.* [1936] 2 K.B. at 280.
[8] (1584) 3 Co.Rep. at 7b, 76 E.R. at 638.
[9] For a fuller statement, see *per* Lord Simon of Glaisdale in *Ealing L.B.C.* v. *Race Relations Board* [1972] A.C. at 361. An interesting example of the working of the rule is *Wycombe Marsh Garages Ltd.* v. *Fowler* [1972] 1 W.L.R. 1156.

Many statutes are the result of recommendations made by Royal Commissions and departmental committees. Can the reports of these commissions and committees be looked at as an aid to construction? In 1935 the House of Lords held them inadmissible for the direct purpose of explaining the intention of Parliament.[10] Yet in an earlier case [11] the House admitted such a report under the rule in *Heydon's* case as showing the mischief against which the Act was directed. If this is once conceded, it seems to follow that these reports are always admissible, for *Heydon's* case applies to every statute. It may be expected that the practice of referring to these reports will extend itself in the future, because they often supply the best commentary upon the wording of an Act.[12]

OTHER MODES OF RESTRICTING THE OPERATION OF STATUTES

Although the judge is supposed to adopt an impersonal attitude to statutes, he is but human and his decision will sometimes be coloured by whether he approves of the legislation or not. The judges approved the policy of the Statute of Treasons 1351, and they extended its scope to cover various " constructive treasons " as a matter of interpretation—disregarding the fact that part of the object of the statute was to clarify and limit the law, in the interest of political liberty. On the other hand the Statute of Frauds 1677 was found to work badly: designed to prevent fraud, it came to be used as an instrument of fraud. Hence the courts limited it somewhat by interpretation, and also by inventing the remarkable doctrine of part performance as an exception to the statute. These are both extreme examples, and generally judicial adaptation will work within narrower limits.

In the past the judges' attitude towards statutes has

[10] *Assam Rys. and General Trading Co. Ltd.* v. *I.R.C.* [1935] A.C. 445.
[11] *Eastman Photographic Materials Co.* v. *Comptroller-General of Patents* [1898] A.C. 571, as explained by Lord Wright in the *Assam Case* [1935] A.C. at 458–459, and followed by the Privy Council in *Dullewe* v. *Dullewe* [1969] 2 A.C. 313.
[12] Cf. *Beard* v. *Beard* [1946] P. at 26–27; *Earl Fitzwilliam's Wentworth Estates* v. *Minister of Town and Country Planning* [1951] 2 K.B. at 310; *Letang* v. *Cooper* [1965] 1 Q.B. at 240.

usually been restrictive. Pollock put this caustically when he said that the courts tend to interpret statutes " on the theory that Parliament generally changes the law for the worse and that the business of the judges is to keep the mischief of its interference within the narrowest possible bounds." [13] Since Pollock wrote the judges' outlook has changed ; but the older attitude has marked the law deeply. In particular, many rules of interpretation have a distinctly restrictive effect. One of these is the *ejusdem generis* rule, according to which, when a series of particular words in a statute is followed by general words, the general words are confined by being read as of the same scope or genus as (*ejusdem generis* with) the particular words. An illustration is one of the Sunday laws (now repealed) which provided that " no tradesman, artificer, workman, labourer or other person whatsoever shall do or exercise any worldly labour, business, or work of their ordinary callings upon the Lord's Day or any part thereof (works of necessity or charity only excepted)." On any rational interpretation, the words " or other person whatsoever " would be taken to mean what they say ; but the courts chose to confine them to persons who were of the same genus as tradesmen, artificers, workmen and labourers ; consequently professional men, such as estate agents, were not covered.[14] The effect was to leave the general words with hardly anything to do. It was no accident that this restrictive interpretation was practised on an Act that was out of harmony with the prevailing mores. At the present day legislation is rarely drafted in this " etc." form ; and, if it were, the courts would be much less inclined to interpret it restrictively. One might imagine some contexts in which general words were not intended to bear the full width of their literal meaning, and then the so-called *ejusdem generis* rule would properly be invoked ; but it would not be used for the purpose of emasculating a modern statute. In short, the " rule " is not a rule at all, in the sense that its use is obligatory ; and for modern legislation its application will probably be the exception rather than the rule.

[13] *Essays in Jurisprudence and Ethics* (1882), p. 85.
[14] *Gregory* v. *Fearn* [1953] 1 W.L.R. 974.

In interpreting statutes, various presumptions may be applied, all of which are of a negative or restrictive character. Some embody traditional notions of justice, such as the rule that a statute is presumed not to be retrospective (except in procedural matters). Others reflect what was almost certainly the intention of Parliament, as that an Act applies only to the United Kingdom unless the contrary is expressed. The most controversial presumptions are those which enshrine the values of a *laissez-faire* or capitalist society—the presumption against interference with vested rights, the presumption against the taking of property without compensation, and the presumption against interference with contract. The last of these now has few followers ; but the first two still retain vitality. So does the presumption against interference with personal liberty.

These few words are perhaps sufficient to enable the student to understand what is involved in the interpretation of statutes. A fuller account of the technical rules will be found in Odgers, *The Construction of Deeds and Statutes*.

CHAPTER 8

WORKING OUT PROBLEMS

I scarce think it is harder to resolve very difficult
cases in law, than it is to direct a young gentleman
what course he should take to enable himself so to do.

—Sir Roger North, *On the Study of the Laws.*

[Since much of the value of this chapter must depend upon
the concrete illustrations it gives, I have been forced to assume
the reader's knowledge of a certain amount of elementary law.
He should postpone reading it until he has made a start with the
study of a case-law subject like Constitutional Law, Criminal
Law, Contract or Tort.]

THE object of including problems in the examination paper
is to discover legal ability. But it is not easy even for an
intelligent candidate in the heat of the examination to show
the calm judgment that a problem requires. It is, therefore,
most important to train oneself in problem answering before
the examination. In doing so the student will not merely
be preparing in the best possible way for his examination:
he will also be developing his mind as a working instrument
and preparing himself for legal practice. As to the latter
point, the technique of solving academic problems is almost
the same as the technique of writing a legal opinion upon a
practical point. The chief difference is that in practical
problems the material facts often lie buried in a much larger
mass of immaterial detail, while the examination problem
contains comparatively little beyond the material facts.

If the student is studying under a tutor or supervisor, or
is attending a university problem class, an adequate number
of problems will be supplied to him. If not, he will have to
buy or otherwise get sight of copies of past examination
papers.

Perhaps the most important piece of advice with problems, as with all examination questions, is to *read every
word of the problem.* Almost every word has been put in

101

for a purpose and needs to be commented upon. In the law of contract, for instance, the word " orally " or " verbally " or " on the telephone," in describing the formation of a contract for the sale of land, will invite a discussion of section 40 of the Law of Property Act 1925. Even if you are of opinion that a fact stated in the problem is immaterial, you should not (in general) pass it by in silence but should express your opinion that it is immaterial, and, if possible, give reasons. However, there is no need to deal in this way with an argument that, if raised, would not receive a moment's serious consideration from the court.

FACTS STATED IN THE PROBLEM ARE CONCLUSIVE

A common query on the part of the novice when he reads an examination problem is: " How could such facts ever be proved? " The teacher's answer is that the student must assume this proof. (Actually, it is surprising how facts often can be proved in practice that at first sight seem to be unprovable if the defendant is prepared to contradict them. But in any case the student is not concerned with this question.)

The student should not assume facts *contrary* to those stated in the problem for the purpose of giving the examiner a piece of information for which he did not ask. Also, there is generally no need to assume facts that go clean beyond those given in the problem: had the examiner wanted a discussion of such facts he would have inserted them himself. Here is an example of a problem in criminal law where the examiner clearly wanted to confine the facts to a narrow compass.

X and Y, discovering that Z intended to commit a burglary in A's house, arranged together to persuade him to steal therefrom certain articles for them. Have X, Y or Z committed an offence?

The fact that the question is thrown into the perfect tense shows beyond doubt that no other facts than those stated in the first sentence are to be assumed. The question is: have they *on those facts alone* committed an offence?

An answer that assumes that X and Y have persuaded Z to steal, or that Z has stolen, will therefore miss the mark. The correct answer to the question is that X and Y are guilty of conspiring to incite (or, indeed, of conspiring to commit burglary), in other words of the ordinary crime of conspiracy. Z is not guilty of anything on these facts; he is no party to the conspiracy and has not committed any act amounting to an attempt.

OMITTED FACTS

Although supplementary facts should not, in general, be added to a problem, the case is different with what may be called omitted facts. One of the marks of a competent lawyer is his ability to know what gaps there are in the facts of his case. The solicitor, for example, when interviewing a client has to draw from him by questions many legally relevant facts that the client has not thought of disclosing. The barrister, too, may find that such facts are missing from his brief, and have to extract them from his instructing solicitor in conference. In order to train the student to look for missing facts a problem may deliberately omit something that is important. Always look for such omissions and state how your answer will be affected by the presence or absence of the fact in question. Here is a simple illustration from the law of tort.

B is A's servant. Discuss A's liability for an accident caused by B's negligence in the following cases:

   (i) B, when driving A's van, picks up his friend C and gives him a lift to the station.

   (ii) [etc.]

Two vital facts are omitted from this casually stated problem. First, we are not told what the injury was. We are to understand that owing to B's negligence an injury was sustained either by C or by some other user of the highway. But the answer may differ according as the person injured was C or some other user of the highway. This distinction should therefore be taken, and each of the two possibilities discussed separately.

Secondly, we are not told whether the station lay on or
near B's proper route, or whether it was so much off the
route that every yard he went was a yard away from his
employment and not to it. This distinction, coupled with
the previous one, yields four possible combinations of fact,
each needing discussion.

Another example of an economically worded problem,
this time taken from criminal law:

A killed his baby thinking that it was a rabbit. Discuss A's
criminal responsibility.

Here A's mistake is so extraordinary that we are justified
in wondering whether he was not insane at the time of the
deed, his insanity being an omitted fact. On the other hand
we are not positively told that he was insane: he may have
been shooting rabbits at dusk, and his baby may have
crawled out of its cot into the garden. Or, more plausibly,
A may have killed his baby in the course of a dream.[1]
The answer, then, again falls into two parts: (i) on the
assumption that A was insane, (ii) on the assumption
that he was sane. However, it is not justifiable to discuss
a problem from the angle of insanity if there is no indication
of insanity in the facts of the problem.

One more example, again from criminal law:

A, a mountaineer, roped to his fellows, cut the rope in order
to prevent them from dragging the leader of the party to death.
Discuss.

Presumably A is being prosecuted for murder; but the
question does not actually say that A's fellows were killed as
a result of what he did. We must assume that they were
killed, or at least injured, in order to create a legal problem.
Presumably, too, A sets up the defence of necessity; but
the question does not expressly say that there was no other
way of saving the leader's life, nor even that there was no
other way of saving the leader's life apparent to A. If A's
conduct was unreasonable on the facts as he knew them the
defence of necessity clearly could not apply. Finally, the
question tells us that A's object was to save the leader; it

[1] As in *H.M. Advocate* v. *Fraser* (1878) 4 Couper 70.

does not tell us whether his object was also to save himself. In other words it does not tell us whether he cut the rope above or below himself. If he cut it below himself his object was presumably to save himself as well as his leader. If he cut it above himself he presumably fell, and in that case his life was evidently saved by something approaching a miracle —at any rate, we know that he was saved because otherwise he would be beyond the jurisdiction and the question would have no legal interest. Perhaps this last doubt is irrelevant ; it may not matter whether A's object was entirely altruistic or partially self-interested. But on the other hand it may, and so the point ought to be taken.

Having thus discussed the interpretation of this problem, you would, of course, go on to consider the law relating to it.

If, as in the last illustration, you decide that a fact can be implied from the problem, though not explicitly stated, it is wise to guard yourself by stating expressly that you assume the fact to exist. For the examiner may not agree that the fact is to be implied from those given ; but he will not mind about this if he sees that your assumption is not the result of carelessness but is your considered interpretation of the question. If you are in any doubt whether a fact can properly be implied from those given you should " play safe " and take the problem each way, that is, first on the assumption that the fact exists and then on the assumption that it does not exist.

Even if all the relevant facts (in one sense of the word " facts ") are stated, what is legally called a " question of fact " may still arise on the problem—*e.g.* a question whether the defendant has, on the facts, been negligent, or whether a lapse of time is " reasonable." In a real case these would be questions for the jury (if the case were tried with a jury), although the judge might withdraw the issue from the jury if satisfied that there was no evidence of negligence or unreasonableness. On such a problem, although the student may venture an opinion as to the proper verdict on the point, and argue his opinion to the best of his ability, he should not, in the last resort, usurp the function of the

jury (or of the judge when there is no jury). In other words
he should again take the facts each way and state the legal
result following on each possible verdict. The following
problem in the law of contract illustrates the importance
of this.

A telegraphed an offer to sell his library to B for £1,000. B
telegraphed in reply: "Will give £900. B." A day elapsed in
which nothing further occurred. Then at 9 a.m. A handed to
the post office a telegram to B: "You can have the library for
£900. A." At exactly the same moment B handed to the post
office a telegram to A: "Cancel my first telegram. I will take
the library for £1,000. B." A received B's telegram at 9.30 a.m.
B received A's telegram at 9.40 a.m. What contract, if any,
exists?

Everything in this problem turns on the unobtrusive
sentence: "A day elapsed. . . ." The question is whether
this was an unreasonable delay on the part of A in replying
to B's counter-offer of £900. If it was unreasonable, the
offer (*i.e.* B's counter-offer) has lapsed, and there is no
contract. If it was not unreasonable, the offer was still alive
when A handed in at the post office his telegram of acceptance, and the contract was therefore completed at that
moment.[2] Now it is not possible to give a confident answer
to the question whether the delay was unreasonable. The
only rule of law is that an offer by telegram raises a presumption that a speedy reply is expected (*Quenerduaine* v.
Cole [3]), and therefore the lapse of a whole day would
normally be too long. But it is to be noticed that in our
problem the telegraphing business was started not by B but
by A. B may have sent his counter-offer by telegram simply
out of politeness, and not because *he* was in any hurry. It is
not certain, therefore, whether the rule in *Quenerduaine* v.
Cole would apply, though on the whole I think it would,
because I do not think that a court would speculate on the
reasons that moved B to telegraph rather than write.

There is more to say about this problem, but the essence
of it is this question of fact.

[2] *Cowan* v. *O'Connor* (1888) 20 Q.B.D. 640. Distinguish the
   Telex case, *Entores Ltd.* v. *Miles Far East Corporation* [1955]
   2 Q.B. 327.
[3] (1883) 32 W.R. 185.

It may be added that where facts are given from which the negligence or unreasonableness (or absence of it) may be inferred, you should argue from these facts in much the same way as if you were addressing a jury. But, as I have said, your opinion on this should not deter you from taking the problem each way.

TWO POINTS OF TECHNIQUE

Some examiners conclude the statement of facts in a problem with the direction to discuss it: others adopt the mannerism of requesting you to advise one of the parties. This second form of question does not mean that you are expected to bias your answer in favour of the particular party; the legal advice you give in your answer will generally be the same whichever party you are supposed to be advising. Do not use the second person in your answer—make the answer impersonal. Thus you should say " X is liable," not " You are liable."

If the examiner has exercised his fancy by using fictitious names, like Tomkins, you are perfectly entitled to abbreviate them to the initial letter—unless, of course, two parties in the same problem have the same initial letter.

RULES AND AUTHORITIES

Next, a few remarks upon the giving of reasons and authorities for an opinion. A bald answer to a problem, even though correct, will not earn many (perhaps not any) marks, because the examiner cannot tell whether the student has knowledge or is just guessing. Reasons and authorities should, therefore, always be given. Pretend to yourself that the examiner will disagree with your point of view, and set yourself to win him over by argument.

One of the most important of a lawyer's accomplishments is the ability to resolve facts into their legal categories. The student should therefore take pains to argue in terms of legal rules and concepts. It is a common fault, particularly in criminal law, to give the impression that the answer is based wholly upon common sense and a few gleanings from the Sunday newspapers. The following illustration of a question and answer in criminal law may show this.

Q.—A fire-engine driven at full speed to a fire knocks down and kills somebody. Discuss the criminal responsibility of the driver.

Student's answer.—" If the driver has been careful he is not responsible. (1) It is a well-known custom that as soon as the bell of a fire-engine is heard, other vehicles should pull up at the side of the road, in order to afford free passage. It is therefore safe for a fire-engine driver to proceed at a higher speed than would be possible for other drivers. Further (2) it is reasonable for a fire-engine to proceed quickly to a fire, for life and property may be in danger. But I do not put much weight on this second ground, for great as may be the importance of putting out a fire, it is not sufficiently great to justify the driver in leaving a trail of destruction behind him."

Upon reading this answer the examiner may well comment: " A commendable effort by an intelligent man who has not read the textbook and knows no criminal law." The answer, to be complete, should have stated the crimes for which the driver may be prosecuted (manslaughter, dangerous driving causing death, or, in the magistrates' court, driving without due care and attention); it should have stated the requirements of each crime, so far as relevant (here, the requirement of negligence in varying degrees); it should have pointed out that the burden of proving these requirements beyond reasonable doubt lies on the prosecution; and it should have cited the case of *Andrews* v. *D.P.P.*[4] It should also have discussed the possible defence of necessity, referring to it expressly by that name, not vaguely as the last two sentences of the answer do. Put into this legal setting the answer would have been first-class.

It is bad style to begin an answer to a problem by citing a string of cases. Begin by addressing yourself to the problem. If the law is clear, first state the law and *then* give the authorities for your statement. If the law is not clear, first pose the legal question and *then* set out the authorities bearing on it.

4 [1937] A.C. 576.

When citing cases, the mere giving of the name is of little use. What is wanted is not only the name but also a statement of the legal points involved in the decision, and perhaps also a consideration of its standing—*i.e.* whether it has been approved or criticised. This is so even though the case directly covers the problem. Still more is it so when the case is not on all fours with the problem. New points often occur in the law, and the lawyer in advising his client must, in effect, predict the probable decision of the court. So also in examinations: a problem is often set upon some point of law that is not covered exactly by authority. No candidate who fails to see this point can get a first class on that question. The late Dr. Coulton, in his autobiography, told a tale of a great mathematical teacher at Cambridge who met a candidate in the College court just after the Tripos. " That was a d——— good answer of yours, A, to the sixteenth question." Yes, sir, but it was a b——— good question, wasn't it? " In order to create this relationship of mutual esteem between yourself and your examiner, pay him the compliment of searching for the point of his problem. Ask yourself what is the point it raises that is not precisely covered by authority.

Failure to follow this common-sense rule is a frequent error of the tyro. Take again, for instance, the " mountaineering " problem already given (p. 104). Most raw beginners think that they have adequately solved this problem if they quote *R.* v. *Dudley and Stephens* [5] (the " Mignonette " case) and declare that necessity is no defence. But if they paused to reflect, they would discover several differences between *R.* v. *Dudley and Stephens* and the facts of their problem. It cannot be asserted with confidence that every, or even any, of these distinctions would find favour with a judge, but at any rate they are possible distinctions which would certainly be made much of by an experienced counsel for the defence. They are as follows:

(1) In *Dudley and Stephens* there was a choice as to who was to die. It will be remembered that *Dudley and Stephens*

[5] (1884) 14 Q.B.D. 273.

was the case where three men and a cabin-boy were compelled to take to an open boat after the wreck of their yacht *Mignonette*. On the twentieth day after the wreck two of the men killed the boy for food; four days later they were rescued. The two men were convicted of murder. It may be said that these facts are materially different from those in our problem, for in our problem there seems to be no choice as to who is to die: it is simply (one supposes) a question of some or all. It is true that in *Dudley and Stephens* the jury found that the boy was in a much weaker condition than the others and was likely to have died before them. But the jury did not find that the boy might not have been revived had one of the others been killed to provide food for him. So long as the boy was alive and had a chance of survival he was as much entitled to retain that chance as the others; whereas in our problem it may be that the men who are cut away have no chance of survival at all.

(2) It is not certain on the facts of *Dudley and Stephens* that the two accused would have died had they not killed the boy. All that the jury found was that had they not done so they would *probably* not have survived to be rescued. It may be that on the facts of our problem the death of the leader is certain, not merely probable, if the rope is not cut. But it must be admitted that this is not a very strong distinction, for in *Dudley and Stephens* the jury also found that " at the time of the act there was no sail in sight, nor any reasonable prospect of relief "; and it would seem that if the law recognises necessity as a defence it should proceed upon the facts as they appeared to the accused at the time.

(3) In *Dudley and Stephens* the cabin-boy was not by his own conduct, voluntary or involuntary, bringing the others nearer to death. In our problem the men whom the accused presumably sends to death are themselves dragging the leader to what will otherwise be his death. It is true that they cannot help it; but does that matter? If a lunatic attacks me, I am surely entitled to defend myself, even though he is not criminally responsible for his conduct. Also,

I am entitled to defend another. Is not our problem a case of defending another?

Another illustration, this time from the law of contract, is as follows:

> A writes to B offering to sell him his horse Phineas for £100.
> B posts a letter accepting, but he misdirects it and in consequence
> it is a week late in being delivered to A. Meanwhile A has sold
> Phineas to C. Discuss.

The ordinary beginner answers this problem simply by quoting *Household Fire Insurance Co.* v. *Grant,*[6] or some other authority to the same effect, and saying that the contract is complete on the posting of the letter of acceptance. But the whole point of the question is whether *Grant's* case applies to a misdirected letter of acceptance. I cannot help thinking that the booby who so completely misses the point of the question is often actuated by some hidden (and mistaken) motive of self-preservation. He really scents the difficulty but thinks it too hard for discussion and so conveniently pretends that he has not seen it. If this ostrich only knew, he would gain more marks *by posing the legal difficulty*, even though he suggested no solution, than he ever could by blinking it completely. If, in addition to posing the difficulty, he could say that there is no authority in point and that *Grant's* case is distinguishable, and could also suggest some reasons why on these facts it ought to be distinguished, he would get a first class on that question instead of a very doubtful pass. In all legal problems, *have the courage to argue.*

If a case falls midway between two authorities, this may indicate that there is a fundamental conflict of principle between the two authorities, and that it is necessary to hold that one of them was wrongly decided. Alternatively, you may come to the conclusion that there is a real distinction between the authorities, and in this event the problem must be looked at from the point of view of general legal principle or public policy to decide whether it should be brought under the one head or the other. This type of situation was

---

[6] (1879) 4 Ex.D. 216.

characterised by Paley, an eighteenth-century divine, as the
" competition of opposite analogies." [7]

To sum this up, when the problem is possibly distinguishable from the authority or authorities nearest in point, a
careful analysis of the possible distinction or distinctions
should always be given. This is particularly important if
the authority in question has been doubted by judges or
criticised by legal writers. It may be that the student does
not feel competent to discuss the various distinctions, but
even so the existence of the possible distinctions should be
pointed out in the answer. Moreover, distinctions should be
pointed out even though in the opinion of the student they
are not material, if it could conceivably be argued that they
are material: of course the student should express his own
opinion that they are not material.

If there is a possibility of the authority in question being
overruled, it is more important than ever to give its status
in the judicial hierarchy, as well as stating any objections
that have been urged against it.

When you have a number of cases to quote, it is generally
best to quote the nearest authority first and to allot it the
most space; the other cases can be brought more casually
into the discussion, as you have time. When you have read
a case in the reports or in a case book, do your best to
convey this fact by referring to some apposite passage
in the judgment or some other relevant detail of the report
which will indicate that you have not merely relied on a
textbook.

If you know that there is no case bearing directly upon
the problem, say so. The fact that the problem is not
covered by authority is in itself a valuable piece of information. If the authority for a proposition is a statute, say
this also, even though you have forgotten the name of the
statute.

A point can often be scored by demonstrating that the
law applicable to a problem may depend upon the court

[7] *Moral and Political Philosophy*, vi, VIII. The classical discussion of Paley's remarks is in Austin's *Jurisprudence*, 5th
ed., ii, 632–633.

before which the case comes. For example, there are some
decisions of the Court of Appeal, like that in *Musgrove* v.
Pandelis,[8] that will be followed by the Court of Appeal but
would quite possibly be overruled by the House of Lords.
Consequently, the " law " on the subject of *Musgrove* v.
Pandelis (strict liability for petrol in the tank of a car)
depends upon the number of appeals that the client is prepared
to take. This illustration shows that English law is, in a sense,
stratified. There is a great deal of law binding upon inferior
courts, a smaller amount binding on the High Court and
Court of Appeal, and less still binding on the House of Lords.
Law, like air, becomes rarefied as you ascend.

PROBLEMS ON STATUTES

A problem may be set on a statute as well as on a case. You
must then recall the words of the statute as best you can,
apply them to the problem and, as in all problems, look for
the " catch." Here is an illustration from constitutional law:

> Longshanks J., a judge of the High Court, is convicted of
> riding a bicycle at night without a light. Can he be dismissed
> from his judicial office, and if so by whom?

The attitude of students towards a problem like this
varies. Some, though knowing the terms of the Act of
Settlement, or of the similar statute now in force, steer clear
of the problem because they are afraid of it. Others write
down simply:

> By the Act of Settlement 1701, " Judges' Commissions [shall]
> be made *quamdiu se bene gesserint*, but upon the Address of
> both Houses of Parliament it may be lawful to remove them." [9]
> Longshanks J. can be removed under this provision.

This is not a bad answer and would win a comfortable
pass. Had the candidate added that dismissal was actually
effected by the Crown he might have risen to a second. To
obtain a first class, one needs to do a little thinking. Long-
shanks J. was appointed " during good behaviour." He has

[8] [1919] 2 K.B. 43.
[9] See now Supreme Court of Judicature (Consolidation) Act
1925, ss. 12, 13.

been convicted of crime, and we shall assume for the moment that he has not behaved himself within the meaning of these words. Clearly he can be dismissed if both Houses present an Address to that effect. But can he not, in this case, be dismissed even without an Address? What the examiner is evidently after is the correct interpretation of the words of the Act of Settlement, or rather of the Act now in force replacing the Act of Settlement. Do these words mean that judges can be dismissed by the Crown *only* upon an Address of both Houses (with a direction to the Houses that they are not to present an Address unless the judge has misbehaved himself)? Or do the words mean that judges can be dismissed by the Crown *either* if they have not behaved themselves (*e.g.* been convicted of crime) *or* on an Address of both Houses? In other words, are the Houses the sole judges of the correctness of the judges' behaviour, or not? The second interpretation can be arrived at by reading the provision in two parts: (1) judges' commissions are to be made for as long as they behave themselves, but if they misbehave they may be dismissed by the Crown; (2) they may be removed by the Crown on an Address of both Houses, even though they have not misbehaved themselves. The first interpretation can be arrived at by reading the provision as a whole. It may be surmised that the correct interpretation is the first; for the object of the Act of Settlement was to make the judiciary independent of the executive, and the second interpretation would tend against this object.[10] A further question that arises is whether a trivial offence like this can be regarded as misbehaviour: for if it is not, the consequence necessarily is that the judge cannot be dismissed except upon an Address.

It is often possible to display the qualities of a good lawyer without knowing much law. Here is another problem in constitutional law to demonstrate this.

A statute is passed giving power to make Orders in Council for the public safety and defence of the realm. Would it be a

---

[10] Yet Maitland, *Constitutional History*, 313, thought that the Crown can dismiss a judge for crime even without an Address. See also the note in (1946) 6 Univ. of Toronto L.J. 464–465.

valid objection to an Order made under this statute that it imposes a tax?

The type of answer to be expected from the Painful Plodder would be as follows:

" A statute similar in terms to that in the problem was DORA,[11] passed in the First World War. By Regulations under this statute the Food Controller was empowered to regulate dealings in any article. Under these powers the Food Controller ordered that no milk should be sold within certain counties except under licence. In *Att.-Gen.* v. *Wilts United Dairies* [12] the question arose whether the Food Controller was entitled to charge for the granting of a licence under this Order. It was held by the H.L. that he was not. The answer to the question is therefore ' Yes.' "

This answer exhibits a common defect; it cites a case without explaining the legal principle involved in it, *i.e.* the legal ground on which the case was decided. Plodder says that in *Att.-Gen.* v. *Wilts U.D.* it was held that the Food Controller could not charge for the licence. This is true, but we need to know why. The facts of the case contained three elements: (1) DORA, giving power to make Regulations for the public safety and defence of the realm; (2) the " daughter " Regulations made under DORA, allowing the Food Controller to regulate dealings in any article; and (3) the Food Controller's Order (" granddaughter " of DORA) that no milk should be sold without licence, coupled with his grant of a licence on condition of receiving payment. Now the decision was that the money promised could not be recovered by the Crown for the reason that (*a*) any prerogative power to tax had been taken away by the Bill of Rights 1689, and that (*b*) as for the statutory powers of DORA, the Regulations under which the Food Controller was acting did not on their wording enable him to impose a tax. The Regulations enabled him to regulate dealings in an article, but regulation of dealings is one thing, taxing another. Order (3) was therefore *ultra vires* [13] the Regulations (2). Had the candidate understood these reasons he would at

[11] The Defence of the Realm Consolidation Act 1914.
[12] (1922) 91 L.J.K.B. 897.
[13] *i.e.* " outside the powers " conferred by the enabling provision.

once have seen that the decision in *Att.-Gen.* v. *Wilts U.D.* did not conclude the question he was asked. All that the case decided was that the Food Controller was acting outside the *Regulations* since the Regulations did not give the power to tax. The question whether a Regulation that expressly gave the power to tax would itself be *ultra vires* DORA was not decided.

Now here is the answer of a gentleman who may be called the Discerning Dilettante. He knows nothing about the Bill of Rights or the decision in *Att.-Gen.* v. *Wilts U.D.*, but he addresses himself to the question and uses his intelligence.

" It may be that the Order is *intra vires* [14] the statute. The statute gives power to make Orders for the public safety and defence of the realm: in other words for the waging of war. Obviously you cannot wage war without taxing. Money, it is said, makes the sinews of war.

" To this it may be objected that although it is necessary to tax in order to wage war, it is not necessary for the Executive to tax without a statute. Parliament is still in being; why not leave taxation to Parliament?

" I think that a valid reply to this objection would be that it is a political objection to the passing of a statute worded in this wide way, not a legal objection to the validity of the Order, if a statute worded so widely has been passed. If the objection were legally valid it could be used to defeat almost all Orders made under this statute, which would be absurd. Suppose that under this defence statute the Government makes an Order requisitioning land for anti-aircraft missile sites. It would obviously be no valid objection to such an Order that the Order is not necessary for public safety because Parliament could have passed it. The object of the defence statute is to delegate to the Executive what in peacetime would be the function of Parliament. Surely the question whether Parliament could have passed the particular legislation is logically irrelevant to the question whether the legislation is for the public safety and defence of the realm.

" At the same time I do not suppose that a court would take the view that I am here expressing. The English tradition that it is for Parliament to do the taxing is so deep-seated that the court would probably brush logic aside and declare that the taxing power cannot be delegated to the Executive except by express words, and that a general formula like that in the statute stated in the question is not sufficient."

[14] " Within the powers [of]."

Or, as Atkin L.J. (as he then was) put it in *Att.-Gen.* v. *Wilts U.D.* in the Court of Appeal, " in view of the historic struggle of the legislature to secure for itself the sole power to levy money upon the subject, its complete success in that struggle, the elaborate means adopted by the representative House to control the amount, the conditions and the purpose of the levy, the circumstances would be remarkable indeed which would induce the court to believe that the legislature had sacrificed all the well-known checks and precautions, and, not in express words, but merely by implication, had entrusted a Minister of the Crown with undefined and unlimited powers of imposing charges upon the subject for purposes connected with his department." [15]

In thus unfavourably contrasting Plodder's answer with Dilettante's, I am not, of course, suggesting that book work is useless. As I have already said, book knowledge should always be used to provide a starting-point. Dilettante's answer would have been better if he could have shown that the *Wilts* case, though apparently relevant, was not conclusive on the question. The point is that although book knowledge is in itself a good thing, it is useless and worse than useless if it deflects your attention from the question that you are being asked.

RELEVANCY

When answering a problem, never preface your answer with a general disquisition on the department of law relating to the problem. Start straight away to answer the problem. Problems are set chiefly to test your ability to *apply* the law you know, and the examiner will speedily tire of reading an account of the law that is not brought into direct relation to the problem. Where the problem contains several persons, say A and B as possible plaintiffs and C and D as possible defendants, the best course is to begin your answer by writing down the heading: *A* v. *C*. When you have dealt with this, write (say) *B* v. *C*, referring back to your previous answer for any points that do not need to be repeated. Then you will deal with *A* v. *D* and *B* v. *D*.

[15] (1921) 37 T.L.R. 884 at 886.

The advice to plunge into the specific problem, on the model of counsel's opinion, applies even where the problem is divided into several parts, all of which are on the same general department of law. For instance, suppose that in criminal law a question consists of a chain of short problems on insanity numbered (i), (ii), (iii), etc. In my opinion it is not advisable to preface the answer with a discussion of *McNaughten's case*,[16] even though *McNaughten's* case is relevant to each of the numbered problems. The examiner is impatient to see you answering the problems, and he may even ignore altogether anything you write before writing down figure (i). You should therefore write the figure (i) at the very beginning of your answer, and begin to tackle problem (i). In the course of doing so you can, of course, set out and discuss *McNaughten's* case. When you come to (ii), (iii) and the rest, it will be easy enough to put a back reference, if necessary, to your previous discussion of the case.

Although a problem is not an invitation to launch out into a general disquisition on the department of law on which the problem is set, it is important in working out the problem to state all the rules of law that are really relevant to it. A frequent blemish upon an otherwise good answer is that the relevant rule of law is not expressly stated but is left to be implied from the candidate's conclusion. Much the better practice is first to state the rule of law and then to apply it to the facts. The following illustration is from the law of tort.

Q.—A, finding B, a tramp, in his shed, locks the door in order to keep B there while he fetches the police. Can B sue A?

Student's answer.—" B can sue A for false imprisonment, because no ' arrestable offence ' has been committed by anyone."

The answer and the reason given are correct, but will not earn full marks because the full rule of law has not been stated. The proper answer is:

Putting aside arrest for breach of the peace, which is not relevant here, a private person could arrest at common law on

[16] (1843) 10 Cl. & F. 200; 8 E.R. 718.

suspicion of crime only if (i) the crime suspected was of the graver class known as felonies (or an attempted felony); (ii) the suspicion was reasonable, and (iii) a felony (or attempt) of the kind suspected had in fact been committed by someone: *Walters* v. *W. H. Smith* [17] [facts]. This power of arrest is continued by the Criminal Law Act 1967, s. 2 (3), with the substitution of "arrestable offence" for "felony": an arrestable offence is defined as one for which a person may by virtue of any statute be sentenced to imprisonment for at least five years, or an attempt to commit such an offence. Theft comes within the definition. Moreover (iv) the person making the arrest must ordinarily inform the person arrested of the act for which arrest is made: *Christie* v. *Leachinsky* [18] [facts]. Here there is no suspicion of any crime—much less of an arrestable offence; nor has any crime been committed. The only legal wrong committed before B's arrest is the tort of trespass. There is, therefore, no right to arrest, and B can sue A for false imprisonment. *Aliter*, if tramps had previously stolen from A and if A reasonably suspected B of such theft; though even then A should as soon as possible communicate the grounds of arrest. This answer does not consider various specific statutory powers of arrest, which are unlikely to affect the position.

The question just considered asked: "Can B sue A?" This formula, very common in law examinations, means "Can B sue A *successfully*?" Examinees sometimes answer it by saying: "B can sue A but he will fail." This displays the writer's common sense but also his lack of knowledge of legal phraseology. It is true that there is virtually no restriction upon the bringing of actions: for instance, I can at this moment sue the Prime Minister for assault—though I shall fail in the action. But when a lawyer asserts that A can sue B, what he means is that A can sue B successfully; if he meant his words to be taken literally, they would not have been worth the uttering.

For much the same reason, you should never write a sentence like: "B can argue that . . . but the argument will fail," or "B has committed such-and-such a crime, but he has a good defence." The proper way to put the last sentence would be to say: "If B is charged with such-and-such a crime, he will have a good defence."

[17] [1914] 1 K.B. 595.
[18] [1947] A.C. 573.

When a problem is based on a rule—*e.g.* the rule in
Derry v. *Peek* [19] or *Rylands* v. *Fletcher* [20]—it is usually
advisable to state the whole rule in a sentence or two, even
though some parts of the rule are not material to the
problem. No further details should be given of parts of the
rule that are not material.

Where the problem turns on an exception to a rule (*e.g.*
an exception to the rule in *Rylands* v. *Fletcher*), there is
usually no need to state any exceptions other than the one
that is relevant.

QUESTIONS DIVIDED INTO PARTS

Questions are frequently divided into two or more parts,
and this division raises difficulties of its own for the inexpert
candidate.

Sometimes the problem begins with a common opening
part before branching out into its subdivisions. The
following is an example:

A writes to B offering to sell him his horse Phineas for £100.

(i) B posts a letter accepting, but he misdirects it and in
consequence it is a week late in being delivered to A. Mean-
while A has sold Phineas to C.

(ii) B, after posting a letter of acceptance to A, sends A a
telegram cancelling " my letter now in the post." The telegram
is delivered to A before B's letter.

Discuss.

It should be obvious that in this type of problem (i) and
(ii) are alternative possibilities, to be dealt with separately;
(ii) is not meant to follow upon and include the facts of (i).
Yet I have known students to suppose that this is all a single
problem, to be disposed of in a single breath.

Another mistake that one student made with this particular problem was to suppose that the opening sentence was
itself a question, inviting a general disquisition on the legal
nature of an offer. This, of course, is not so.

A different type of two-part problem is one in which the

[19] (1889) 14 App.Cas. 337.
[20] (1868) L.R. 3 H.L. 330.

second part begins: "Would it make any difference to your answer if . . . ?" This means that the second part of the question is the same as the first part, except for the variation expressly stated. An illustration is as follows:

(i) A is firing with an air gun in his garden at a target on a tree. The shot glances off the tree and hits A's gardener, B. Can B sue A?

(ii) Would your answer be different if the shot had been fired by A's son, C?

Most students assume that (ii) is a question as to the liability of C. Clearly on its wording the question is the same as in (i), namely, as to the liability of A.

Sometimes a problem is so worded as to involve two successive questions, but the second question logically arises only if the first is answered in a certain way. Suppose that the student has answered the first question in the *other* way; is he now to answer the second? The answer is "Yes." For the purpose of answering the second part of the question he should state that he is assuming that he is wrong in his answer to the first. An example from the law of contract:

Pickwick, who manufactures cricket bats, affixed a signboard on the boundary of the field belonging to the Dingley Dell Cricket Club, stating that if any batsman hit the signboard with a batted ball during the course of a match Pickwick would pay him the sum of £5. Podder hit the board whilst batting in a match between Dingley Dell and Muggleton, and afterwards orally requested Pickwick to pay £5 to Mrs. Jingle, to whom Podder was indebted for board and lodging. Mrs. Jingle demands payment of the £5 from Pickwick but it is refused. Discuss the rights of the parties.

This problem involves two issues: (i) whether there is a contract between Pickwick and Podder, resulting in a debt owed by Pickwick to Podder; (ii) whether Podder has validly assigned the debt to Mrs. Jingle. Issue (i) turns on the difficult distinction between consideration and the performance of a condition precedent to a gratuitous promise,[21] or if you like on the equally difficult question of intent to contract. It may well happen that the student in considering

[21] See Salmond and Williams, *Contracts* (1945), 100 *et seq.*

this comes to the conclusion that there is no contract between Pickwick and Podder. If this view is correct, issue (ii) does not really arise. All the same, it should be dealt with. It may be that the examiner disagrees with the candidate in his answer to (i), and although that may not affect the candidate's marks on (i), the candidate will lose the marks on (ii) if he does not deal with it. Even if the examiner agrees with the candidate in his answer to (i), the examiner must have meant (ii) to be dealt with, or else he would not have troubled to put it in.

A fourth kind of two-part question consists of a book-work question followed by a problem. The difficulty here is often that it is not clear whether the problem is meant to bear a relation to the book-work question or not. No universal rule can be stated, because examiners differ in their practice, but nearly always there is meant to be a connection, at least if the two parts of the question are not subdivided by numbers or letters. I am conscious that this may not sound very helpful advice. But some examinees fail to search for a connection between the book-work question and the rider, thus missing the point intended by the examiner, while other examinees, finding no connection between the two (in fact there being none), avoid the question altogether. The student must be left to steer his own course between this Scylla and Charybdis.

THE OVERLAPPING OF SUBJECTS

In a problem on criminal law, make no statement as to the law of tort, unless of course the question whether a crime has been committed involves a question of tort. Similarly, in a problem on tort make no statement as to the law of crime, unless again the existence of a tort depends on the law of crime.[22]

This mutual exclusiveness of subjects does not hold between tort and contract. Where a problem is set in a tort

---

[22] As in a problem of false imprisonment (above p. 118), or on the rule that the imputation of a crime punishable by imprisonment is actionable without proof of damage.

paper or in a contract paper involving both a possible tort and a possible breach of contract, both aspects of the matter should be discussed. This is because a tort and a breach of contract can be proceeded upon in the same action; the distinction between criminal and civil law is more deeply marked. The overlap between tort and contract should be looked for particularly in problems involving the negligent carriage of passengers by rail or sea, and the sale (or repair) of goods or houses that turn out not to be of merchantable quality or reasonably fit and that cause physical injury to the buyer (or owner).

In problems on tort and criminal law the student is expected to enumerate and discuss all the possible torts or crimes that may have been committed on the facts given in the problem, and also all the possible defences that may be raised. In this respect the answering of an examination question differs somewhat from the giving of an opinion in legal practice. A practitioner will not argue legal points unnecessarily. He will not, for example, argue the question whether there exists a tort of offensive invasion of privacy, if his client has a clear remedy in defamation. But an examiner will usually be disappointed if, in an appropriate problem, both points are not discussed. In other words, if a point is *relevant*, discuss it, even though it be not necessary.

THE ANSWERING OF PROBLEMS IN CRIMINAL LAW

Always consider all the possible crimes that have been committed, by all possible persons,[23] and all the possible defences open to them. By " possible " I mean " seemingly possible to an ignorant person." If you consider that such-and-such crime has not been committed, or that such-and-such defence is not available (though an ignorant person might think it is), do not pass it by in silence but state your opinion expressly. You should also give the reason for your opinion as shortly as the importance of the point seems to require. The reason for this advice is that quite possibly

---

[23] Unless, of course, the problem specifically asks for the criminal responsibility of some only of the *dramatis personae*.

the question was set as a trap, and if you refrain from commenting upon the trap the examiner may think that you have avoided it by good luck rather than good management.

Never come to the defences until you have stated the crime for which the defendant is in your opinion being charged. Start with the responsibility of the perpetrator, taking secondary parties afterwards.

If you think that the problem leaves open some question of fact, state the law according as the fact is present or absent.

If the outcome is clear you can say so—*e.g.* " D is guilty of burglary." But if the application of law to fact is not clear, you need not state a definite opinion or even " submit " that the position is so-and-so. Instead, consider whether there is any evidence for the jury (sufficient to require the judge to leave the case to the jury); if there is, explain how the judge would direct the jury, and state whether a verdict of guilty would be likely to be upheld or upset on appeal. It is at these points in a jury trial that the legal opinion is important: a lawyer is not *directly* concerned with the work of the jury.

Often the problem will be found to fall short of one of the major crimes. In such a case it will very frequently involve a lesser or lesser-known crime. The student should note these lesser or narrower crimes very carefully when they are mentioned in his book. Here is a short list of them.

An act that falls short of:	may be:
Manslaughter	Assault and battery (O.A.P.A. 1861, s. 47).
	Offences under Road Traffic Act 1972;
	section 1, causing death by dangerous driving;
	section 2, dangerous driving;
	section 3, careless driving;
	section 5, driving " under the influence."
	Excessive speed (Road Traffic Regulation Act 1967, s. 78A, inserted by Act of 1972, s. 203).

An act that falls short of:	may be:
Murder	Abortion (O.A.P.A. 1861, s. 58).
	Child destruction (Act of 1929).
	Concealment of birth (O.A.P.A. 1861, s. 60).
	Infanticide (Act of 1938).
	Manslaughter (O.A.P.A. 1861, s. 5).
	Manslaughter on account of diminished responsibility (Homicide Act 1957, s. 2).
Attempted murder (O.A.P.A. 1861, s. 15)	Assault and battery.
	Wounding, etc., with intent to maim, etc. (O.A.P.A. 1861, s. 18 as amended by Criminal Law Act 1967, Sched. 3).
	Malicious poisoning resulting in danger to life, etc. (O.A.P.A. 1861, s. 23).
	Malicious wounding, etc. (O.A.P.A. 1861, s. 20).
	Occasioning actual bodily harm by an assault (O.A.P.A. 1861, s. 47).
	Malicious poisoning with intent to injure, etc. (O.A.P.A. 1861, s. 24).
	Robbery (Theft Act 1968, s. 8).
	Offence under Prevention of Crime Act 1953 or Firearms Act 1968.
Criminal Damage (Criminal Damage Act 1971)	Cruelty to animals (Protection of Animals Act 1911).
	Theft (Theft Act 1968).
Burglary (Theft Act 1968, s. 9)	Theft.
	Going equipped for stealing (Theft Act 1968, s. 25).
	Being found in a building, or in an enclosed yard or garden, for any unlawful purpose (Vagrancy Act 1824).
Theft (Theft Act 1968, s. 1)	Removal of articles from places open to the public (Theft Act 1968, s. 11).
	Taking motor-vehicle or other conveyance (Theft Act 1968, s. 12).
	Obtaining property by deception (Theft Act 1968, s. 15).
	Obtaining pecuniary advantage by deception (Theft Act 1968, s. 16).
	False accounting (Theft Act 1968, s. 17).
	Fraudulently retaining a letter (Post Office Act 1953, s. 55).
	Unlawful pawning (Pawnbrokers Act 1872).

An act that falls short of:	may be:
Robbery (Theft Act 1968, s. 8)	Assault and battery: aggravated assaults; carrying weapons. Blackmail (Theft Act 1968, s. 21). Threatening letters (O.A.P.A. 1861, s. 16).
Obtaining property or pecuniary advantage by deception (Theft Act 1968, ss. 15, 16)	False accounting (Theft Act 1968, s. 17). Offences under Trade Descriptions Act 1968.
Forgery Coining (Coinage Offences Act 1936)	Theft, obtaining property by deception. False trade description (Trade Descriptions Act 1968, s. 1).

When several crimes appear to emerge from the facts of a problem, it is best to start your answer with the gravest crime that seems clearly to have been committed. For it would be absurd to open your answer by considering some summary offence of which the defendant is guilty, and then to wind up with the conclusion that he has also committed, say, murder! The murder should come first, and the summary offence as a rather casual postscript. If the defendant is clearly guilty of a crime like wounding with intent, and only doubtfully guilty of murder, it is sensible to start with the clear crime before coming to the doubtful one.

Problems in criminal law often start with an inchoate crime—conspiracy, attempt or incitement. Even though the problem shows that the full crime was consummated, the culprits may be convicted of attempt or incitement, so that it may be relevant to mention these crimes—though normally, of course, the indictment would be for the completed crime, not for a mere attempt or incitement. If you mention the possibility of a conspiracy charge, it would be wise to add that the judges frequently disapprove the addition of conspiracy counts when the crime is consummated. As for incitement, if the crime is actually committed the inciter becomes an accessory to it. In other words, the difference between (i) incitement and (ii) being a participant in a crime as one who has counselled or procured it is that in (i) the main crime has not been (or need not have been) committed by the person so incited, and in (ii) it has.

THE ANSWERING OF PROBLEMS IN TORT

As in criminal law, look for all the possible torts that may have been committed, and consider whether their essentials have been satisfied. Draw into your net all possible defendants, and then turn round and consider all the possible defences open to them on the facts given.

There are not so many " obscure " torts as there are obscure crimes, but a considerable overlap occurs between some of the leading torts. The following are the chief examples:

Nuisance.	Negligence.
Rylands v. *Fletcher.*	Contractual duty to use care.
Negligence.	
	Negligence.
	Breach of statutory duty.
Defamation.	
Offensive invasion of privacy	
[—at present non-existent.]	Conversion.
Slander of title.	Detinue.
Malicious falsehood.	Trespass to goods.

In the tort of negligence, it is frequently necessary to consider the machinery as to proof of negligence—the burden of proof, functions of judge and jury, *res ipsa loquitur.* Questions of negligence, contributory negligence and remoteness of damage are frequently wrapped up together, and so are questions of contributory negligence and *volenti non fit injuria*, and of necessity and private defence.

If the problem appears to be a novel one, it may raise the theory of general liability in tort.

CHAPTER 9

ANSWERING BOOK-WORK QUESTIONS

> He that knows, and knows not that he knows, is
> asleep—wake him.
>
> —Anon.

THIS chapter is chiefly concerned with the answering of
questions other than problems, though some of the remarks
apply also to the answering of problems. Like the last
chapter it is not meant for hasty consumption immediately
before the examination. The wise student will at the outset
of his course buy copies of his examination papers for the
past few years (unless he is supplied with a digest of them by
his instructor), and, whether compelled to or not, will write
out the answers to some questions (even though only in brief
note form) in order to gain practice in self-expression. Past
examination papers will also show him the probable lay-out
of the paper that he will be expected to answer, and the
amount of time likely to be allowed on each question.

SUBDIVIDED QUESTIONS

If your question is expressly divided into several sub-
questions, answer each sub-question separately ; and if the
sub-questions are numbered (i, ii, iii) or lettered (*a, b, c*)
number or letter them in the same way in your answer. A
question may be divided into parts even though numbers or
letters are not used. For instance, the question—

Summarise the provisions of, and the changes introduced by,
the Misrepresentation Act 1967.

—invites an answer in two parts: (1) the provisions of the
Act ; (2) its impact on the previous law. It would be wise
to write your answer under these two headings. Always
model your answer to conform to the question ; do not, for
instance, on this particular question adopt the chronological
order of (1) the pre-Act law, and (2) the Act. The reason is

that if the examiner is reading your script quickly (and he
may have hundreds of scripts to mark) he may be puzzled
and annoyed by your departure from the order of his question. Besides, he may have set the question like that with
the object of seeing whether your mind is sufficiently
adaptable to vary the order of what you have learnt.

RELEVANCY

In answering a question you should, of course, give as much
detail as you can within the limits of the question. It is
sometimes possible to answer a question literally in a couple
of sentences, but this will not always impress the examiner.
The extreme example of this kind of answer is the story
told by Mark Twain, in his *Life on the Mississippi*, of his
piloting lesson.

" Presently Mr. Bixby turned on me and said: 'What is the
name of the first point above New Orleans?'
" I was gratified to be able to answer promptly, and I did.
I said I didn't know."

Not many candidates would attempt this frankness in the
examination room, but they often do suppose that an
accurate answer directed to the very words of the question is
all that is required. This is frequently a mistake. For
instance, in the law of contract the question, " What is the
difference between void and voidable contracts? " can be
accurately answered by saying that a void contract is an
apparent contract that is in truth no contract at all, while a
voidable contract is a contract that is capable of being
avoided at the option of one party. This, though accurate,
would not score many marks. It is an accurate statement
of the difference of *definition* between void and voidable
contracts, but it says nothing of their different *effects*. The
candidate should, therefore, add, as a minimum, a discussion
of such cases as *Cundy* v. *Lindsay* [1] and *Lewis* v. *Averay* [2]
in order to illustrate the effect of each kind of contract (or
apparent contract) upon third-party rights. To put this

[1] (1878) 3 App.Cas. 459.
[2] [1972] 1 Q.B. 198.

advice generally, if you are asked to distinguish between two legal concepts or institutions, you should give not only the difference of definition but also the difference of legal effect.

It need hardly be added that the examiner *always* wants reasons and authorities for the answer, even though he does not expressly ask for them.

To say that a question should be answered fully is not to say that irrelevant matter should be introduced into the answer. Questions are often worded to cover only a fragment of a particular subject; in that case the examiner does *not* want the whole of it.

This question of relevancy is often the examinee's greatest headache. Often he has to interpret a badly worded question, with no hope of redress if his guess as to the examiner's meaning should turn out to be wrong. My advice is this. If the question is reasonably clear do not wander outside it. If there is a doubt as to its meaning, the question will usually have at least a central kernel of meaning that is relatively clear. Answer this to begin with. Then, as to the doubtful " shell " of the question, if you still have time to write on the question, you should expressly point out the doubt in your mind as to what you are being asked, and proceed to write on the doubtful part of the question for the rest of the allotted time. If, on the other hand, you have no time left for the doubtful part of the question, declare your doubt whether the question was intended to have any further scope, and leave it there. The fact that you have been able to spend your whole time on the core of the question is itself some indication that the question was not intended to have any wider scope.

For instance, suppose that a question in the law of contract is:

Discuss the maxim, *In pari delicto potior est conditio defendentis.*

Clearly this invites a discussion of the general rule preventing recovery of money paid or property transferred under an illegal contract, and this rule, with its exceptions

and quasi-exceptions, should therefore be discussed first. The
problem then arises: does the question cover also the general
rule against suing for damages for breach of an illegal
contract? However you decide this conundrum, you should
state your decision in the answer. If you rule this second
topic out of order, and the examiner wished it to be included,
the examiner will at least see that you have had the point
present in your mind, and will probably also be brought to
see that he was at fault in his wording of the question. In
any case, the proper limits of time for the question should
not be exceeded.

If in doubt whether a particular matter is relevant, a
good test is to ask yourself whether, if the examiner had
wished you to discuss it, he would naturally have framed an
extra question upon it.

Once the limits of the question are settled, do not canter
beyond them. The examiner cannot give credit for irrele-
vancy, because that would be unfair to others who have
answered only the question that they were asked. There is,
however, a clever way in which matters otherwise irrelevant
may be lightly introduced. This is by the method of com-
parison. For instance, if in constitutional law you are
directed to write a note on the " kangaroo " (a method of
curtailing discussion in the House of Commons), a discussion
of the closure and guillotine (two other methods of curtailing
discussion) would generally be out of order. But a com-
parison of the kangaroo with the closure and the guillotine
would be admissible, and credit would be given for it.

Many students begin an answer with a prologue. Cut it
out. Thus, if you are asked the history of the action of
assumpsit, do not begin with a paragraph on the medieval
precursors of *assumpsit*—debt, detinue and account. If the
questioner had wanted these he would have said so. If
you are asked to discuss, say, *Nordenfelt's* case,[3] begin by
setting out the facts and decision—do not start in the
Middle Ages. Having stated the case you may legitimately
put it into its historical setting in order to show what

[3] [1894] A.C. 535.

advance it made on the previous law; and you may also
indicate the trend of development that it started. But all
this depends on the time you have left after giving your
attention to the centre of the question.

Students (particularly advanced students) are frequently
vexed by doubts as to the amount of detail that they should
put into their answer. The best advice is: aim at concen-
trating all your intelligence on the specific question, and bring
in your knowledge only so far as it is relevant. If you show
that you are a master of the *relevant* knowledge, the examiner
will readily give you credit for knowing the rest of the
subject. An example would be the question: " ' The jury is
a historical anachronism.' Discuss." This is not an invitation
to give the whole history of the jury system: the question is
whether the jury *is* a historical anachronism. Are there any
features of the modern jury that can be explained only as
historical survivals, which are out of place in modern
society, or has the jury been so adapted that it is a truly
modern institution?

Again, should you assume that your examiner is an
ignoramus and explain everything to him, or can you assume
that he is a lawyer so that a hint is sufficient?

The answer lies somewhere between these two extremes.
On the one hand, the examiner wants to be told *nothing* that
is irrelevant to the question. On the other hand, he is
suspicious of nutshell knowledge and footnote knowledge,
and he wants as full an explanation of everything that *is*
relevant as is possible in the time allowed. More specifically,
the following rules may be laid down.

(a) If a legal concept is mentioned in the question, do not
attempt a full explanation of it unless explanation is
requested or necessitated by the question. For instance, on
a question involving a law of wagers, there is generally no
need to discuss what is a wager. Had the examiner wanted
such a discussion he would have asked for it in a separate
part of the question. On the other hand, a question in the
form of a quotation with a request for discussion normally
requires an explanation of everything in the quotation. Thus
the question—

—demands a detailed explanation of impeachment as well as of the convention of ministerial responsibility and of the reasons why the second replaced the first.

(b) If the legal concept is not mentioned in the question but is first introduced by the candidate in his answer, it should be explained. Take, for instance, the question: " When will the right to avoid a voidable contract be lost? " It is not enough, in the course of answering this question, to mention that the right will be lost if *restitutio in integrum* ceases to be possible. You must not assume that the examiner knows what *restitutio in integrum* means. Tell him what it means, and when such *restitutio* ceases to be possible.

GETTING AT THE POINT

Before unmuzzling your wisdom on any question, ponder the question carefully. Very often the examiner will have worded it in a particular way in order to enable you to show a little originality of treatment. Take, for example, the following question in criminal law.

" The use of impeachment at law as a method of control of the Executive by the Commons has been replaced by the convention of ministerial responsibility to Parliament." Comment.

Discuss the decision in *R. v. Dudley and Stephens* from the standpoint of the purposes of criminal punishment.

This is not simply a question on the decision in *R. v. Dudley and Stephens*, as most men seem to think, nor even is it simply a question on the defence of necessity in general. It is a question, primarily, on the purposes of criminal punishment. You are requested to set out the different theories of the purposes of criminal punishment (general and particular deterrence, incapacitation, reformation, ethical retribution) and to consider whether any of these theories can be used to support the conviction in *R. v. Dudley and Stephens*.

Another " angle " question, this time from constitutional law:

What parallels may be drawn between royal prerogative and parliamentary privilege? Examine, in particular, the attitude of the court in questions concerning (a) their exercise, and (b) their extent.

I have marked hundreds of scripts in which the answer offered to this question was a formless mass of cases and propositions concerning prerogative and privilege. These candidates simply vomited over the page everything they knew upon the two topics; they made no attempt to bring their knowledge into relation with the question, and did not even divide off their answer by the (a) and (b) of the question. The following is a skeleton of the answer that an examiner wants. It should be within the competence of every student of moderate ability who has worked properly and who directs his mind to what he is being asked:

Prerogative and privilege are somewhat similar in definition. Prerogative may be defined as the exceptional position of the king at common law. Privilege is the exceptional position of the two Houses of Parliament and of their members at common law *and by statute*. There is, of course, a difference of content between prerogative and privilege.

Turning to (a) in the question, the rule is that the court will *not* inquire into the *mode of user* of an undoubted prerogative or privilege. [Demonstration of this by decided or hypothetical cases.]

As to (b), the rule is that the court *will* inquire into the *limits* of both prerogative and privilege. [Similar demonstration of this.]

Both prerogative and privilege are subject to statute. [Demonstration.]

It may seem unnecessary to add: if given a choice, do not attempt to answer a question that you do not understand (unless, of course, your plight is such that there is no other you can do instead). This may seem obvious advice, but it is often ignored. The following, taken from a constitutional-law paper, is a good example of the " wrapped-up " question.

" Much of the structure of the Constitution is now mere form; it is tolerated only because in practice its form is no indication of the way it functions."
Comment.

What does this question mean? If it conveys no clear meaning to you, avoid it. For if you attempt to answer

it and miss the point, the examiner may not be able to
give you any marks, because you will not have answered
his question. Actually the question is on our old friends,
the conventions of the constitution. It is an invitation to
enumerate the conventions and to contrast them with the
law. Once the meaning is penetrated, the writing of the
answer is easy.

Often the answer to a fearsome-looking question can be
divined by a little patient thought. Here are two specimens,
again from constitutional law.

What is the constitutional importance of the power to dissolve
Parliament?

Very probably you have never given a moment's thought
to this question. But that does not mean that you must
stand mute to it. Just ponder for a moment. Probably
you know that, under the Parliament Act, Parliament lasts
for five years unless sooner dissolved by the Crown, and
that the Crown acts on the advice of the Government of
the day. We are asked to state the constitutional importance
of this power possessed by the Government. Very well: to
find the importance of x, the obvious thing to do is to
consider what would happen if x were not present. Let
us consider what would happen if the power to dissolve
did not exist. Clearly Parliament would last its full five
years and the Government could not bring it to a premature
end. One result would be that the Government could not
time a general election to its own advantage, going to the
country at the moment when it feels most popular ; so
Governments might change more often. More important
would be the effect on private members. Suppose that
within the five-year term the Government were defeated
in the Commons on a topic so important that it regarded
it as a matter of confidence in itself. As things are the
Government has the choice of either (a) resigning or (b)
advising a dissolution—*i.e.* going to the country. If there
were no power to dissolve it could only resign, and a new
Government would have to be formed from the ranks of
the existing House of Commons. What would be the

consequence of that? A moment's reflection will show that it would make private members more independent. Government back-benchers do not like elections; they prefer a quiet life. It is the fear of an election that at present prevents them in many instances from disobeying their party whip. If they knew for certain that a vote of censure could not result in a general election, but would simply bring about a reshuffle in the Government, their conduct would probably change. Governments would have to give way more often to the opinions of back-benchers, and not force every measure through as a matter of confidence. But it might occasionally happen that, rather than give way, the Government might prefer to reconstruct itself as a Coalition Government with the support of some middle-of-the-road members of the Opposition. This might cause a fragmentation of the present essentially two-party system, though in time our electoral system would probably cause the re-emergence of two opposing parties.

If you happen to know that it is the Prime Minister personally who advises the Queen to dissolve Parliament, you will realise that this gives him the whip hand over other members of the Cabinet—who fear the cataclysm of an untimely election as much as back-benchers do. Without power to dissolve Parliament, the Prime Minister could more readily be induced to resign in favour of a rival within the same party. Is it too imaginative to suppose that all these consequences would follow an abolition of the power to dissolve? If they would, we have demonstrated the importance of the power. It is the existence of the power that ensures the supremacy of the Cabinet and of the Prime Minister within the Cabinet. Whether they are *too* supreme is another question.

The second conundrum is:

What evidence is there that in the early eighteenth century there was lacking a true realisation of the problem of responsible government?

This sounds appalling. But many of my readers know the answer, if they will but think hard enough. The eighteenth century was born in 1700. An obvious expedient

is to run through the years after 1700, and to stop and
consider when one of them rings a bell in the memory.
1700 . . . 1701 . . . 1701 was the year of the Act of Settlement. What did the Act do?   Among other things, as every
student of constitutional history knows, it provided that
no person with an office or place of profit under the King
was to sit in the House of Commons, and that everything
done in the Privy Council should be signed by those taking
part.[4] Both those provisions were aimed against the Cabinet
system. . . . There you have the answer to the question.

CRITICISM

When the question quotes a statement and asks for a discussion of it, do not be afraid to criticise the statement if
you think it is open to criticism.   As often as not the
examiner will have disagreed with the statement himself ;
that is why he thought of setting it.

DOUBT

Where the law is doubtful, a categorical statement that the
rule is one way or the other will earn few, if any, marks.
This is particularly important in answering problems.   If
the answer to the problem is doubtful, say so, and then
suggest what the answer ought to be.   It is a mistake to
simulate confidence where you have no certain knowledge.

Conversely, to state the law as doubtful when it is not
doubtful will also be penalised in marks.   Excessive caution
is therefore as much to be avoided as excessive dogmatism.
This may seem obvious, but I have known students repeatedly
use the phrase " I respectfully submit " before some trite
proposition or other, purely out of affectation.   Even words
like " seemingly " or " probably " are out of place if the
law is clear.

Strictly, a submission (" I submit that . . . ") is an
argument advanced in court.   Lawyers grow so accustomed
to the phrase that they use it even in legal writing, where it
is somewhat absurd.   A writer need not pay the exaggerated

[4] Maitland, *Constitutional History*, 292, 390.

deference to his reader that an advocate does to a judge.
Some writers carry humility even further: when they wish to
express an opinion but feel that the first person singular is
too assertive, they use the plural (" we submit "). It is not
proposed to discuss the aesthetics of this usage for the text
writer [5]; all that I wish to say is that it should not be
copied by the student, for in his mouth it sounds too grandi-
loquent. Naturally, one desires to suppress the personal
element so far as possible, but if one has an opinion to
express there is nothing to offend anybody in a straight-
forward " in my opinion." Alternatively, expressions like
" it is thought that " or " there are good grounds for saying
that " or " it follows from the authorities that " can be used.

THE ARRANGEMENT AND WORDING OF THE ANSWER

Try to make your answer attractive. Examiners are human
beings, and they are easily bored. If a question is capable
of being answered in a sentence, answer it immediately in
that sentence and proceed to explanation afterwards. Within
limits, it is permissible (and often desirable) to divide up
the answer into numbered " points," with subheadings under-
lined. This both saves your time and enables the examiner
to see without effort how you have treated the subject. But
the process of subdivision should not be pushed too far.
An answer that is excessively divided and subdivided gives
an unpleasant impression that the candidate has simply
learned a crambook or correspondence course by heart.

Lecturers and text writers often indulge in what R. L.
Stevenson called " a little judicious levity." The student,
who usually cannot distinguish between the judicious and the
injudicious sorts, should avoid levity altogether. He should
likewise shun all colloquialisms and colloquial abbreviations
(" it's," " isn't," etc.). In short, the student should write his
script upon the model of a counsel's opinion or judge's
judgment, with gravity and decorum.

A few remarks may be made about citing authorities.

[5] But I cannot forbear to record the observation that the use
of " we " should be confined to kings, editors and women in
the family way.

Never quote the textbook for an established principle of law. A sentence like " Every simple contract needs consideration to support it, as Cheshire and Fifoot point out," is infantile. Textbooks should be quoted only if they express an individual opinion, and the lecturer (*qua* lecturer) not at all. When quoting authors, if the author is dead he may be referred to by his surname only, but if he is still with us it is polite to give him a handle—Sir or Prof. or Dr. or Mr. As regards judges the customary J., etc., should be used irrespective of whether they are alive or dead.

If you cross out some words and subsequently wish to restore them, the accepted way of doing it is to put dots underneath the words so deleted and to write " *stet* " [6] in the margin.

The commonest grammatical error (if it is an error) is the split infinitive. Fowler divided the English-speaking world into (1) those who neither know nor care what a split infinitive is ; (2) those who do not know, but care very much ; (3) those who know and condemn ; (4) those who know and approve ; and (5) those who know and distinguish. Most examinees belong to the first class, most examiners to the third. Whatever the merits of the dispute, the safe course for the student, as for every writer who does not wish to risk offending the susceptibilities of his readers, is to avoid splitting infinitives. A split infinitive occurs when a word (usually an adverb) is placed between the word " to " and a following verb, as in " to really understand." On grammar and style in general, Fowler's *Dictionary of Modern English Usage* is an invaluable guide ; a more recent competitor (excellent value at 45p) is Eric Partridge's *Usage and Abusage*. Other useful works are H. W. and F. G. Fowler's *The King's English*, and *Good English* by G. H. Vallins.

Lastly, a word on handwriting and orthography. Some people write atrociously. If you feel apprehensive on this, give a page of your notes to a friend and ask him to tell you which letters or words in your handwriting gave him difficulty in reading. Make a special effort to improve them.

[6] " Let it stand."

If you have reached the stage of your university or professional examinations without being able to spell you probably never will be able to spell, but at least observe the correct spelling of the words commonly used in legal discussions. The following passage contains a number of misspelt words taken from examination scripts. If you feel weak in this respect, pick out the words which you think are misspelt and write your own version. Compare your effort with the key on page 141.

" The Homocide Act does not effect this problem, for the Act has not superceded the common law on the point. The question that ocurrs here is whether responsibility is deminished because there is a likelyhood that the provokation would have lead a reasonable man to loose his self-control and inflict this grievious harm. The correct answer is difficult to gauge. An analagous case is *Brown,* where something like these facts occured. The acussed alledged that he could not forsee the harm he would do, and proceeded to argue that since he acted inavertently, he did not committ the offence. The prosecution tried to rebutt this defence by offerring evidence of an admission by the accused. There was a legal arguement on this, and the evidence was ajudged not to be admissable. The defendent appealed but the judgment of the court was against him. On the principle question in the case, the concensus of the judges was that the authorities against the existance of the defence were irresistable, but perhaps this payed too little regard to the paralell rule for the priviledge of self-defence. I beleive it would be indefensable to assert that the court leant it's authority to the test of reasonableness. In any case, it is permissable to observe that one cannot regard the same problem as occuring here. As to the wife, she is now treated seperately from her husband, and her responsibility is independant of his. Her ommission to help the victim definately does not mean that she abetts the crime, or is an accessary to it. In the absense of other facts, she is not guilty."

Key to spelling test on page 140: Homicide affect superseded occurs diminished likelihood provocation led lose grievous analogous occurred accused alleged foresee inadvertently commit rebut offering argument adjudged admissible defendant principal consensus existence irresistible paid parallel privilege believe indefensible lent its permissible occurring separately independent omission definitely abets accessory absence.

The rule for verbs ending in the sound *-er*, such as *offer*, *prefer*, *occur*, is to double the *r* for the *-ed* and *-ing* endings if the accent is on the *-er* syllable, but not otherwise. Thus *prefer*, *occur*, make *preferred*, *preferring*, *occurred*, *occurring*, but *offer* makes *offered*, *offering*.

To express the sound *ee*, the rule is: *i* before *e*, except after *c*. So: *achieve*, *believe*, *grievous*; but *deceive*, *receive*.

The word *foresee* takes an *e* in the middle, but you can write either *forgo* or *forego*. *Judgment* is spelt correctly, but an alternative spelling is *judgement*. The rule generally followed in dictionaries is that mute *e* is dropped before suffixes beginning with a vowel (*e.g. deplorable*, *likable*, *movable*, *notably*, *ratable*, *milage*), but not before suffixes beginning with a consonant. (*statement*). Statutes do not altogether follow the former rule: " rateable value " is an established statutory spelling. Mute *e* is generally retained after soft *c* or *g* (*e.g.* unenforceable); so *judgement* should really be the preferred spelling.

Gauge and *appealed* are spelt correctly; note also *appeal*, *appellant*, *appellate*.

The adjectives *dependent* and *independent* take an *e* in the final syllable, but the noun *dependant* (meaning one who is dependent on another for his bread and butter) takes an *a*.

Note that *criteria*, *data* and *dicta* are plural words: the singulars are *criterion*, *datum* and *dictum*. Say " this dictum," not " this dicta." Treating *data* as singular (as many Americans do) makes it difficult to speak clearly of " this particular datum " as opposed to " the rest of the data."

CHAPTER 10

IN THE EXAMINATION ROOM

Examinations are formidable even to the best prepared; for the greatest fool may ask more than the
wisest man can answer.

—C. C. Colton, *Lacon*.

BEFORE starting to write, read through the whole of the
examination paper and jot down in the margin the names of
plaintiffs in any relevant cases you remember, the dates of
statutes and any other details that are likely to elude you
when you come to write out the question. You thus give
your memory two chances of recalling the elusive details.
Also, if during the examination you think of any fresh
authorities that you do not propose to incorporate at once
in your script, make a similar note of them on your question
paper. Some men (and more women) leave the examination
room complaining that at one stage they remembered a
case, but later forgot to cite it. The practice above
suggested should obviate this.

The most important general piece of advice on examinations is that every question in the paper that the student
is expected to and can answer should be answered. He
should not spend all his time on a few only of the questions.
There is nothing more tedious for the teacher than to hear
one of his best men saying, after the examination: " Oh,
I did very well, but I only had time to answer half the
paper." In nearly all examinations the scripts are not
judged simply on the questions that the student has answered,
where he has not answered all he was expected to answer.
On the contrary, the total possible marks are divided
equally among all the questions, and no answer can earn
more than the appropriate marks for that question. The
result is that a student may have answered half the paper
in a manner worthy of a Law Lord, and yet obtain a third

class because he has not answered the other half. Another point to be remembered in this connection is that an examiner is much more willing to give the first 50 per cent. of marks on a question than the second 50 per cent., and full marks are practically never given. A man may, therefore, get 50 per cent. on the whole paper if he answers all the questions moderately well, whereas he certainly will not get 50 per cent. if he answers half the questions almost perfectly. For the good man, therefore, there is nothing more important in examination technique than dividing up his time as equally as may be between all the questions.

The same remark applies to questions containing two or more distinct parts. Here the examiner will probably have divided up the possible marks in his mind among the component parts, and an answer to one part, be it ever so brilliant, can earn only the appropriate total for that part. It is, therefore, most important to search for all the possible angles to a question, and this involves reading the question with meticulous care.

THE CHOICE OF QUESTIONS

All law examinations give a certain choice of questions.

Sometimes questions of enormous width are found in the paper. They are meant for the pass man. If the first-class man attempts them, he will usually find that the answer required is so long that it will throw his whole script out of balance.

Where there is a choice between problems and book-work questions, there are two reasons why the better candidate should prefer the problems, First, they are usually shorter to answer, and so save time. Secondly, an examiner tends to be grudging in his marks for book-work questions, which he knows do not require much intelligence in the answering. A good answer to a problem, on the other hand, at once evokes his admiration.

There is, it is true, a certain danger in problems, for if the point of the problem is completely missed the result may be catastrophe. But a good man should be able to sense whether he is getting the point of the problem or not. If the problem to his eyes appears " pointless," he had better exercise his choice elsewhere in the paper.

Perhaps I should add a corrective to the foregoing paragraph. I said that if the point of a problem is completely missed the result may be catastrophe. This is true, but on the other hand it must be said that to give the wrong answer to a problem is not necessarily to miss the point of it. If the point is seen and well argued, the fact that the examiner does not agree with your conclusion will not seriously affect your marks. In legal matters there is always a certain room for difference of opinion, and even though there be positive authority against your view, the examiner is anxious not so much to test the details of your knowledge as to assess your ability to argue in a lawyer-like way. A safe course to adopt if in any doubt is to present the argument for both sides—to turn yourself successively into counsel for the plaintiff (prosecutor), counsel for the defendant, and finally the judge. If then the examiner disagrees with your judgment, it will hardly matter because you will have presented (even though you have also rejected) the argument for his point of view. Incidentally, you will have shown your ability to accept a brief on either side, or even to be promoted to the Bench.

THE PRESSURE OF TIME

Abbreviations of technical words and expressions should be used only very sparingly in an examination. If, however, you find that time has run short for the last answer, the best course is to reduce the answer to bare note form, using as many key headings as possible and abbreviating freely. You may head such an answer with the words: " (In note form)." This course should be adopted only in case of absolute necessity, and you should be able to plan out your time so that it is not necessary.

It is no use writing " unfinished " at the bottom of your answer. Some candidates send in meagre scripts in which every answer is carefully labelled " no time to finish." Let me assure them that the phrase has no mark-getting capacity whatever. There is all the difference between an *incomplete* answer labelled " no time to finish "—when marks can be given only for what is written down—and a *complete* though condensed answer labelled " in note form "—when the examiner may of his charity overlook defects of style, excessive abbreviation and lack of full detail.

The legitimate way to save time in an examination is normally not by extensive abbreviation but by omitting windy phrases, such as " first it is necessary to consider whether." Long before the examination the student should have practised and perfected a clear, incisive style in which every word is made to count.

SELF-CONTRADICTION

There is a story of a party of Americans who stood by the Porters' Lodge at King's College, Cambridge. One of them pointed north and said: " That's the chapel." They turned round and another pointed south. " No, that's the chapel." " No," said a third, pointing west, " that's the chapel." " Anyway," they said, as they turned to go, " we've seen the chapel." Many examination scripts are guided by the same philosophy. The candidate will start with one version of the law and then gradually veer round to a contradictory version—thus making sure that the right rule is there some-where, even though he cannot pick it out. Perhaps he hopes by this means to get the best of both worlds; actually, of course, he gets the worst. If you find yourself changing your mind in the course of an answer, either cross out what you have written and start afresh, or, if there is no time for that, say frankly that you have changed your mind. You must show not only that you have seen the chapel, but that you can identify it.

Chapter 11

MOOTS AND MOCK TRIALS

" In my youth," said his father, " I 'took to the law,
And argued each case with my wife;
And the muscular strength which it gave to my jaw
Has lasted the rest of my life."

        —Lewis Carroll, *Alice in Wonderland.*

MOOTS

THERE is no finer training for the young advocate in the argument of points of law than taking part in moots. Moots are legal problems in the form of imaginary cases, which are argued by two student " counsel " (a leader and a junior) on each side, with a " bench " of three " judges " (or perhaps only one) representing the Court of Appeal. The arrangement of the moots is usually the responsibility of the students' law society,[1] though a law teacher or practising lawyer can usually be persuaded to set the moot and preside on the " bench." If no one else is arranging them, organise one yourself. Mooting not only gives you practice in court procedure but helps to develop the aplomb that every advocate should possess.

Counsel should notify opposing counsel of the main points and of all the authorities on which they will rely. (To exchange authorities before the hearing is a practice of the profession.) The Master of Moots or other organiser should also be informed of the authorities to be cited, in order that he may arrange for such reports or case books as are available to be brought to the court-room.

Since the moot is attended by an audience it is important to confine the proceedings to a reasonable length. Between half an hour and 40 minutes for each side (to be divided

[1] Moots are held by students' law societies in the universities and Inns of Court, by the Law Society (*i.e.* the official one) at its Hall in Chancery Lane, and by some provincial Law Societies.

between leader and junior as they think fit) is enough time. The appellant has a right of reply, and it is therefore a good plan to " sandwich " the two counsel for the respondent (or Crown) between the two for the appellant. The order of speaking is then: leading counsel for the appellant; leading and junior counsel for the respondent; junior counsel for the appellant.

After counsel have concluded their arguments the presiding judge may invite members of the audience to express their opinions upon the legal problem as *amici curiae*. The members of the court then confer, and may deliver their judgments in turn. If there are two student members on the bench they may be asked to deliver their judgments before the senior member. (My own opinion is that the moot is most efficiently conducted if the senior member alone gives the judgment of the court.) After the judgment or judgments the opinion of the audience may, if desired, be tested by a vote.

Both counsel and judges follow the punctilios of court procedure and conduct, and a few words may be said on these. Counsel rise to their feet when addressing or being addressed by the court. If your opponent interrupts you with a lengthy submission, resume your seat while he is speaking. If you have occasion to refer to your colleague he is your " learned junior " or " learned leader," as the case may be, and your opponent is " my learned friend," or occasionally, informally, " my friend " (*not* " the opposition "!). " It has been argued on the other side that " is permissible.

Do not interrupt anyone, ever, if this can be avoided. If you must interrupt, do so as gently and courteously as possible.

Beginners sometimes get confused between the two polite ways of addressing a judge—" My Lord " and " Your Lordship." The difference is that " My Lord " is the mode of addressing a judge in the vocative case, while " Your Lordship " is the mode of referring to the judge in the course of a sentence, *i.e.* as a polite substitute for " you." [2] The

---

[2] As in Richard Bethell's famous piece of rudeness to the judge who, after hearing the argument, said he would reserve the point in order to turn it over in his mind—" May it please

formula for opening a case is: " May it please your Lord-
ship(s), I am appearing with Mr. —— for the plaintiff
(prosecution) (appellant), and my learned friends Mr. ——
and Mr. —— are for the defendant (respondent) (Crown).
The claim (charge) is . . ." Other counsel will begin
by saying: " May it please your Lordship(s)." The formula
for submitting to a ruling of the judge during the case is:
" If your Lordship pleases."

In referring to the Queen as prosecutor in the course of a
case one speaks not of " the Queen " but " the Crown."

The most common breach of etiquette committed by
the enthusiastic beginner when arguing a moot case is the
expression of a personal opinion on the merits of his case.
Counsel may " submit " and " suggest " as strongly as he
likes, and he may state propositions of law and fact, but
he should not express his own belief or opinion. It is
disrespectful to the Bench to say: " My Lords, in my opinion
the law is so-and-so," still more to say: " My Lords, in my
opinion this man is innocent." Questions of law and fact
are for the court to decide, not counsel; counsel's function
is simply to argue.

Begin your address to the court by stating quite briefly
what you wish to show. Speak slowly and get as soon as
possible to the core of your case. Your time is much more
limited than it would be in a real case, and you cannot
afford to waste it; on the other hand, it is no use gabbling
what you have to say, for then it will not be understood.
Establish eye contact with the judge, and do not read out
your argument if you can possibly avoid it.

A frequent fault is to read out passages from textbooks
as though they represented the last word on the law.
Although textbooks and treatises are not taboo in court,
they should be used sparingly and cautiously. What the
judge wants to hear are the relevant cases (and, of
course, statutes), not the views of writers. If a writer is

your Lordship to turn it over in what your Lordship is
pleased to call your Lordship's mind? " (It is said that the
nearest approach Bethell ever made to politeness was in his
reply to a judge who corrected him: " Your Lordship is quite
right, and I am quite wrong—as your Lordship usually is.")

quoted, the case that he cites in support of his opinion should be read out and referred to. Read slowly, with proper periods and emphasis. You want what you read to sink into the judges' minds.

There used to be a rule that a writer was not an " authority " until he had gone the way of all flesh [3]: whereas dead authors could be cited in court without apology, living ones could be cited only by the subterfuge of " adopting " what they said as part of counsel's argument. Nowadays, however, living authors are cited in the ordinary way. If you meet a judge who cavils at this, you can usually pacify him by stating that you are not treating the writer as an authority but are merely adopting the writer's words as part of your argument. It is always desirable, at least in the superior courts,[4] to refer the court to the cases cited by the writer for his propositions.

If at all possible, the reports of cases cited should be produced at the moot. If the reports are not available, case books should be used for the cases contained in them. Case books should also be available for the use of the Bench. When citing cases the reference should always be given ; and it should be pronounced in full, not in abbreviated form.[5] For instance, [1944] A.C. 200 is: " reported in the

---

[3] Hence when Salmond died it was said that he had at last beaten his friendly opponent Pollock (who was then still with us); for Salmond had become an authority.

During Pollock's lifetime Lord Wright remarked in one of his judgments:

" The matter is very clearly stated in a work, fortunately not a work of authority, but to which we are all as lawyers indebted, Sir Frederick Pollock's *Law of Torts* " (*Nicholls* v. *Ely Beet Sugar Factory Ltd.* [1936] Ch. at 349). The printer of the case in the Law Times Reports misunderstood the subtle compliment and turned " fortunately " into " unfortunately " (154 L.T. at 533).

[4] In magistrates' courts a treatise may be used as an authority in itself: *Boys* v. *Blenkinsop* [1968] Crim.L.R. 513.

[5] There is an old tale of a junior who cited the Law Reports to Lord Esher M.R. as " 2 Q.B.D." " That is not the way you should address us," said Lord Esher. The learned counsel protested that he merely meant to use the brief and ordinary formula for the second volume of the Queen's Bench Division Reports. " I might as well," retorted his Lordship, " say to you, ' U.B.D.' " Norton-Kyshe, *Dictionary of Legal Quotations*, 57.

150 Moots and Mock Trials

Appeal Cases for 1944 at page two hundred"; and 2 B. &
Ald. 6 is: " in the second volume of Barnewall and Alderson's Reports at page six." The facts of cases should be
read, unless the case is relied upon only for an obiter dictum.
Usually it is sufficient to read the headnote and the passage
you want; but if the case is an important part of your
argument you would, in court, read what you consider the
essential facts in full. Refer to judges by their full title
(see pp. 64–65).

Citing cases, though usually a necessary part of the
moot, tends to take a long time and to be boring for the
audience. Try, therefore, to pick out the cases that are
most apt for your argument, and rely on them. In professional practice it is the duty of the advocate to call the
attention of the court to all decisions that are in any way
against the submissions he makes; but this may not be
possible under moot conditions. It is not a bad plan to
have a positive rule that not more than, say, six cases shall
be cited on each side. The object of a moot is to provide
practice in developing an argument, and while the reading
out of decided cases is often the necessary foundation of
an argument, it should not constitute the whole of it.
Remember that your primary object as an advocate is to
persuade: the citing of cases is only a means to this end.[6]

Just as you should not overload your argument with
cases, you should not load it with too many separate points

[6] The observation of Lord Greene on this matter is worth
quoting. If one compares, he says, the student arguing a
moot case with the experienced practising lawyer arguing in
court, " it will be found (at least that is my own experience)
that the student builds up his argument on authorities which
he refers to in great profusion, whereas the experienced advocate builds up his argument out of his instinct for legal principle and only uses his authorities to substantiate his points or
to convince a judge who declines to accept a proposition unless
it is supported by authority. Some of the best legal arguments which I have heard on points of difficulty and complication have been conducted with surprising economy of
reference to authority. And the reason is that the advocate's
instinct for law and its principles has enabled him to present
in an attractive and logical way an argument which convinces
by its own inherent strength and does not require at every
point to be propped up by references to authority": (1936)
J.S.P.T.L. 12.

of law. " Mooty " as the case may be, it is unlikely that
there are many *good* points to be made for your side.
All first-class advocates concentrate on what they consider to
be their good points ; they do not run the risk of alienating
the judge's affections by producing obviously bad ones.

Consider the timing of your moot. Half an hour is the
minimum for each side ; so if the moot starts at 8.30 p.m.,
and if three judges each take ten minutes to give judgment,
it is 10 p.m. even if not a minute has been lost—and this does
not allow time for the presiding judge to invite the audience
to comment before judgment is given. It would be much
better to hold the moot, say, between 2 and 5 p.m. The
presence of an audience is relatively unimportant. Far better
have many moots with a small or even no audience than one
moot with a large audience.

You cannot improve the beauty of your countenance,
but you can, if you wish, add greatly to the attractiveness
of your speech. For all who have to speak regularly—and
this includes all lawyers—a few pounds spent on elocution
are well worth while ; but some bad habits can be cured
by self-help. Many experienced speakers mar their conversation as well as their orations with a profusion of ums
and ers which distract attention. Other bad habits are using
" I mean " and " you know." The simplest way to cure these
defects—which probably exist in your own speech, although
you are unaware of them—is to tape-record your conversation with some other person on a serious subject in which
you are both interested. Probably you will be surprised at
the imperfections in your own expression when you play
back the record. Only by means of a tape-recorder can
you hear yourself as others hear you. Try to eliminate all
the " filled pauses " in your speech—moments of silence
are far more impressive than meaningless noises. Mumbling
or lack of clarity in articulation is another common defect.
Many people's vowels are so badly formed that they are
hard to distinguish from each other. Do you speak like
this? *Open your mouth* when talking, particularly when
making a speech : even exaggerate the opening. Some not
only fail to speak up but talk with their hands wandering

to cover their mouth. When you make your first public speeches of any kind, ask a close friend to attend and to comment to you on your performance.

It is an excellent thing to take part in debates. Here are a few hints for speech-making of any kind.

Plan your speech under a number of points so that it has a definite structure. Write it out in full, reflect on it overnight and polish it the next day. Then summarise the main headings on a small card or cards about the size of a postcard. Include in the card any figures, quotations, names, key phrases or other material which you wish to state exactly. Read through your full speech several times, preferably aloud and preferably into a tape-recorder, but do not try to memorise it word for word. You will probably not succeed in being word-perfect, and there is danger in reciting a memorised speech either of appearing unnatural or of forgetting a complete section or even coming to a dead halt. If you play back a recording of the rehearsal, consider whether you spoke at the right pace, and particularly whether you made an impressive pause at the right moment.

When on your feet before the audience, have the outline card or cards in your hand and, with this aid, speak naturally in the way you have planned.

Speak slowly. The commonest fault among inexperienced speakers (and even many experienced ones) is to speak too fast. All good advocates speak with great deliberation and force. Tell yourself before you begin that you are going to speak slowly, and keep reminding yourself to do so. Of course you must not be monotonous, and your matter should be good enough to stand deliberate presentation.

Don't hide behind any furniture if you can help it, and don't fold your arms or fiddle with anything. Look at the audience as you speak, and turn to different sections of it. You may use your hands to emphasise points—not in too exaggerated a way, but sufficiently to show that you are putting your whole being into it. If you make a joke, practise getting the timing right—and let the audience know that humour is about to enliven the proceedings by enjoying it yourself beforehand.

If you are nervous, console yourself with the thought that the initially nervous speaker often performs far better than the stolid chap with no nerves. And remember that the audience are on your side. They want to be engrossed by your speech ; they want the occasion to be a success. They are not there to criticise you, unless you force the criticism on them.

MOCK TRIALS

A mock trial differs from a moot in that it is a mock jury-trial, with jury and witnesses, not an argument on law. The proceedings may be somewhat humorous ; witnesses may dress themselves up, and court and counsel wear robes (if procurable). The audience may consist of non-lawyers, who, of course, come simply to be entertained. Since the trial is unrehearsed, it requires a high standard of forensic ability on the part of the student " counsel "; and the proceedings should either be leavened by humour or present an intellectual problem of the " whodunit " type.

There are two way in which the " case " may be got up. It may have been enacted beforehand by the witnesses, so that they testify to what they have actually witnessed ; alternatively, the organiser of the mock trial may simply have given to each witness a statement of his evidence, which he is expected to remember. The former method requires some effort, but it makes the case more realistic when it comes to cross-examination, and it enables the preliminary proceedings, including the interviewing of witnesses and briefing of counsel, to be done by student " solicitors." The actual trial is, of course, a valuable experience for budding advocates who take part in it as counsel.

It is a good plan to set the scene of the case (*e.g.* the murder) in some place known to the audience (*e.g.* the College or Law School). Alternatively, the case can be modelled upon an actual case in one of the Trials Series (below, p. 207). Try to depart from your model trial just sufficiently to prevent counsel using the same speeches and the same

questions to witnesses. Keep the number of witnesses down
to five or six. See that the legal participants have attended
real trials in order to learn how things are done; the
clerk of the court in particular should know his job. If
your are at all doubtful about the success of the evening, do
not advertise the event outside your Law Society.

A variant of the mock trial is the flitch trial.[7] A flitch
of bacon is offered to the married couple who shall be
adjudged to have been the happiest in the bonds of
matrimony. Married couples are thus induced to submit
themselves to examination, cross-examination and re-examina-
tion upon their private lives. One or two " counsel "
defend the flitch, and one or two represent all the applicant
couples. It is obvious that very great tact is required of
counsel for the flitch if the applicants are not to wish from
the bottom of their hearts they had never applied for it.

As another diversion from the serious business of moots,
the students' law society may like to try one evening the
game of " Alibi." The gathering divides into groups of four,
each group being composed of two prosecuting counsel and
two defendants. It is assumed that the two defendants have
committed some crime at a stated time—say between 10
and 11 p.m. last Wednesday—and have set up an alibi.
They go out of the room for not more than ten minutes
in order to prepare their story. They then return, one at a
time, for cross-examination by the prosecuting counsel.
Counsel's aim is to break down the alibi by asking
unexpected questions and so getting contradictory answers
from the two defendants. After the two cross-examinations,

---

[7] Originating at Dunmow in Essex. The monks of the priory
there made a standing offer of a flitch of bacon to any pair
that could, after a twelvemonth of matrimony, come forward
and make oath that, during the whole time, they had never
had a quarrel, never regretted their marriage, and, if again
open to an engagement, would make exactly that they had
made. The first claim was made in 1445, and there was a
revival (though not connected with the priory) in 1855. See
F. W. Steer, *The History of the Dunmow Flitch Ceremony*
(1951). During the last war a trial was held with National
Savings Certificates substituted for the flitch. The provision
of a genuine flitch was later made possible by a gift from
New Zealand.

lasting perhaps ten or fifteen minutes in all, the two counsel put their heads together for a minute, and then one of them addresses the rest of the gathering, who have acted as jury, and submits that the alibi has been broken down because of this and that discrepancy. The jury signify their verdict by a show of hands, the opinion of the majority being taken.

A master of ceremonies is needed to dispatch successive pairs of defendants out of the room, in order to keep the game going continuously.

Would-be lawyers will find this game not at all a bad test of their powers of advocacy. No training for would-be defendants is intended.

A somewhat similar game called " False Evidence " was played in radio programmes in 1951. Three masked " defendants " are interrogated on their day-to-day lives by two counsel. One of these defendants has assumed a completely false name and occupation, and it is the jury's task to decide which. Each defendant must submit to counsel a week in advance a couple of hundred words summarising his life, and this enables counsel to prepare their questions. Each defendant calls a witness who has also submitted a statement with the facts of his or her life, particularly where that life crosses that of the defendant. In the case of the innocent parties they must have known each other for at least two years. The witness is not in court during the interrogation of the defendant, and counsel try to shake the evidence and establish discrepancies between the defendant and his witness. Each defendant and his witness are given a limited time—say fifteen minutes altogether—in the box. The judge sums up briefly to the jury, who consider and announce their verdict. The imposter then declares himself, and it is interesting to see if the judicial process has succeeded in ascertaining the truth of the matter. It may be mentioned that the written statements do not contain sufficiently specific information to enable counsel to identify who the person is. Two or three trials may be held on the same evening.

Yet another variant is " Third Degree." One member of the party is selected as the defendant: he is told the outline of an alibi defence and has to fill in the details impromptu under questioning. For example, he may be told that his alibi relates to a period between 2 and 5 p.m. last Thursday, when he left the refectory after lunch and took a train to a named neighbouring town and visited a friend in time for tea. The defendant on being told this alibi must immediately amplify it under questioning, and can be " gonged " for undue hesitation in answering or for any vagueness in answering (he must not say " I think so " or " That is probably what I would have done "). He can also be gonged for self-contradiction. The object of the rest of the company, who question him for fifteen minutes, is to establish a self-contradiction. Leading questions may be asked: for example, if the defendant says that he was not carrying a mackintosh, he can later be asked whether his host put his mackintosh on a peg in the hall or where else? If the defendant is gonged, or runs for the allotted time without mishap, another outline alibi can immediately be supplied to another volunteer defendant. A beauty of this game is that it can be played by two players only, and it may help you to bring out unsuspected ability as an implacable interrogator.

BIBLIOGRAPHY

For illustrations of moot cases, see *The Moot Book of Gray's Inn*.

Books on advocacy are referred to in Chap. 13 (p. 177). For the procedure at a mock trial, consult any book on criminal or civil procedure. " Counsel " should make themselves acquainted not only with this procedure but with the main rules of evidence —*e.g.* those relating to leading questions.

CHAPTER 12

LEGAL RESEARCH

First there's the Bible
And then the Koran,
Odgers on Libel
Pope's Essay on Man.
—Mostyn T. Piggott, *The Hundred Best Books.*

GEORGE III is reputed to have said that lawyers do not know much more law than other people, but they know better where to find it. This chapter is written to help the reader to a more intimate knowledge of his law library, and also to guide the first steps of the research worker.

LOOKING UP PRACTICAL POINTS

The only type of legal research that most practising lawyers want to do is research into the law relating to a case that they have on hand. A convenient place in which to start looking is frequently Halsbury's *Laws of England*. First look up the main volume, and note the number of the paragraph printed in heavy type. Then turn up the current Supplement to find the most recent annotations. You cannot look up the Supplement directly.

Often Halsbury will give the answer without further trouble, but if further detail is needed it may be necessary to turn to a specialised treatise. The experienced practitioner carries in his head the names of the best works on the subjects with which he usually deals, and the sooner the student gets to know some of them the better. Consult *Where to Look for Your Law*, together with the latest catalogues published by Butterworth and Sweet and Maxwell, or a publication of the Institute of Advanced Legal Studies entitled *A Bibliographical Guide to the Law of the United Kingdom, the Channel Islands and the Isle of Man.* An American counterpart is *Law Books in Print*, ed. J. Myron

Jacobstein and Meira G. Pimsleur, which covers books in English published throughout the world.

There are five ways of tracing whether a statute has been repealed or amended. (1) Turn up the statute in Halsbury's *Statutes*, and then check the same reference in the current Cumulative Supplement, which shows how it has been affected by later legislation; to bring this even more up to date, consult the current numbers of *Current Law*. (2) An alternative is to use the cumulative *Current Law Citator*, which is published annually; then bring it right up to date with *Current Law Statutes*, which is published, usually, in six or seven parts during the course of each year, containing the statutes passed in that year, with, in the Statute Citator, a table of those statutes' effect on earlier legislation. These, however, give only amendments and repeals since 1947 (the year when *Current Law* began), which is satisfactory if your main statute was passed after 1947, but otherwise not. (3) Yet another method is to use the official work called *Chronological Table of Statutes*, which is also published annually. This will show amendments and repeals up to the date of last publication, so for very recent statutes you will still be driven back to one of the first two methods. (4) When the official *Statutes in Force* is further advanced in publication than it is at the time of writing, it will be the best method of establishing the current text of legislation. (5) A very convenient source for some statutes is the Local Government Library, which publishes statutes and statutory instruments on certain topics in loose-leaf form with annotations and indexes. The subjects covered are: Factories, Shops and Offices; Highways; Housing; Planning; Compulsory Purchase and Compensation; Public Health; and Road Traffic. There are also the *British Tax Encyclopedia*, the *Encyclopedia of Value Added Tax* and the *Industrial Relations Encyclopedia*; the *Encyclopedia of European Community Law* is to be published in 1973.

It may be mentioned that the Statute Citator in *Current Law Statutes* includes statutory instruments issued under rule-making powers, cases decided on the construction of statutes, and legal literature dealing with statutes, as well as all statutes of any year that are affected by legislation during the years covered. If a statutory instrument is wanted, it can generally best be looked up in Halsbury's *Statutory Instruments*, the annual supplements stating any changes that may have been made.

If the question is one of common law, much assistance can be got from the *English and Empire Digest*. This digests practically every reported case, and is well arranged and well indexed. It also gives the subsequent history of the case—whether it has been approved, overruled, and so on. The Case Citator in the *Current Law Citator* similarly shows what has happened to every case in the period since 1947.

A valuable aid to the interpretation of legal expressions is *Words and Phrases Legally Defined*. This is a collection of words and phrases in statutes which have been interpreted by the judges, together with statutory definitions of terms and definitions advanced by legal writers. Another excellent work of the same type is Stroud's *Judicial Dictionary*.

Further information is given in Derek J. Way, *The Student's Guide to Law Libraries* (1967).

RESEARCH PROPER

The ordinary practitioner will not need to dig any deeper than this—apart, of course, from references to the statutes and law reports. I should, however, add a few words for the benefit of any student who wishes to research into the history of some branch of legal doctrine. The *English and Empire Digest* is undoubtedly the best basis from which to begin. Pre-1865 cases should be turned up in the English Reports rather than in the original reports, because the former adds many cross-references. In order to prevent cross-references from becoming unmanageable it is important to devise a card index system.

When the material supplied in this way has been exhausted, it is useful to turn first to Petersdorff's Abridgement and then to Viner's Abridgement. Assuming that the particular topic that is being investigated has a long history, Viner will take it back to the Abridgements of Rolle, Brooke and Fitzherbert, and from these it is easy to take yet another step backwards to the black-letter Year Books. In reading the Year Books it is necessary, in order to distinguished judges from counsel, to have at hand Foss's *Tabulæ Curiales*, or his *Biographia Juridica* (Biographical Dictionary of the Judges of England). For the reading of law-French, Pollock's *First Book of Jurisprudence*, 6th ed., 297 *et seq.*, and Winfield's *Chief Sources of English Legal History*, Chap. 1, will set one on the right track. To the bibliography on medieval Latin given in Winfield's book there must now be added the important *Medieval Latin Word List,* by Baxter and Johnson.

Cases in the Year Books and the earlier reports are dated according to law term (Hilary, Easter—otherwise called Paschal—Trinity and Michaelmas) and regnal year. The correct conversion of this into the calendar year may give the beginner a little trouble. A useful list, giving the order of terms in each reign, is in Beardsley and Orman, *Legal Bibliography and the Use of Law Books* (2nd ed., Brooklyn, 1947), 305. Other good guides are Nicholas's *Chronology of History* or Powicke's *Handbook of British Chronology* or a little volume entitled *English Regnal Years and Titles*, by J. E. W. Wallis, in the series *Helps for Students of History*, or C. R. Cheney, *Handbook of Dates* (1948). A table of regnal years appears in Sweet and Maxwell's *Guide to Law Reports and Statutes*, but unfortunately it does not give the rules for finding the dates of commencement and termination of law terms, as the four former works do. There is a rough but simple guide to the dates of the law terms in Wambaugh, *Study of Cases*, (2nd ed., 1894), 319 ; and see *Manual of Legal Citations* (Institute of Advanced Legal Studies), Part I, 18–19. Information on chronology can also be obtained from the Appendix to the *Oxford Companion to English Literature*, 2nd ed.

Sometimes the old reports give two dates for a case. Thus *Matthew* v. *Hassel,* Cro.Eliz. 144, 78 E.R. 401, is case 2 in a batch attributed to Mich. 31 and 32 Eliz.; but immediately under the title appear the words " Michaelmas

Term, 30 & 31 Eliz.Roll 49." This means that the case was entered on the plea roll in that term; nevertheless the date of judgment, and therefore the date of the case, is that given by the reporter at the head of the page—Mich. 31 and 32 Eliz. To convert this date into the calendar year, turn up a table of regnal years and find when the 32nd year of Elizabeth commenced. That was on November 17, 1589, and 1589 is therefore the date of the case. (On November 17, 1589, Michaelmas term had already been running for some time and before that date the term had, of course, belonged to Elizabeth's 31st regnal year. Hence the term belongs to 31 & 32 Eliz. and is so referred to.)

An invaluable guide for the legal historian is Winfield's *Chief Sources of English Legal History*, and, of course, Holdsworth. The textbooks, old and new, can be traced through Sweet and Maxwell's *Bibliography of English Law*. A bibliography on judicial and official records is given in Pollock, *Essays in the Law* (1922), 239.

For periodical literature, consult the *Index to Legal Periodicals* and *Index to Foreign Legal Periodicals*, published for the American Association of Law Libraries; there is also an *Index to Periodical Articles Relating to Law* which is supplementary to the *Index to Legal Periodicals*. A list of American and other periodicals in English libraries is published by the Institute of Advanced Legal Studies. See also W. A. Friend, *Anglo-American Legal Bibliographies* (1944).[1]

In preparing a script useful advice on citations will be found in Part I of the *Manual of Legal Citations* published by the Institute of Advanced Legal Studies.

---

[1] The finding of an undated Command Paper may give trouble unless the following table is known. There are five series. From 1833 to 1869 they were numbered " 1 " to " 4222." From 1870 to 1899 they were numbered " C.1 " to " C.9550." From 1900 to 1918 they were numbered " Cd.1 " to " Cd.9239." From 1919 to 1956 they were numbered " Cmd.1 " to " Cmd.9889." The new series is numbered " Cmnd.1 " consecutively.

There is a rather vexatious custom of referring to some reports of commissions and committees by the name of the chairman instead of by the proper title. A dictionary of these informal citations will be found in *Where to Look for Your Law*.

Much useful work can be done by comparing legal development in the various common-law countries. Part II of·the *Manual of Legal Citations*, referred to before, explains the mode of citation of Commonwealth material. Australian cases can be traced through the *Australian Digest*,[2] Canadian through the *Canadian Abridgement*, New Zealand through the *Abridgement of New Zealand Case Law*. There are various Irish Digests. The Institute of Advanced Legal Studies, 25 Russell Square, London, WC1B 5DR, publishes a Union List of Commonwealth legal literature in English libraries. See also Reynold Boult, *A Bibliography of Canadian Law* (1966), and Paul O'Higgins, *A Bibliography of Periodical Literature relating to Irish Law* (1966).

Turning to American material, the Middle Temple possesses an excellent collection of American reports, and a certain number of American textbooks. The libraries of the Inns of Court have a duplicated list showing which American reports are in which libraries. The Middle Temple has the American equivalent of Halsbury, the *Corpus Juris Secundum*. Copies of the American *Restatement* are fairly common. The Institute of Advanced Legal Studies, already mentioned, is also building up a library of American law. Useful guides to American law reports and digests are Hicks, *Materials and Methods of Legal Research* (2nd ed., 1942), and the work by Beardsley and Orman already cited. There is an *Annual Survey of American Law*, an *Annual Survey of Commonwealth Law*, and an *Annual Survey of South African Law*. Chambliss and Seidman have compiled a reseach bibliography called *Sociology of the Law* (1970) ; this is based largely on American materials.

The libraries mentioned above are, of course, private libraries, and non-members of the bodies to which they belong must obtain permission to use them. In addition the Libraries of the Commonwealth Relations Office, Downing Street, S.W.1, the Privy Council, Old County Hall, Spring Gardens, S.W.1, and the Colonial Office, Church House,

---

[2] For Australian sources in general see Enid Campbell and Donald MacDougall, *Legal Research: Materials and Methods* (1967).

Great Smith Street, S.W.1, possess some series of reports of other Commonwealth countries. Members of the public are permitted upon application to consult them.

Those reading French law may be helped by A. W. Dalrymple's *French-English Dictionary of Legal Words and Phrases* (2nd ed., 1948); there is also a companion English-French volume. Similar dictionaries for German have been compiled by Erdsiek, Dietl and Weil, and for Spanish by Louis A. Robb.

Those working in London may be helped by Irwin and Staveley, *The Libraries of London* (2nd ed., 1961).

If the reader's research carries him beyond familiar legal fields into a large general library, he will find E. J. Dingwall's *How to Use a Large Library* a useful guide. Much the most important of general works of reference is the *British Museum Subject Index*, which classifies books according to their subject-matter. Where a book is not in a library, the librarian may be willing to apply to the National Central Library for a copy on loan.

Two hints may be given on the preparation of the finished script. (1) Frequently the date of decision of a case is a year before the date by which it is cited in the Law Reports. It is customary to take the date of the volume of the Law Reports as the date of the case. (2) If the case is reported in the Law Reports it may be thought sufficient to cite only the Law Reports; but if it is not in the Law Reports the ideal is that all the " collateral " reports should be cited in which the case appears. A list of references can be obtained from one of the Digests.

Those who are troubled by questions of style and grammar would be well advised to read *Complete Plain Words*, by Sir Ernest Gowers. A revised edition by Sir Bruce Fraser has been published by H.M.S.O. in elegant hardback for £1.

CHAPTER 13

FROM LEARNING TO EARNING

No Wind makes for him that hath no intended port
to sail unto.
—Montaigne.

IN this chapter I shall speak chiefly to the University student;
the man studying for professional examinations will already
have his future mapped out.

Many Art graduates (and even Science graduates) now
find it impossible to obtain a post that matches their training
and ability, unless they are willing to teach. Law graduates
are in a happier position, but the state of the market changes
continually.

PRACTICE AT THE BAR

What qualities go to make the successful barrister? I will
not depress the aspirant by dwelling on all the attributes
that my predecessors in this field of writing have required.
One of the most formidable lists was that compiled by that
long-winded but entertaining writer, Samuel Warren. On
the physical side he demanded a melodious voice, a com-
manding appearance and an iron constitution; on the
mental, a long list of qualities, including perseverance, logical
thought, quick perceptions, a retentive memory, sound
judgment, presence of mind, self-reliance, self-control, and
" that ductility, elasticity, activity; that expansive and con-
tractile power of mind which can adapt itself to everything,
and pass in a moment from one engagement to another, of
the most different character, from labyrinth to labyrinth—
with unwearied energy, with a mind unconfused." [1] Among
all these desirable qualities the most important are quickness
of thought, a good memory and a sound constitution. As
to the first, cases on the common-law side are usually won
not through counsel's addresses to the court, which there

[1] Warren, *Introduction to Law Studies*, (2nd ed., 1845), 60–69.

is usually a little time to prepare in advance, but through the effective examination of witnesses. Now cross-examinations cannot be prepared, because you can never be quite sure what the other side's witnesses are going to say until they are actually in the box. A certain nimbleness of wit is therefore essential. There are some men who are very sound, but who can formulate opinions only after prolonged consideration. That type of mind is no use for advocacy.

A good barrister must also be able to assimilate facts quickly. He may have a brief with correspondence numbering two or three hundred letters delivered to him the night, or two nights, before the case begins, and all the facts must be mastered before he goes into court. The best advocates have had prodigious memories, enabling them to retain the details of one complicated case after another for presentation in court. Lord Alverstone recorded that when at the Bar he was able to read the sheets of correspondence almost as fast as he could turn them over, and he never required to read them twice. Hawkins, one of the most powerful leaders of the common-law Bar in the nineteenth century, used to give the following advice. " Never examine or cross-examine from your brief. Know your brief and examine from your head." The student can best test and foster his powers of advocacy by making full use of his debating society.

The need for a sound constitution can be realised from the following passage from Gilchrist Alexander's *The Temple of the Nineties*. Anyone who has seen a busy barrister at work will bear out the truth of the picture.

" Few people realise under what pressure successful barristers live. . . . The busy barrister is on the *qui vive* all the time. In court he has to be on the alert every moment and is watched by a highly trained expert on the other side who pounces upon his slightest mistake. Out of court he has to work far into the night, night after night, working hard and continuously at a mass of detail. He cannot, like the head of a big business, delegate to subordinates the actual carrying out of his work. His ' devils ' prepare for him notes of his material, but once he has gone into court he has to take entire responsibility on his own shoulders."

On the Chancery side the chief qualifications are, I think, patience and thoroughness. There is not such a great deal of advocacy to be done ; much of the work is non-litigious (such as drafting documents and advising on title), and the cases that do get into court tend to turn upon techicalities of company law, property and wills, or upon questions of company finance, rather than upon controversial questions of fact. Also, a good deal of litigious work is disposed of not in open court but before a judge or master in chambers. To some types of mind work at the Chancery Bar appears dull and repellent, because it tends to lack human interest. On the other hand, existence is more placid than on the common-law side.

It is hardly necessary to emphasise the necessity of probity for all members of the Bar. A barrister must have the confidence of the Bench. Any kind of sharp practice or dishonest dealing will infallibly ruin his career.

Formerly, the entrant to the Bar had to finance a long period of waiting before the briefs began to come in. But with the increased work provided by legal aid and the volume of crime, young barristers in general common-law practice now make a living immediately. Indeed, it may be said that too many people of indifferent quality are succeeding. The fledgling is allowed to take his own cases after only six months' pupillage, and the clerk will probably be waiting with briefs at the end of that time. Young men in the right chambers make £1,500 to £3,000 gross with small cases in the first year. Out of the gross receipts must be paid various expenses to be mentioned later, plus the cost of travel (not large within London, but travel and hotels elsewhere can be quite an item). The amounts in the fee-book do not represent actual income, because some solicitors, disgracefully, take years to pay counsel's fees ; but payments for legal aid cases are comparatively prompt, and they represent much of a young man's earnings.

On the Chancery side, the immediate prospects are not nearly so good; but since there is a great shortage of Chancery barristers, a sound lawyer who can find a seat in chambers can make his living two years after pupillage.

In specialist chambers (such as taxation, local government law, town and country planning, rating, shipping, restrictive practices, and patent) the young barrister will again have to wait a couple of years or more before he pays his way, but his prospects then are better than in general practice. His life is likely to be less hectic, and his income distinctly greater. There is no official limit to the fees chargeable by barristers, so that when practitioners in a particular speciality are in short supply, their fees rise.

It was said in 1964 that competent juniors could expect to earn £3,000–£10,000, and successful Queen's Counsel could also expect to earn the latter figure.[2] The amount could now be doubled. Rewards at the Chancery Bar are probably somewhat less, while at the specialist Bars they can be several times as great.

The Bar sets notions of social security at defiance. There is no pension, no goodwill to sell, no partner to help earn your money if you are ill. Even if you succeed in building up a good practice as a junior your troubles will not be at an end, because at that point in your career you will have to decide whether to apply for silk. These expressions need a word of explanation. A " junior " means any barrister who has not taken silk ; and some highly successful barristers (especially on the Chancery side) remain juniors all their lives. " Taking silk " means obtaining the right to wear a silk gown by becoming a Q.C. or (to use the language of lawyers) a leader. Whereas a junior does both advocacy and the preliminary paper work, a leader confines himself to advocacy (apart from the giving of oral and written opinions, an activity common to both grades).

The grant of silk is entirely in the discretion of a political officer, the Lord Chancellor ; and the grounds on which he makes his selection are, as *The Times* wrote in an unusually critical vein, " shrouded in mystery." Many juniors who are qualified do not succeed in their application. No doubt, the Lord Chancellor weighs the needs of the various circuits and branches of law. But, whatever his good intentions,

[2] See Abel-Smith and Stevens, *Lawyers and the Courts* (London, 1967), 426–427.

successful leaders are in such short supply, and consequently are able to charge such high fees, that the cost of fighting an important case in the High Court is a public scandal. One day the whole silk system may be reconsidered. Why should it not be left to individual members of the Bar to decide whether they wish to specialise in advocacy? [3]

Anyway, the position now is that if you do not take silk at the right moment, it may mean that you have to continue working much too hard for your time of life; on the other hand some barristers who take silk repent it, for they find too late that their services in the more expensive class of advocacy are not in demand. Once you have taken silk there is no going back to a junior's practice. It seems a perverse arrangement to add this hazard to a profession that is already too full of risks for our comfortable age.

Should you be interested in the Bar as a career, do not go any further without reading Sir R. E. Megarry's *Lawyer and Litigant in England* which gives a fair picture of the hazards and rewards of the profession. You do not need to make your decision until the beginning of your second year at the University; but you must, according to the quaint custom, eat dinners for two years at your Inn of Court as well as passing the Bar examinations before you can be called, so it is wise to commence to " keep terms " at your Inn not later than your fifth University term.

Consult your University tutor or lecturer, because he may be able to give you helpful advice. Some barristers will receive students from their old University in their chambers for a couple of weeks during University vacation, in order to introduce them to the barrister's life and enable them to make a more informed choice of chambers for pupillage. Others will give impartial advice on this very important choice. Of the various arrangements that exist, the only one that has been publicised as open to all is the Student Sponsorship Scheme of the Northern towns. Any University student who thinks he may wish to go to the Bar and may wish ultimately to practise in the North can be

---

[3] For a less radical suggestion see Blom-Cooper in 121 *New Law Journal* 367.

allocated a sponsor who will advise him generally. The student should send his name to Mr. Rhys Davies, 43 King Street, Manchester M2 7AT, or Mr. Michael Wolff, 27 Dale Street, Liverpool 2.

If you are not at the University, you may be glad to know that many local authorities award grants to students reading at the Bar on the same basis as University awards. But they do not pay during pupillage.

Assuming that you decide to take the plunge, you should if possible determine at the same time whether you are going to practise on the common-law or on the Chancery side. For the latter you will probably join Lincoln's Inn, for the former one of the three other Inns. (This is the usual course, but there is nothing to prevent a member of any Inn from practising on either side of the profession.) As between the three common-law Inns the choice does not really matter: you can quite well be a member of one Inn, become a pupil in chambers belonging to a second, and in due course attain a seat (*i.e.* a room, or share of a room) in chambers belonging to a third. It has already been explained that for the ordinary person who has no special connections it is easier to get started on the common-law side. This is largely because on the common-law side there is a great deal of small work, in county courts and the criminal courts; on the Chancery side there is no criminal work and all the civil work tends to be fairly important. A second point to be remembered is that the common-law side is larger and has more work than the Chancery side; it can, therefore, do with a greater annual intake of new recruits. In the third place, the Chancery side is much more concentrated in London than the common-law side. This leads me to your second choice: between practice in London and practice in provincial chambers. Efforts are now being made to encourage the localisation of the Bar, and quite a number of towns have their own chambers. It is no longer necessary for the local barrister who takes silk to move to London.

There is no need to enter into the details of dinners, examinations and fees. The Consolidated Regulations of the

Inns of Court, together with particulars of the scholarships and prizes available, can be had by applying to the Sub-Treasurer at the Inner Temple or to the Under-Treasurer at the other three Inns.[4] The total fees up to and including call (including the cost of dinners) are about £400, less a returnable deposit of £75. The cost of robes and wigs is an additional and expensive item.[5] Attendance at the Part II course at either the Council of Legal Education or the College of Law is now compulsory for those who intend to practise in England and Wales. After or shortly before taking his call the student who intends to practise will read in the chambers of a junior barrister. This is called pupillage. A year's pupillage is compulsory for those who intend to practise in England, except that the Masters of the Bench of the Inn may waive six months of this period on the condition of participation in one of the Practical Training Courses organised by the Council of Legal Education. Take one of these courses (generally called the Post-Final Courses) by all means; it will give you valuable training in advocacy and draftsmanship; but do not try to shorten your period of pupillage, for twelve months is the minimum in which you can acquire the rudiments of professional skill. The fee for pupillage is the very modest sum of 100 guineas for the year plus 10 guineas for the clerk (half these figures for six months). The Inns of Court have funds available for able students who need help in this respect. The reason for the modesty of the fee is that it became fixed by custom at the beginning of the practice of pupillage, in the latter half of the eighteenth century, and has remained at the same figure notwithstanding the fall in the value of money.[6] Some barristers do not charge for pupillage.

Sir Harold Morris Q.C., recommended first six months' pupillage with a man who has a good criminal-law practice

---

4 See also Sweet and Maxwell's *Guide to a Career in the Law*, 7th ed. (paperback).
5 The Bar Council acts as agent for the sale of second-hand (and therefore well-ripened) robes and wigs.
6 A. D. McNair, *Dr. Johnson and the Law*, 45–46, quoting Campbell, *Lives of the Lord Chancellors,* ix, 143; the same fee is mentioned by Warren.

and then 12 in a mixed practice. Some prefer to spend six months in Chancery chambers before turning to the common-law side.

The advice is sometimes given not to read in the chambers of a man with a specialised practice, as in the case of those who practise exclusively at the Admiralty, Bankruptcy, Commercial, Divorce, Patent, Parliamentary,[7] or Probate Bar. It may be the theoretical ideal to obtain a broad training first, but, all the same, a man is far more likely to establish himself in a specialist practice if he starts at it as a pupil. There is great pressure on places in specialist chambers, and a pupil in the chambers who has commended himself to the members is likely to be favourably placed for obtaining a seat in the chambers after pupillage is over. It must be understood that a set of chambers is rented by one of its members (called the head of the chambers), in London from one of the Inns of Court, and he sub-lets rooms to his colleagues; thus the head of the chambers will not necessarily be the same person as your pupil master.

For those who have an eye to practise eventually at the Parliamentary Bar a scientific qualification is a help, and in patent work it is a necessity.

Selection of the right chambers is enormously important, calling for the best advice that can be got. But the pressure on the Bar (and its conservatism in sticking to the purlieus of the Inns) means that it has become quite difficult to arrange pupillage and subsequently a seat in chambers, so you will not have much if any choice. It is in these matters of finding a place that the element of luck still determines success at the Bar. Your master will not promise you a seat when he takes you on (indeed, he is likely to tell you firmly that there will be no seat); and during your pupillage you must do your level best to please him (and the clerk) if you want to be invited to remain. So great is the pressure on space that some members of chambers have to make shift

---

[7] Members of the Parliamentary Bar are concerned with the passage of private Bills through Parliament. Planning inquiries are now of greater importance than Parliamentary work, and practitioners (as at most of the specialised Bars) are doing very well.

with a seat in the hall entrance, borrowing a colleague's room for conferences. Fortunately, the accommodation problem in the provinces is less acute.

How does one find a barrister who will accept one as a pupil? There is no fully organised system. Many barristers take a pupil on the recommendation of a friend at the Bar (particularly a former pupil), or a solicitor; and this is the best method of approach if you can work it. The Council of Legal Education has an advisory service. Oxford and Cambridge undergraduates receive the benefit of advice from special committees of old University men in choosing chambers. Those who give unsparingly of their time and effort to this most laudable purpose do so as a matter of University loyalty. Unfortunately, to the student from a modern University it looks like favouritism. The remedy would be for a few well-established barristers from modern Universities to give the same kind of advice to men from London and elsewhere; and perhaps if this were done the various committees would one day fuse and forget their University allegiances.

The difficulties of the student in arranging pupillage make it rather theoretical to give advice on the assumption that he can pick and choose. If you have the opportunity of an introduction to a particular barrister, find out as much about him as you can. There are two dangers to be avoided, if you can avoid them, in the choice of chambers; reading with someone who is too busy, who cannot spare the time to give you instruction, except possibly over a snack lunch, and reading with someone who has not enough work to give you proper experience. The ideal type of man, if he can be found, is the young man in good practice who is rapidly rising and who may take you up with him. A man, in other words, who is likely to take silk, but likely to take it at a time sufficiently far in the future to give you a chance of stepping into part of his practice as a junior. If your master is in general practice, he should not be above doing the humbler type of work (in the county court or before magistrates) with which you will have to start in your own practice. Unless you have competent advice elsewhere, consult the Dean of the Inns of Court School of Law.

You may make your pupillage contract for only six months, varying your experience afterwards by moving to other chambers if you are lucky enough to be able to arrange this. You may, for example, spend six months in London and six months with a local barrister if your intention is to join the local Bar.

Other things being equal it is much better to read with someone who will give you a seat in his own room than with a man who sets you apart in a pupil room.

A pupil has a right, which he should exercise to the full, of reading his master's papers and accompanying him to court. He may be asked to take notes of the evidence. There is a temptation on both sides for the pupil to spend his time doing this, but it soon becomes rather profitless. The pupil spends his days far better drafting a pleading or writing an opinion and having his master criticise his work afterwards.

When listening to cases in court the student should do so not passively, like the spectator of a play, but with active thought, as though he were himself taking part; framing in his mind during the examination-in-chief the questions that he would put to the witness if the cross-examination fell to him. If possible, the cases he attends should be those cases in which he has contrived to read the papers beforehand: the educational value of hearing them is then much greater.

By the way, barristers usually talk about cases by identifying themselves with their lay client. " I am a girl who was assaulted," etc.

It need hardly be said that the Bar Final should be got out of the way before pupillage commences, for a man cannot do two things at once. To pay a fee for pupillage while spending the day working for an examination is simply a waste of money, besides being an abuse of the system designed to prepare you for the responsibilities of the profession.

Pupillage in itself does not give experience in the art of advocacy, and it is therefore highly desirable to attend one of the Post-Final Courses already mentioned, which give an opportunity to take part in moots and mock trials under the eye of a tutor. Take part, also, in the moots held at your Inn of Court.

To go back a little, there is something to be said for spending six months to a year (no more is allowed) in a solicitor's office before pupillage. This would, indeed, be a useful way of spending one of your Long Vacations while you are at the University. It gives extra experience, and it gives an understanding of the solicitor's difficulties and requirements. The Consolidated Regulations somewhat foolishly provide that a man cannot be called to the Bar until six months have elapsed from the date of his leaving the solicitor's office. The hope presumably is that this will give his new friends among the solicitors time to forget him.

When pupillage is over the young barrister may emigrate at once to one of the local Bars that exist in most big towns, such as Manchester, Birmingham, Bristol, Liverpool, Leeds, Cardiff and Swansea, or he may stay in London. The Bar Council keeps a register of tenancies and of chambers requiring devils, both in London and in the provinces.

During the early years, expenses are a factor to be taken into account. The rent of a seat in chambers will vary according to the type of chambers, *e.g.* whether general or specialist, and may be anything between £200 and £400 at first. Rents in provincial chambers are usually rather higher than in London as chambers in the provinces are let on a commercial basis. Then there will be a share of the clerk's guaranteed salary, and the expenses of telephone, stationery and books. A car, though not essential, is a very great convenience.

If the young barrister has any spare time in his early years he should use it to prolong his pupillage in fact if not in name. Perhaps his former master will allow him to continue to read his papers; or he may be permitted to read the papers of another in his own chambers with whom he is on friendly terms. There are many gaps in his legal knowledge that he now has an opportunity to make good, as he never will again. When his own practice begins he will find that his clerk has arranged conferences for him, and before

the conference he will often know nothing of the questions
that are likely to be put to him. If, for instance, he is on
the common-law side, the case that he is asked to consider
may turn on the Landlord and Tenant Acts, the Rent Acts,
the Consumer Protection Act, the Sale of Food Act, the
Town and Country Planning Acts, the Arbitration Act,
income tax, separation, divorce, bankruptcy, conflict of laws,
carriage of goods, insurance, and many other topics which he
may never have studied at the University or for his Bar
examinations. He will not be expected, and will not need, to
have every detail of all these subjects in his mind. But
complete ignorance of their general structure will not raise
him in the esteem of his professional clients.

On top of all this there is the possibility of " devilling "
for fellow members of the Bar. This means giving them
assistance in their cases, and even (with the client's consent)
taking cases for them in court if owing to some clash of
appointments they find themselves unable to appear. It
is now obligatory to pay the devil a share of the fees
(usually half) and the work therefore helps one's livelihood,
as well as providing experience and (sometimes) bringing
one to the notice of the professional client. But the possibilities of devilling must not be exaggerated. On the
common-law side only the busiest barristers have any devilling to give: they will themselves do all that they possibly
can. On the Chancery side there is rather more, because of
the amount of drafting work to be done. But drafting
for a fellow-barrister, though desirable for experience, does
not bring one into contact with the instructing solicitor,
and so does not nurture one's own practice.

If you have a social conscience you can satisfy it hand-
somely by taking part in your local Legal Advice Centre;
and the same remark applies, of course, to solicitors.

When your own practice starts it is of the utmost
importance to give your cases the most meticulous attention
of which you are capable, and particularly, before going into
court, to familiarise yourself with the various procedural
contingencies. When you ask for damages on a continuing
cause of action, do you know precisely the period for which

you are claiming, so as to help the judge in framing his judgment? When you ask for costs, do you know the relevant Rule stating the power of the judge or master in this matter? It is quite wrong to expect to be prompted by the judge. Take with you to court all the authorities that you may possibly require: leave them in the robing room if you think they will probaby not be needed, but have them ready to back you up in case they are. Otherwise you may land your client in a quite unnecessary appeal.

A few remarks on addressing your colleagues and your betters. Every barrister is entitled and expected to address other practising barristers of whatever eminence by their surnames. High Court judges and circuit judges are addressed by barristers out of court as " Judge " (not " Judge Smith "), a Law Lord as " Lord Smith," and other judges as " Lord Chancellor," " Lord Chief Justice " (or " Lord Chief "), " Lord Justice," " Master of the Rolls," " President," " Common Sergeant," and " Recorder." These conventions are followed both in speech and in correspondence.[8] Members of the public, on the other hand, would speak to a judge as they would to any other knight or peer—Sir John, or Lord Smith. (All judges of the High Court and Court of Appeal are knights, if they are not peers.)

In court, address all judges from the High Court upwards (including those acting as High Court judges, and including also all judges sitting at the Old Bailey, and the particular persons who were formerly Recorders of Liverpool and Manchester Crown Courts) as " my Lord." Circuit judges and bankruptcy registrars are called " your Honour," Masters are called " Master," magistrates are called " Sir " (or " your Worship "), and all other judicial officers (like recorders and registrars) are called " Sir."

A lively book of advice which all young barristers should read is Henry Cecil's *Brief to Counsel* (2nd ed., 1972). Of the many biographies and autobiographies of barristers giving some information about life at the Bar perhaps the most informative is Sir Harold Morris's *The Barrister* (1930). The seamy side

[8] On the envelope, write " His Honour Judge Smith " (circuit judge), or " The Hon. Mr. Justice Smith " (High Court judge), or " The Rt. Hon. Lord Justice Smith," as the case may be.

of the legal profession is revealed with gusto by John Parris, in his book *Under my Wig* (1961). This makes some grave charges against solicitors, but it may be questioned whether the author should not have brought them to the attention of the Law Society, instead of merely putting them into a book of reminiscence. Also on the critical side, see C. P. Harvey's frank and entertaining little book *The Advocate's Devil* (1958). On advocacy, see Leo Page, *First Steps in Advocacy* (1943); also: Hilbery, *Duty and Art in Advocacy* (1946); J. E. Singleton, *Conduct at the Bar* (1933); F. J. Wrottesley, *Letters to a Young Barrister* (1930) and *The Examination of Witnesses* (3rd ed., 1961); Parry, *The Seven Lamps of Advocacy* (1923); R. Harris, *Hints on Advocacy* (18th ed., 1948); Lord Macmillan, *Law and Other Things* (1937), 200 *et seq.*; J. H. Munkman, *The Technique of Advocacy* (1951); Richard Du Cann, *The Art of the Advocate* (Pelican Books, 1964). Some notion of the nature and difficulty of cross-examination may be derived from E. W. Fordham's *Notable Cross-Examinations* (1950). On drafting, Piesse and Smith, *The Elements of Drafting* (2nd ed., 1958), is to be warmly commended. A useful general work is *The Young Lawyer* by Clay, Frankenburg and Baker (1955). For the rules of etiquette see W. W. Boulton, *Conduct and Etiquette at the Bar*. A copy of this is presented to everyone upon call.

THE BAR AS A STEPPING STONE

There are some 5,000 names of counsel in the *Law List*, but only something over 3,000 are in actual practice. This does not mean that the rest have failed. Many of them will have used the Bar as a stepping stone or crutch leading them on to other things. There is, in fact, a glittering array of dignified and sometimes very lucrative offices open to members of the Bar. I shall proceed to describe some of them, prefacing the list only with the warning that for the more attractive of them there is, of course, considerable competition.

For the brilliantly successful or the politically fortunate there are the offices of Attorney-General and Solicitor-General and about eighty superior judgeships, the latter carrying stipends of £15,750 a year and over, plus pensions. As consolation prizes there are many posts worth £9,350 a year or less, with pension. These include the positions of circuit judges, recorders, stipendiary magistrates, official referees, bankruptcy registrars, and Industrial Injuries

Commissioners and Deputy Commissioners, as well as certain Parliamentary and Court of Protection appointments, and the office of Registrar of Companies. Offices like those of the Masters of the Queen's Bench Division, Clerk of the Crown Court, Registrars of the Family Division, and Registrars of the Court of Appeal (Criminal Division) should also be mentioned. A list of most of the offices referred to in this paragraph, and others, will be found in the *Law Society's Handbook*, and in Halsbury's *Laws of England*, 3rd ed., iii, 29–33. A barrister who applies for any office may now reckon as part of his qualification period any time he has spent in practice or in employment as a solicitor.[9]

There is no more important, exciting and intellectually rewarding work for a lawyer than that of drafting legislation. The post of Parliamentary Counsel is open to both barristers and solicitors, and candidates of adequate intellectual quality are in short supply. My little book will have performed a useful function if it persuades one or two of the best of its readers to take up this career.[10]

For all these posts a certain amount of actual practice is essential. In addition, most Government Departments make appointments from professional lawyers, and here, although practical experience is an important qualification, it is not always regarded as essential. Barristers and solicitors are appointed in about equal proportions. (Even when the head of the department is a barrister, he may be known as the department's solicitor.) A list of the Departments concerned will be found in the *Law Society's Handbook* and in Halsbury. Legal assistants start in inner London at £2,436 at age 24, and senior legal assistants rise to £5,525 a year. There are also occasional higher appointments, as to the post of Assistant Solicitor (open to barristers as well as solicitors). The posts are pensionable. There is no examination; vacancies are advertised in the legal weeklies (*Law Society's Gazette*, *New Law Journal*, *Law Times*, *Solicitors' Journal*), and in *The Times*. Since it is hard to change departments

---

[9] Barristers (Qualification for Office) Act 1961.
[10] For the work of Parliamentary Counsel see Sir Granville Ram in (1951) 1 J.S.P.T.L. 442; Sir Noel Hutton in (1967) 64 *Law Society's Gazette* 293.

once you are in, choose the department in which you think you will be able to settle down. You can write to the Establishment Officer of the department of your choice and ask for an interview in expectation of the next vacancy. In this case you will probably join as temporary legal assistant with a view to establishment later. Alternatively, you may be immediately recruited as an established legal assistant through the Civil Service Commission, the address of which is Alencon Link, Basingstoke, Hants, RG21 1JB.

Those who have worked in the legal civil service report that it is much more interesting than appears at first sight. The work is not purely legal, and in no department is it solely specialist. The Board of Inland Revenue, for example, has many problems wholly unrelated to tax law. A barrister who left the Inland Revenue for practice at the Bar summed up his opinion of the service in the following words: " I enjoyed it, they enjoyed me, and I would always consider returning if the Bar did not prove satisfying."

The above information concerns the professional class of the civil service. Other classes will be discussed later.

Many private concerns also employ a legal staff of barristers and solicitors. Banks, for instance, have executor and trustee departments. The work involves the legal processes of obtaining probate of wills and the winding up of a deceased person's affairs so that the wishes expressed in those wills may be carried out. This entails such transactions as the settlement of business contracts, the purchase and sale of stocks and shares, house property and lands, provision for beneficiaries under wills and other trust instruments. It may mean managing an estate worth several millions of pounds. Appointment to these departments is not confined to those with professional qualifications or a knowledge of law; it is not uncommon for men and women to read for the Bar or for an external University degree after appointment. But naturally a person who already has these qualifications starts with an advantage. It may be added that there seems to be no prejudice against women. Similar remarks apply to the legal departments of transport

undertakings and big insurance companies, which deal
principally with claims for damages, and the legal departments of large business firms and combines. It was reported
in 1972 that the average earnings in the upper quartile were
£7,900.[11] All the big newspapers employ a legal staff to read
proofs in order to minimise the risk of libel actions, and
also to watch the interests of the newspaper generally.
Finally, there is law reporting. Information on these careers
in business is given in a booklet published by the Bar
Association for Commerce, Finance and Industry entitled
Barristers in Business: address to B. S. Russell, 4 Verulam
Buildings, Gray's Inn, London W.C.1.

SOLICITORS

The life of a successful solicitor is not so exacting as that
of his opposite number at the Bar: the solicitor has his
clerks and junior partners to do some of his work for him.
He misses the *camaradérie* of life at the Bar and the
exhilaration of forensic battle in the exalted courts, but
his work is generally more varied than the barrister's,
and offers closer contact with the life of the ordinary
man.[12] True, it does not lead to the same wealth and fame
as does great success at the Bar; but in normal conditions
there is much better assurance of reasonable success. The
Prices and Incomes Board reported that the mean remunera-
tion of solicitor-principals in private practice was £5,373
in 1968, which was more than architects and much more than
dentists.

The type of work done by a solicitor is well known. On
the property side he investigates title to land, prepares contracts of sale, conveyances and wills, obtains probate of
wills, and frequently acts as executor and trustee. He interviews clients, advises them generally on their legal position,
and writes letters. He pilots company promoters through

---

[11] 122 *New Law Journal* 279.

[12] "Starting as client," said Mr. Martineau, "many become life-
long friends, whose inmost thoughts one gets to know, and
there is a great satisfaction in realising that there are people
who rely on one's judgment and turn to one whenever they

the legal technicalities of forming companies. On difficult questions he takes the opinion of counsel, and he also prepares briefs for counsel in legal proceedings in which counsel are employed.

As in the United States, English lawyers are now distinctively class-structured. A few very large and affluent City firms have adapted themselves to act as the agents and advisers of commerce and industry; they have modern offices with every aid and convenience, and the partners specialise intensively. These firms may even have overseas branches. Next come medium-sized firms with about ten partners, specialising in some particular field of commerce or industry such as shipping or insurance or property development, and other smaller but still highly-specialised firms, all of them mainly in London. But the great majority of solicitors continue in their traditional ways, making their staple living from conveyancing, probate, advising middle-class clients in minor disputes and business affairs, and litigation—though some firms prefer not to do the last if they can help it. Business is booming to such an extent that this is all the work that solicitors need for their own prosperity.

The qualities required of a country-town solicitor appear clearly enough from the foregoing description of his work. He should have a knowledge of human nature, practical wisdom, and the ability to dictate a good letter. Naturally he needs a working knowledge of property and company law and the law of procedure ; and the better his knowledge, the better he is at his job. It is a great mistake to suppose that a solicitor can get along without having mastered the legal topics with which he is called upon to deal. However, the

are in difficulties, and also regard one as a confidential friend and adviser. Some of my clients are the best and dearest friends I possess. You become a member of the family. You see the children grow up, and they in their turn very often look to you as their guardian and counsellor. The charm of a solicitor's business is, therefore, in the clients he possesses and the friendship he makes amongst them. It was Lord Hannen, one of the greatest of our judges, who said that an honourable solicitor is a family blessing." (1932) 29 *Law Society's Gazette* 123.

finer points of such subjects as tort can with relative safety be left to repose in his books of reference.

The traditional argument for our bifurcated profession is that barristers are the professional advocates, but in fact solicitors conduct much the greater number of cases in the lesser courts—county courts and magistrates' courts. So if your talents run to advocacy you will have ample opportunity to display them as a solicitor; and if you later wish to change over to the Bar you will be able to do so. Proposals are being discussed in dilatory fashion for a joint basic training for solicitors and barristers, which will make change-over easier. One day we may see the artificial division of the profession reduced still further, so that everyone will begin as a solicitor and, after gaining experience, will be able to elect to specialise in advocacy with a minimum of formality.[13]

The future will undoubtedly see an increase in specialisation among solicitors, and a corresponding increase in the size of partnerships. Medium-sized firms are now common. The spate of new legislation imposes a great strain upon the smaller firm. One client will have a problem under some recent Act relating to divorce or maintenance; another will need advice on capital gains tax, or redundancy payments, or VAT, or company law, or leasehold enfranchisement, or agricultural tenancies, or rent control; another will be enraged by a refusal of planning permission, or the threat of a motorway through his garden. Each of these subjects involves a highly intricate body of law, and it is not to be expected that any one man or even three or four men can master them all. At present, many solicitors simply fail to give adequate advice, and this is not because of any immediate fault on their part but because they are operating in units that are too small.

It seems likely that conveyancing will cease to occupy its present share of solicitors' attention. The spread of registration of title will greatly reduce the complexity of the transaction and make the solicitor's monopoly hard to defend.

[13] See the proposals of the Young Solicitors Group of the Law Society, *Tomorrow's Lawyers*.

A breach in the monopoly has already been made *de facto*
by Mr. Sydney Carter's National House Owners' Society,
with whom the Law Society is at present doing battle.

Those of my readers who are already in articles will
know the technicalities of becoming a solicitor, and I can
therefore address myself to those who are not yet in articles
but who have or hope to have a University degree. The
Law graduate who has gained full exemption from Part I
of the Qualifying Examination may take his Part II before
entering articles, and it is a considerable advantage to get
them over in order to avoid distraction later. Besides,
solicitors think more highly of the clerk who has passed
the examinations, and the period of articles is reduced to
two years. However, if you are not good at examinations
it will be better to postpone your Final until you have
completed your articles, because you will acquire experience
in such matters as conveyancing and probate which will
help you with the examinations.

Fees (for the student with a Law degree who is exempted
from Part I of the examination) are £52. Virtually no
firm now demands a premium for articles. Nearly all pay
a bare living wage—say £1,000 for the Law graduate, rising
to £1,200 when he takes Part II of the examination. Sometimes the pay is better, sometimes worse; a non-Law
graduate is generally paid less. The Law Society administers
a number of bursaries to assist articled clerks.

Finding a suitable firm for articles is not easy if you have
no friends or relatives who are in a position to help. The
Law Society keeps a register for those seeking articles, but
many applicants fail to be placed in this way. You can put
an advertisement in the *Law Society's Gazette* or write to
firms at random, but if this method produces an offer you
will need to take all possible steps to sound opinions upon
the standing of the firm. Advice may be obtained from the
Law Society or the teaching staff of your law school.

Let me now assume that you are being favourably considered by a prospective principal and are seeing him for
the first time. A number of important questions need to be
asked, with all the tact at your command; some of them may

be best addressed to an articled clerk who is already with the firm. Will you be allowed to sit in with your principal or another solicitor, and if so about how often? (A survey showed that only 17 per cent. of articled clerks are allowed to sit in often.[14]) Will you have to do your own typing or will you be allowed to use the office typists? Will you be able to attend courts? (One in three articled clerks never attends court, which implies a serious omission from his training.) If in local government, will you attend committee meetings?

How wide will be the experience you will receive in the firm? The survey already mentioned showed that most prospective solicitors gain some practical experience of: registered and unregistered conveyancing, landlord and tenant, matrimonial causes, probate and succession, family law, criminal law, accident claims, litigation generally and briefing counsel. Most of them never have experience of: town and country planning, administration of trusts, company law, partnership law, tax planning, book-keeping and accounts, commercial law, or (doubtless) advocacy. The law has become so complex that it cannot be expected that the solicitor will be proficient in everything, and we shall undoubtedly move more and more towards the large firm with specialised partners. All the same, it is important that the prospective solicitor should have as broad a base as possible, particularly if he is not certain which field is likely to offer the best opening. Large firms generally arrange for the articled clerk to move around from one department to another—a very satisfactory arrangement.

Will you have the opportunity of spending some time with London Agents, and if so what are the financial terms likely to be? Will you be paid while attending an examination course? (Most are not.) If you can attend any practical exercises or advocacy training courses provided for those in articles (*e.g.* in London or Birmingham), do so.

It is probably too delicate to ask the principal the final question: How much of your time will you give to instructing

---

[14] *The Prospective Lawyer—Blue-Print for the Future*, published in 1968 by the Associate Members' Group of the Law Society.

me?—but you may be able to find out the probabilities from any other articled clerks in the firm. Lamentably, one in three articled clerks receives no instruction whatever from his principal, and about one in four receives no instruction from anyone in the office—truly a scandalous state of affairs. When you are qualified, remember your own difficulties in starting and try to do better for the next generation.

An all-round practice gives better training than a specialised one—but it may be well worth taking articles in a specialised firm if you are assured that they are looking out for a bright young man like you to be a partner.

The Law Society announced in 1969 that it was no longer in favour of articled clerkship. Plans have been made to commence a system in 1975 whereby a limited number of Law graduates will be able to take a practical course in place of articles.

Not long ago, immediate prospects in the profession were very good. Now, however, things are filling up. There is still a shortage of good solicitors but not a shortage of solicitors in general. This is owing to a large increase in recruitment: whereas between 600 and 700 new solicitors qualified in 1960, the number in 1972 was about 2,000. Good entrants are still highly successful, and even the less good find it easy, at the time of writing, to get employment as assistant solicitors (*i.e.* salaried employees of a firm). But it is quite possible that in another couple of years the profession will have filled to such an extent that some new entrants will not find an opening in private practice.

Newly qualified men who obtain appointments may expect a salary of £2,000 or so, and they should not stay too long at that if they are any good at all. It may, however, be better to stay on in your existing firm even at a lower salary than this if there seems to be a real prospect of a partnership.

Getting a partnership is still not easy, but it is easier than it was, partly because solicitors generally carry super-annuation policies which make it less necessary for them to raise money by selling goodwill on retirement, and partly because they have come to realise that young men nowadays do not command the capital to pay substantial sums for goodwill. An increasing practice is to establish a retirement benefit scheme, whereby the younger partners, instead of paying an initial sum for goodwill, contribute to the pensions of the senior partners as they go. Another plan is for new partners to be admitted merely on undertaking to contribute their share of the partnership capital, and this may either be raised by borrowing from an insurance company or even left to be paid over a period of years by deduction from their share of the profits.

Instead of going into private practice, or after some years of practice, the solicitor may seek an appointment. The most favourable field is in the local government service, which will be described in the next section. In addition, solicitors are eligible for appointment to the legal departments of Government Departments as described in the previous section, though not always to the head positions. In some cases, by law or practice, the chief appointments are confined to solicitors, as in the Public Works Loan Board and the Department of the Environment. Within the judicial system solicitors are appointed as Masters and Registrars of the Chancery Division, Taxing Masters, Official Solicitor, Bankruptcy Registrars, District Registrars of the High Court, Registrars of County Courts,[15] Stipendiary Magistrates, Recorders (and, by way of promotion, Circuit Judges), Justices' Clerks and as various kinds of clerk in the Supreme Court, the last with opportunities of promotion (see later, under Civil Service). Then again, various public utility undertakings offer important positions to solicitors. Details of the foregoing can be seen in the *Law Society's Handbook*, or in Halsbury's *Laws of England*, 3rd ed., xxxvi, 52–55. Solicitors may also enter the Oversea Civil Service.

Although both solicitors and barristers may be appointed to positions in industry, there is a tendency to prefer solicitors. It was said in 1967 that a salary of between £5,000 and £8,500 could be expected by the age of 50—at least by barristers, and presumably the same was true for solicitors.[16]

---

[15] See (1964) 61 *Law Society's Gazette* 669.
[16] See 117 *New Law Journal* 995 for further details.

Most legal departments in industry merely do the work that would ordinarily be entrusted to a solicitor; sometimes it is largely confined to routine conveyancing and the drawing of contracts, but a much wider field may be touched, including the formation of subsidiary companies, company finance, insurance and employers' liability, patents, trade marks—there is, in fact, hardly any limit to the economic activities upon which a large corporation may engage. Some corporations entrust their routine legal work to outside solicitors, but have legal advisers whose task is to give advice at high level within the industry; these advisers organise the legal work which is to be executed by the outside solicitors—perhaps in many countries. The position of legal adviser to a large and growing industry can be of high importance and interest. At the same time, the highest rewards in industry are not yet available to even the most brilliant lawyer whilst he continues to practise the law.

In view of the difficulty of obtaining articles with a reasonable salary in private practice, the prospect of obtaining a salaried position and free articles in the legal department of a company is attractive. Do not do this, however, unless you are keen to make your career in industry. You will only be taken on if you can convince your employer of this keenness. Articles in industry are in any case not the best preparation for private practice, and unless a man has a fairly fixed intention to make his career in industry or commerce he may find it difficult to settle down even for only two or three years in the atmosphere of a company's legal department.

Solicitors are frequently appointed not only in the legal departments but in the secretarial departments of large concerns; but a man who intends to go for a secretarial department would be better advised to obtain a secretarial rather than a legal qualification (to have both would, of course, be best of all).[17] To these possibilities must be added miscellaneous positions not capable of concise description, in building societies, insurance companies, and so on.

[17] See R. A. Lynex, " The Role of the Employed Lawyer in Industry." (1954) 2 J.S.P.T.L. 214.

It is now quite easy for a solicitor to transfer to the Bar: all he generally needs to do is to spend six months in pupillage.

A highly specialised profession, open to barristers and solicitors and indeed to those who are neither, is that of Parliamentary Agent, whose work lies in promoting and opposing Bills and Departmental Orders. A description of this work will be found in (1964) 7 *The Lawyer* 21.

Further information on the technical details of becoming a solicitor can be obtained from the Secretary, Law Society's Hall, Chancery Lane, London WC2A 1PL. The Law Society publish and will supply free two good brochures: *Becoming a Solicitor* and *A Guide for Articled Clerks*. Descriptions of the work of a solicitor are given in a series of booklets published by the Solicitors' Law Stationery Society called *The Doorstep Series*, and in an highly entertaining book by G. A. L. Burgeon, *This Ever Diverse Pair* (1950). Fictionalised accounts will be found in the various books by Julian Prescott, such as *Both Sides of the Case* (1958), and in an entertaining story by John Malcolm entitled *Let's Make it Legal* (1966). Useful hints are given in H. O. Lock's *Advice to a Young Solicitor* (1946), and, on conveyancing, in Edward Moeran's *Practical Conveyancing* (5th ed., 1971). In addition to the books on advocacy previously given, there is F. J. O. Coddington's *Advice on Advocacy to Solicitors* (2nd ed., 1954). Sir Thomas Lund has written a *Guide to the Professional Conduct and Etiquette of Solicitors* (1960).

LOCAL GOVERNMENT

Local government offers in many ways an attractive field for the lawyer. Every borough, county council, urban district council and rural district council has a Clerk, who is generally either a solicitor or (in a small and decreasing number of cases) a barrister In a borough the head of the Clerk's department is called the Town Clerk.

After 1974 there will only be county councils and district councils. The great reduction to be made in the number of authorities—from about 1,400 to about 400—will mean that channels of promotion will be better than at present; there will be fewer top positions, but they will be at a higher level.

The work of a Town Clerk or Clerk to a County Council can best be described in the words of Professor Robson:

" The nature of the Town Clerk's work has changed considerably, for the simple reason that the nature of local government has itself changed. The main concern of the town council is no longer the maintenance of law and order among the local inhabitants, the policing of the city or the repair of its highways. These perpetual necessities continue to exist and to demand attention, but the real centre of gravity has shifted to the vast body of social services which the local authority is called upon to provide. Public health in all its branches, education, housing and town planning, maternity and child welfare, lunacy and mental deficiency, public utilities and transport services—these are the functions which dominate modern local government, and it is these questions which demand the attention of the leading official of the county borough or county council." [18]

Realisation of this has broken the lawyers' monopoly of the head administrative position in local government. It is now common for advertisements for the position of principal officer to be worded to invite applications from all with administrative experience, and not merely from lawyers.

What is likely to happen is that the legal department will have its own chief officer who will be a lawyer; the salary range at present scales would be £4,000–£5,000. In addition there will be the chief executive who will be the head of the paid service but not necessarily a lawyer. Even so, a lawyer within the service will stand a good chance of promotion to the chief administrative office provided that he has administrative ability. If he has been properly trained, he has been given an opportunity to see all sides of local government, and, given good intelligence and the right personality, he should be in a strong competitive position.

As to the method of entry, the young lawyer who wants to go in for local government work had better become a solicitor, not a barrister, for it is difficult to obtain the requisite experience at the Bar. Service need not be with

[18] Robson, *The Development of Local Government* (1931), 264–265.

the chief legal officer himself, for duly qualified assistants also can grant articles. It is now customary to pay a salary during articles; graduates receive at least £1,311 a year to start, and this can rise to more than £1,500. Assistance is often given towards the cost of examinations and the courses for them.

Vacancies are advertised in the *Municipal Journal*, the *Local Government Journal*, and the *Justice of the Peace*, besides the ordinary newspapers.

As for financial prospects, there is at present a considerable scarcity of qualified applicants for the post of Assistant Solicitor, and a newly qualified graduate should have no great difficulty in obtaining a post on Senior Officer grade (starting at £2,661) or even Principal Officer grade (starting at £3,102). After two years' service the officer will probably move to a more senior grade in another town. The salary of the Clerk depends on the population; as an example, the Clerk for a population of 100–200,000 has a minimum salary range of £5,712 to £7,098, with annual increments. Also, these positions are pensionable.

General information as to conditions of service is given in T. E. Headrick, *The Town Clerk in English Local Government* (1962). A readable account of the work done by local government authorities is W. Eric Jackson's *Local Government in England and Wales* (Pelican Books). H. Victor Wiseman's *Local Government at Work* (1967) is a case study of a county borough. Considerable changes will be introduced in 1974 as a result of the Local Government Act 1972. If you wish to be articled in local government, you can obtain advice and assistance by writing to that effect to T. Foord, Esq., Hon. Sec. of the Society of Town Clerks, Town Hall, Worthing, Sussex, or R. E. Millard, Esq., Hon. Sec. of the Society of Clerks to County Councils, County Hall, Aylesbury, Bucks.

WOMEN

Practice at the Bar is a demanding task for a man; it is even more difficult for a woman. Her trouble starts when she tries to arrange pupillage and a seat in chambers. Pressure

being what it is, nearly all barristers who have a vacancy
would prefer to give it to a man; and even when she has
found a seat the clerk may prefer to " build up" a man.
In my view, it would be folly for a woman to read for
the Bar with the intention of practising without first establishing that someone already in practice will help her. She
would be better advised to become a solicitor, perhaps
transferring to the Bar when acquaintances have been made.

In building up her practice at the Bar a woman has
a double prejudice to conquer: the prejudice of the solicitor,
and the prejudice of the solicitor's lay client. It is not easy
for a young man to get up and face the court; many
women find it harder still. An advocate's task is essentially
combative, whereas women are not generally prepared to give
battle unless they are annoyed. A woman's voice, also, does
not carry as well as a man's.

Notwithstanding these disadvantages, some women
succeed. A married woman may not mind that her practice
is slow at building up, when small children are making
demands on her. Greater success may coincide with greater
domestic freedom. We have had our first woman High
Court judge, county and Crown Court judge, recorder and
metropolitan magistrate. Moreover, the technical Bar
qualification enables many women to take legal positions in
banks, industry, commerce and government.

There is no longer any reason why a woman should not
succeed as a solicitor. A few years ago a survey found that
there were over 400 women practising as solicitors. Women
have a special qualification in matters of divorce and nullity,
since married women frequently prefer to confide the details
of their married life to a member of their own sex. In a
certain city, married women solicitors have established a
" corner " in matrimonial matters before justices; they are
said to be far more aggressive than their male rivals in
cross-examining men as to their sex life!

THE CIVIL SERVICE

For the man or woman with a first-class academic brain
the administrative posts in the Home Civil Service have great

attraction, above all because they give the satisfaction of doing work of paramount social and national importance. There is the interest of being " in the know " when important governmental decisions are being made, and at the rank of Assistant Secretary there is real governmental power. In order to indicate the importance of this *corps d'élite* of the Civil Service one cannot do better than quote the words of Sir Ivor Jennings, written in 1966.

" The citizen meets it [the process of administration] at many points, the local post office, the telephone exchange, the employment exchange, the office of the inspector of taxes . . . . The most important part, however, is that with which he is not directly in contact but which really influences his environment even more because it assists ministers in reaching the decisions which determine the policy of the country. This ' administrative class,' as it is called, is very small. It contains only about 3,300 people, while Government employees of what are called non-industrial classes number over 600,000 of whom about 250,000 are commonly designated as ' civil servants ' by ordinary citizens. These 3,300 men and women, however, occupy the key positions in the administrative system. Some of them are so important that their names get into the newspapers in spite of the service practice of anonymity. These are among the most eminent of the administrative class; but that class includes also the young men and women who came straight from the Universities at the latest examinations." [20]

Since Jennings wrote, the civil service has been reorganised into three groups of staff—the General Category, the Science Category and the Professional and Technology Category. The last, as it affects lawyers, has already been dealt with (p. 179). A graduate may join the General Category either as an Administrative Trainee or as an Executive Officer. Selection is by qualifying tests (meant to assess general ability) and interviews.[21] An alternative mode of entry is available for the Tax Inspectorate. If you are undecided whether to apply, you may visit a government department during vacation in order to see what goes on, your reasonable expenses being refunded.

[20] Jennings, *The British Constitution*, 5th ed. (1966), 131.
[21] The technique of the Civil Service Selection Board interview is explained in a pamphlet entitled *Recruitment to the Administrative Class of the Home Civil Service and the Senior Branch of the Foreign Service*, Cmnd. 232 of 1957.

The mode of entry described above covers not only the administrative class of the Home Civil Service, but also certain clerkships in the House of Commons, the administrative class of the Northern Ireland Civil Service, and the diplomatic service. There is a shortage of suitable recruits in the diplomatic service, which offers varied experience abroad and a good career structure.

Finally, special examinations are held for the executive and special departmental classes of the Home Civil Service. The salaries are not so good as those in the administrative class. University education is not essential.

Intending candidates for any of the above examinations should obtain further information as soon as possible from the Secretary, Civil Service Commission, Alencon Link, Basingstoke, Hants, RG21 1JB.

The various public corporations (such as the National Coal Board, the Airways Corporations, the Railways Board, and the Development Corporations under the New Towns Act 1946) require some lawyers on their staffs, but there is no standard method of recruitment. Vacancies are generally advertised in *The Times*.

FURTHER READING

A good impression of the work of the higher civil service is conveyed in John Carswell's witty book, *The Civil Servant and his World* (1966). See also the volumes in the *Whitehall Series* (published by Putnams), each devoted to a different Government Department, and Frank Dunnill's provocative book: *The Civil Service: Some Human Aspects* (1956).

TEACHING

I need say very little about this, because the kind of life led by a law teacher is well known to the student, and if he aspires to it himself he will not lack advisers. A man who wants to teach and has a good degree stands a good chance of appointment—though not necessarily, of course, in his own University. There are many opportunities of teaching in Polytechnics and Technical Colleges where Law is taught at every level from " O " level to degree courses.

Research work is an important qualification, and it can

be profitably combined with a visit to another University, preferably abroad. Several scholarships and fellowships are available for study in the U.S.A. Some of these require the holder to read for a particular degree; some require assistance with teaching; some are unfettered. The following are bodies offering the main American awards.

American Council of Learned Societies (American Studies Program), 345 East 46th Street, New York, N.Y. 10017, U.S.A. (research in U.S.A.).

English Speaking Union Fellowships (General Fellowships, and University of Michigan Fellowship in Comparative and International Law and post of Instructor); apply to Miss L. Moore, 37 Charles Street, London W1X 8AB.

Harkness Fellowships of the Commonwealth Fund of New York, 38 Upper Brook Street, London W1Y 1PE.

Henry Fund: Secretary, University Chest, Oxford.

Rotary Foundation Fellowships (open to all; inquire at local Rotary organisation).

St. Andrew's Society, New York (for male Scots who are graduates of Oxford, Cambridge or Scottish Universities).

University of California School of Law, Berkeley, Calif., U.S.A. (Fellowships: address to Dean of Graduate Division).

Columbia University, New York, N.Y., U.S.A. (Ford Fellowships in International Law; University Fellowships).

University of Chicago, Chicago, Ill., U.S.A., awards British Commonwealth Fellowships (apply to Secretary of the British Commonwealth Fellowship Program) and Bigelow Teaching Fellowships (apply to Dean of Law School).

Harvard Law School, Cambridge, Mass. 02138, U.S.A. (Graduate Fellowships: address to Chairman of Committee on Graduate Studies. Also Frank Knox Fellowships: address to the Secretary, Knox Fellowships Committee, Association of Commonwealth Universities, 36 Gordon Square, London WC1 0PF).

University of Illinois, College of Law, Champaign, Illinois 61820, U.S.A. (Law teaching Fellowships).

New York University School of Law, New York 10012, N.Y., U.S.A. (Graduate Fellowships).

Northwestern University School of Law, 357 East Chicago Ave., Chicago, Ill. 60611 (Fellowships: address to Chairman of the Graduate Committee).

University of Pennsylvania Law School, 3400 Chestnut Street, Philadelphia 19104, U.S.A. (Fellowships). Also Thouron Awards, for which address to the Registrar, The University, Glasgow G12 8QQ, who deals with these awards on behalf of the University of Pennsylvania.

Rutgers University School of Law, 53 Washington Square, Newark, N.J. 07102, U.S.A. (Teaching and Research Associates).

Tulane University School of Law, New Orleans, La., U.S.A. (Fellowships).

University of Virginia Law School, Charlottesville, Virginia 22901, U.S.A. (Fellowships for graduate study; address to Secretary of the Graduate Committee).

Walter G. Meyer Research Institute in Law, 435 West 116th Street, New York, N.Y., 10027 (grants for research in law: address to the Director).

Yale Law School, New Haven, Conn. 06520, U.S.A. (graduate work and visiting research scholars).

Except where otherwise stated, address the Dean of the Law School. State your position, achievements, proposals for U.S. study (research, reading for degree), and whether you would like to teach. If you are contemplating an academic career, say so. Make your inquiries well in advance, otherwise you may be caught by closing dates. The Cultural Office of the U.S. Embassy, 41 Grosvenor Square, London, W.1, will answer most queries. Anyone who has secured dollar support in the U.S. is eligible to apply for a Fulbright Travel Grant, which covers transportation. Apply to U.S. Educational Commission, 71 South Audley Street, London, W.1.

Commonwealth scholarships and fellowships are tenable at Universities in Australia, Canada, Sri Lanka, Ghana, Hong Kong and India; write to the Secretary, Association of Commonwealth Universities, Marlborough House, Pall Mall, London, S.W.1. Research scholarships are offered by the Australian National University, Research School of Social Sciences, Box 4, G.P.O. Canberra, A.C.T., Australia.

With our association with Europe, it is vital that some lawyers should interest themselves in the law of the EEC and improve their contacts with European lawyers. A booklet *Scholarships Abroad* is available from the British Council, 65 Davies Street, London, W.1, and details of overseas Universities are given in *The World of Learning*, published annually. There is also a flow the other way: the British Institute of International and Comparative Law, 32 Furnival Street, London, E.C.4, offers Research Fellowships in Public International Law to students from overseas, and lawyers from African and Asian countries may apply for Research

Fellowships to the University of London Institute of
Advanced Legal Studies, 25 Russell Square, London WC1B
5DR. The University of Cambridge offers Humanitarian
Trust Studentships in International Law (write to the
Secretary, Faculty Board of Law, The Old Schools, Cam-
bridge). Irrespective of the place of study, senior workers
may apply for Leverhulme Research Fellowships and grants,
particulars of which may be obtained from the Secretary,
Union House, St. Martins-le-Grand, E.C.1. The British
Academy, Burlington House, London W1V 0NS awards
grants and a Fellowship for research. The Social Sciences
Research Council, State House, High Holborn, London,
W.C.1, awards studentships for research in socio-legal topics.
A list of further awards in this country will be found in
United Kingdom Postgraduate Awards, published each year
by the Association of Commonwealth Universities, 36 Gordon
Square, London, W.C.1. This also includes a few awards
tenable abroad.

Experience in the practice of the law is also regarded
very favourably by appointing bodies.

In addition to university teaching posts there are lectureships, tutorships and examinerships offered by the Council
of Legal Education, and tutorships, assistant tutorships, and
examinerships at the Law Society's School of Law.
Vacancies in the Inns of Court lectureships (which are part-
time) are advertised in the legal papers and in *The Times*;
they are also announced on the notice boards in the Inns.
Vacancies in the Law Society's teaching staff are advertised
in the *Law Society's Gazette*.

There are many teaching opportunities overseas, where
you will be paid more highly than in England. Certainly go
to a teaching post in Canada or Australia or elsewhere if you
are unmarried and can easily return to England later on to
look for your first post here; or go intending to make a new
life in a new country; but do not go, severing your connections with England, intending to make this a step to advance-
ment in England. It is very difficult to transfer to a teaching
post in this country from one overseas, because the appointments committee will rarely appoint without interview, and

will not be able to pay travel expenses for candidates who
are abroad.

ACCOUNTANCY

Few law students go in for accountancy, even though a
knowledge of law is useful both for the examinations and for
practice. In present conditions the practice of the law is at
least as attractive and remunerative as that of accountancy.
It is true that accountants have become advisers to industry,
and that many accountants are to be found on the Boards
of large public companies. But as many salaried posts are
advertised for lawyers as for accountants; and unless you
have a special bent for figures you will probably find the law
a more interesting profession.

OTHER CAREERS

In these pages I have written only of those careers for which
a knowledge of law is distinctly a qualification. There are
others for which a legal knowledge is no hindrance and may
be some help. The *Careers Guide*, published by H.M.S.O.,
may prove helpful.

Since the last war, large industrial and business concerns
have found many places for Arts graduates—an expression
which for this purpose includes law graduates. One attraction is that salaries are paid even during training; and a
career in the world of manufacture and commerce is attractive
to those who want to do something " real," to tackle a
variety of problems and jobs and to have a chance to
organise and administer, and perhaps to travel. The general
impression of investigators is that the great majority of the
graduates, in spite of certain difficulties, enjoy their work.
At the same time, the vast output of Arts graduates from
the Universities, coupled with high unemployment, means
that competition for vacancies is acute.

If you are being interviewed for any post, here are some
questions you may ask, by way of a change from being
asked questions. How has the vacancy arisen? Is training
provided for? What will be your relationship to others
in the department? Can you meet them before joining?

What are the working conditions and fringe benefits? What are the prospects of promotion, and who decides upon promotion?

I can say things in print that might naturally give offence (or at least cause distress) if I were speaking to you personally. In print my remarks are obviously indiscriminate. I should not have chosen in a personal conversation to mention the matter of slurred vowels and meaningless noises, as I did on p. 151. Now here are some words of wisdom, after the manner of Polonius, on the delicate matter of your appearance. It is accepted that students can dress comfortably in jeans and pullovers, or in garb expressing a more extravagant fancy (though there is no reason why the portions of the body remaining visible should appear unwashed and unkempt). What I want to say is that by the time you are thinking of a career you should be prepared to relinquish these carefree ways. Your acceptance and progress in any walk of life depends upon the judgment of an older generation (to which you will yourself shortly belong), and they will value conspicuous cleanliness, neatness and absence of undue ostentation in dress and hair style. It is folly to let your appearance handicap your career.

On a less personal subject, why not learn to type? Admittedly, you may be given a secretary to whom you can dictate, and this is a great convenience ; but often you will find that the draft you want in a hurry is still in her notebook or on her tape. Anyway, it is much easier to compose a difficult draft by typing it yourself than by dictating it. You can learn to type by touch in only one day, as I did. I bought an instruction book with a chart of the keyboard showing the proper fingering, and I tied an apron round my neck and over the keyboard so that I could not see the keys. (This is essential.) Then I practised the exercises for one day. After that I could remove the apron without having the temptation to peep, and I knew all the finger-stretches and could type by touch. It was far and away the best day's work I ever did. I grievously lacked accuracy at first, but that improved with practice.

For general advice I have seen nothing better than some remarks of Mr. A. D. Bonham-Carter.

" I would say to every ambitious and able young man who is choosing to make his career in industry: first, you must realise that the way to the top is something which has to be worked out with your employer, and although you have to fight your way up in the face of keen competition your employer is not one of your competitors but is just as keen that you should reach the top as you are. Secondly, you will best get there by squeezing all you can out of every position you hold and out of the experience of every man you serve or meet: pick their brains, study their successes and their failures; never be afraid to ask questions or put new ideas, but do not get upset or angry if they are not accepted at first, and do not assume that the other man's judgment is wrong. Maybe it is, but it is just as likely that your idea was not quite right. Finally, look after your health—if you are really going to the top enormous demands are going to be made on your time and strength and you cannot afford to be careless."

GENERALLY

The University student should not neglect his University Appointments Board or Committee, which can often give him valuable assistance. Solicitors can obtain help from the Law Society's Appointments Officer. Anyone looking out for a public appointment should keep his eye regularly on the Public Appointments column of *The Times*. There is an annual publication by the Cornmarket Press called *Directory of Opportunities for Graduates*.

CHAPTER 14

GENERAL READING

A lawyer without history or literature is a mechanic,
a mere working mason; if he possesses some knowledge of these, he may venture to call himself an
architect.

—Scott, *Guy Mannering*, Chap. 37.

No one wants to read law all the time; but some of the
hours not spent on serious legal reading may be devoted with
profit and pleasure to lighter literature touching upon the law,
and to works that set the background in which the lawyer
lives. The following, which is hardly more than a list, may
be of assistance not merely to the beginner at law but to
the practitioner in his leisure moments. What is offered is
a collection of titles that may come the reader's way at
intervals during his life, and that are worth reading if they
do. Not all the books included are in print.

DRAMA

The number of legal references in Shakespeare has given rise
to a theory that he was a trained lawyer. This thesis would
be more attractive if the internal evidence had not also been
used to assign him to a number of other walks in life.

> The bard play-writing in his room,
> The bard a humble clerk,
> The bard, a lawyer, parson, groom,
> The bard, deer-stealing after dark,
> The bard a tradesman—and a Jew—
> The bard a botanist—a beak—
> The bard a skilled musician, too—
> A sheriff and a surgeon, eke! [1]

In fact, modern research has shown that there are as
many references to legal concepts among the lesser Elizabethan dramatists as in Shakespeare, and that there is no

[1] W. S. Gilbert, *The Bab Ballads.*

reason to suppose that Shakespeare possessed any unusual knowledge. Much the best discussion of the plays from the legal point of view is G. W. Keeton, *Shakespeare's Legal and Political Background* (1967). See also the very learned study by Professor O. Hood Phillips, *Shakespeare and the Lawyers* (1972). A specialised work comes from America, entitled *The Law of Property in Shakespeare and the Elizabethan Drama*, by Paul S. Clarkson and Clyde T. Warren (1942). It need hardly be added that, as any commentator will allow, the plays themselves are worth a shelf-full of commentaries; commentaries are for those who know the plays. There is endless fascination in picking out the legal allusions in Shakespeare without the help of commentaries.

Among dramatists of the present century, three of Galsworthy's plays have a direct interest for lawyers—*The Silver Box*, *Justice* and *Loyalties*, the last involving a strict application of professional etiquette. A performance of *Justice* was witnessed in 1911 by Mr. Winston Churchill, then Home Secretary, and he was so moved by it that he made a long-overdue reform in prison administration by drastically curtailing the period of solitary confinement.[2] It is of interest to note that Galsworthy was called to the Bar in 1890; but he never practised.

FICTION

Dickens started life as (among other things) a lawyer's clerk and court reporter, and most of his novels contain legal characters or legal references. The famous trial scene in *Pickwick* (written when the author was only 24) shows the working of the system of advocacy in a common-law court at its worst. We have moved far since those days, not least because, since 1851, the parties to the suit have been allowed to testify on their own behalf. Students of the reports may like to know that Dickens's Mr. Justice Stareleigh was

[2] He reduced it to one month for all but recidivists. Such a reform had been advocated by a Departmental Committee as long before as 1895. See S. and B. Webb, *English Prisons under Local Government* (1922) 223, n. 1.

modelled upon the real Mr. Justice Gaselee,[3] while Serjeant
Buzfuz was Serjeant Bompas.

Less widely read but even more engrossing for the
lawyer is the description of the appallingly inefficient proceedings of the Court of Chancery in *Bleak House*. Space
forbids extended discussion of Dickens's works, but a
good commentary is Holdsworth's *Charles Dickens as a Legal
Historian* (1929). See also Sir Gerald Hurst's *Lincoln's Inn
Essays*, p. 109.

An earlier writer, Henry Fielding, must occupy a special
place in the esteem of the lawyer and the law-abiding citizen,
for it was he who, with his blind half-brother, sitting as
London magistrates, founded the Bow Street Runners, the
ancestors of our present professional police.[4] His *Tom Jones*
deserves to be read for its own sake, and not merely for the
incidental legal allusion.

Thackeray entered the Middle Temple (though he did
not get much further), and his experience there is pictured
in Chapter 29 of *Pendennis*.

The name of Samuel Warren is no longer known to the
general public. He was a snob and often a bore, but withal
quite a sound lawyer, and his legal novel, *Ten Thousand a
Year*, is assured of immortality within his own profession.
It is somewhat over-long, and may be commenced without
loss at Chapter 7. The plot involves an action in ejectment
which succeeded because the judge refused to admit in
evidence an ancient deed on which there appeared an erasure
(Chapter 13). The refusal was based on the ancient rule
that a material alteration in a document after execution
renders it void. Unfortunately Warren is guilty of bad law
in this particular: the rule is that there is a presumption in
the case of a deed or other document *inter vivos* that any
alteration appearing in it was made before execution ; and

---

[3] It is pointed out in (1923) 1 Can. Bar Rev. 631 that in *Brooke
v. Pickwick* (1827) 4 Bing. 753, 130 E.R. 753, the defendant
was the coach proprietor of Bath from whom Dickens took
the name of his hero, and one of the judges was Gaselee J.
For the legal purlieus of London as they survive since
Dickens's time see 120 *New Law Journal* 492.
[4] Anthony Babington, *A House in Bow Street* (1969).

on the facts supposed in the novel there was no evidence to
rebut this presumption. Also, the rule avoiding deeds for
material alteration does not apply to deeds of conveyance,[5]
as the deed in Warren's novel was. It is said that the
character of "Mr. Sterling" was intended to represent
Pollock C.B.; Mr. Subtle was Scarlett, Mr. Quicksilver was
Brougham, Mr. Crystal and Mr. Lynx were Cresswell and
Wightman, Mr. Chaffanbrass was Serjeant Ballantine, Sir
Charles Westenholme was Lord Lyndhurst, Lord Widdring-
ton was Lord Tenterden, and Mr. Justice Grayley was
Bayley J.[6]

Galsworthy's *Forsyte Saga* has a solicitor as one of the
principal characters, a libel action conducted on somewhat
irregular lines,[7] and a will that neglects the Thellusson Act.
Someone brought the latter mistake to the author's attention,
and in the sequel, entitled *On Forsyte 'Change,* the point is
admitted but ingeniously evaded.[8]

Outside the field of English law there are the works of
Sir Walter Scott and Honoré de Balzac—both lawyers, and
both prolific in legal allusion. Scott combined novel writing
with the practice of a busy Scottish advocate and judicial
duties. His rather boyish romances do not appeal to all;
but the reader may like to know that the two with the
strongest legal flavour are *Guy Mannering* and *Redgauntlet.*
Students of Scots law will find instruction in *Sir Walter Scott
and Scots Law*, by David Marshall (1932). R. L. Stevenson
became qualified as a Scottish advocate, though he never
practised. His unfinished *Weir of Hermiston* gives an arresting picture of a coarse and cruel Scottish judge, Lord
Braxfield (in the story called Lord Hermiston).[9]

[5] *Bolton* v. *Bishop of Carlisle* (1793) 2 H.Bl. 260 at 263–264.
[6] See J. B. Atlay in *Cornhill*, October, 1907.
[7] See (1927) 5 Can. Bar Rev. 500.
[8] (1931) 50 *Law Notes* 68.
[9] The number of novelists with legal connections is surprising,
and it may be of interest to add a note on two others.
Charles Reade was a barrister and read in chambers (though
he never practised); but although he wrote novels bearing
upon the law they are disappointing. His only worthwhile
novel (*The Cloister and the Hearth*) is non-legal. Wilkie
Collins, another nominal barrister, is notable as the fore-
runner of the modern detective novelists.

It is not only the lawyers, real or nominal, who have written novels with a legal angle. Trollope is best known for his descriptions of ecclesiastical life in the *Barchester* series; but lawyers will remember him for his account of their own profession in *Orley Farm*.[10] Emily Brontë's *Wuthering Heights* shows an accurate knowledge of the law of entails fifty years before her own time.[11] George Eliot's *Felix Holt* has an ambitious legal plot turning on a base fee —though the legal reader will want to know why the owner in possession of a base fee, with constant legal advice, did not take steps to bar the remainder.

Present-day novelists deserve a paragraph to themselves. Judge Gordon Clark wrote detective novels under the pseudonym of " Cyril Hare," and the plot of several of them turns on a point of law. Thus his *Tragedy at Law* involves an unobtrusive subsection (now repealed) of an Act of 1934; it is of interest for its detail of circuit life. *That Yew Tree's Shade* requires for the solution of the mystery a rule of law stated in Chapter 7 of the present book. *When the Wind Blows* is inspired by a bad old rule of the law of marriage. English law is steadily becoming more rational, and the rule in question was abolished in 1960. All these novels are reprinted as Penguins. Another County Court judge, H. C. Leon, now retired, has written under the pen-name of " Henry Cecil." My own favourite is his first book *Full Circle*; but he has written many other humorous best-sellers about judges and lawyers.

BIOGRAPHIES

From the many biographies of lawyers one should perhaps put first the lives of two great reformers: C. H. S. Fifoot's *Lord Mansfield* (1936) and Mary L. Mack's *Jeremy Bentham*

---

[10] Those who wish to pursue the legal errors (which do not spoil the tale) will find them unsparingly attacked by Sir Francis Newbolt, K.C., in (1924) 95 *Nineteenth Century* 227, reprinted in his *Out of Court* (1925). Trollope's views on the ethics of advocacy are discussed in E. B. V. Christian's *Leaves of the Lower Branch* (1909), 65–66. See also Henry S. Drinker, *The Lawyers of Anthony Trollope*.

[11] See C.P.S[anger], *The Structure of Wuthering Heights* (Hogarth Essays, 1926).

(Vol. 1, 1962). The achievement of Sir Samuel Romilly can best be read in Sir Leon Radzinowicz's monumental *History of English Criminal Law*, Vol. 1, Part V. Romilly and Bentham also figure, with Beccaria, in Coleman Phillipson's *Three Criminal Law Reformers* (1923). Mention may also be made of Lord Birkenhead's *Fourteen English Judges* (1926), and Catherine Drinker Bowen's biography of Coke C.J. called *The Lion and the Throne*.

The interest in these works is largely historical, and many readers will be more attracted by biographies of successful lawyers living nearer to our own time. The apex of success is traditionally the Woolsack, and the careers of those who have reached it are given by R. F. V. Heuston in scholarly detail in his *Lives of the Lord Chancellors, 1885–1940* (1964). Edward Marjoribanks's *Life of Sir Edward Marshall Hall* (1929) [12] may be recommended for its portrayal of the last of the flamboyant advocates, and the same writer's *Life of Lord Carson* (1932) is fit to take its place among the best modern biography.[13] Derek Walker-Smith's *Lord Reading and his Cases* (1934) and H. Montgomery Hyde's *Norman Birkett* (1964) are also worth reading.

There is a plethora of autobiography. The late Lord Justice MacKinnon, in his book *On Circuit* (1940), said that most books of legal reminiscence are bad; and he named only two exceptions, in which I hesitate to follow him.[14] My own list of the best legal autobiographies would include one by a successful advocate of the last century, one by a judge who made his name on the criminal side, and one by a country solicitor. The first of these is *Some Experiences of a Barrister's Life*, by William Ballantine

---

[12] Reprinted in condensed form by Pelican Books.
[13] The author had written the first of what were intended to be two volumes when he died, and his work was then published. It was later completed in a further two volumes by I. Colvin; but those who have only Marjoribanks's volume will find that it gives a satisfying account in itself.
[14] The two exceptions made by MacKinnon L.J. were "*Pie-Powder*," by "A Circuit Tramp" (J. Alderson Foote, K.C.) (1911), and *As I Went on My Way*, by Arthur J. Ashton, K.C. (1924). The former is little more than a collection of anecdotes (chiefly humorous), though the anecdotes have merit.

(1882)—better known as Serjeant Ballantine's *Experiences*. Its gossipy pages are crowded with Victorian personalities who are still alive to students of the law reports. Ballantine was retained on behalf of Orton, the false claimant in the Tichborne case, and his book gives shrewd advice on advocacy. A more recent work in the same vein is Sir Travers Humphreys (Humphreys J.), *Criminal Days* (1946). This is an autobiography full of good stories, with reflections upon the criminal law. Reginald Hine's *Confessions of an Un-Common Attorney* (1945) is a revelation of the interest that can be won from life by a country solicitor who observes his fellow creatures and is an antiquarian and *littérateur* to boot. Not one of these is a " must " book, though each is good in its own class.

Finally, it is convenient to mention here the remarkable *Pollock-Holmes Letters* (2 vols., 1942), the correspondence of two men who became the *doyens* of English and American law, carried on over a period of 58 years. This may well be read with Mark deWolfe Howe's two-volume biography, *Justice Oliver Wendell Holmes* (1957, 1963).

TRIALS

The historian, the devotee of detective fiction, the student of advocacy, and the novelist in search of a plot, should not ignore the very full collection of trials that may be found in some libraries. Cases of historical interest are reported at length in the 34 volumes of Howell's *State Trials*, such, for example, as Coke's virulent prosecution of Sir Walter Raleigh (vol. 2, p. 1). A selection from these trials was published in three volumes by J. W. Willis-Bund. Other series are the Notable British Trials Series, the Famous Trials Series, and the Old Bailey Trials Series ; all these give a full transcript of the cases, so that each step in the evidence can be studied. The series presently running is called Celebrated Trials. Perhaps the most remarkable of the nineteenth-century *causes célèbres* was that of *The Tichborne Claimant*; Douglas Woodruffe's book under that title is noteworthy. Illustrations of the technique of famous advocates are given in Edgar Lustgarten's *Defender's Triumph* (1951). There is also an inexpensive series of Famous Trials in Penguins, each volume containing condensed accounts of a number of trials.

As a matter of interest it may be recorded that R. L. Stevenson's *Kidnapped* is based in part on the famous Appin murder case—*R.* v. *Stewart* (1752) 19 Howell's State Trials 1. This is itself the subject of a study by Sir William Mac-Arthur (*The Appin Murder*, 1960). The *Annesley Case*, retold in the Notable English Trials Series (a series that later became Notable British Trials), supplied material for parts of three novels.[15] Another novelist who used these Trials was Nathaniel Hawthorne.[16]

ESSAYS

It would be possible to compile an anthology of essays bearing upon the law, beginning with Bacon's essay " Of Judicature," and passing through Selden's *Table Talk*, Lamb's " Old Benchers of the Inner Temple," [17] Bagehot's " Lord Brougham," [18] Hazlitt's portrait of Eldon,[19] and several by Maitland, to modern examples such as John Buchan's " The Judicial Temperament " (in his *Homilies and Recreations*), Lord Justice MacKinnon's *Murder in the Temple* (1935), Theo. Mathew's *For Lawyers and Others* (1937), and Lord Macmillan's *Law and Other Things* (1937). (John Buchan, be it noted, started at the Bar and wrote a book on the taxation of foreign income). Some of the best legal essays are to be found in no other place than the law reports, in the judgments of such men as Mansfield, Bowen, Macnaghten and Sumner. The speech of Lord Macnaghten in *Gluckstein* v.

---

15 Tobias Smollett's *Peregrine Pickle*, Chap. 98; Scott's *Guy Mannering*, and Charles Reade's *The Wandering Heir*. See David Marshall, *Sir Walter Scott and Scots Law*, 48–57.

16 See Alfred S. Reid, *The Yellow Ruff and the Scarlet Letter* (University of Florida Press, 1955).

17 Included among the *Essays of Elia* and republished with notes by MacKinnon L.J. in a limited edition (1927), and again in the same writer's *Inner Temple Papers* (1948).

18 Republished in *Collected Works*, ed. N. St. John-Stevas (London, 1968) iii, 159.

19 Included in his essays entitled *The Spirit of the Age*, first printed in 1825.

Barnes [1900] A.C. at 255 is a brilliant example of pungent wit, which was thought worthy of inclusion in the *Oxford Book of English Prose* ; and Atkin L.J.'s judgment in *Balfour* v. *Balfour* [1919] 2 K.B. 571 also deserves honourable mention. Mr. Louis Blom-Cooper has published his own selections of best legal writing under the titles *The Law as Literature* (1961) and *The Language of the Law* (1965).

HUMOUR

Collections of anecdotes are usually poor things, but an exception is Sir Robert Megarry's *Miscellany-at-Law* (1955), an entertaining collection of judicial wit and wisdom. The best book of humorous reminiscence comes from Ireland: it is Maurice Healey's *The Old Munster Circuit* (1939). W. S. Gilbert's libretto to *Trial by Jury* is a joy to read: but then, Gilbert was by training a lawyer! The *Complete Forensic Fables* by " O " (Theo. Mathew) is well known. Sir Alan Herbert's even more famous *Misleading Cases* are now collected together under the title *Uncommon Law* (1935) with its sequels *Codd's Last Case* (1952) and *Bardot, M.P.?* (1964). A selection is published as a Pelican under the title *Wigs at Work*.

HISTORY

Legal histories are generally outside the scope of this chapter, but three are so clearly entitled to rank as literature that mention may be made of them. They are Maine's *Ancient Law* (which should be read in Pollock's edition), Maitland's *Constitutional History*, and Holmes's *The Common Law*.

The lawyer must feel a sense of shame about the part played by the legal mechanism in repressing the poor in the eighteenth and nineteenth centuries. J. L. and Barbara Hammond's *The Village Labourer* (Pelican ed.) is good and necessary medicine to cure us of too much professional pride, and from the literary point of view it is by no means unpalatable. It is a study in the government of England before the Reform Act, the impoverishment of the agricultural labourer through enclosures and the Game Laws, and the use of poor relief as a means of avoiding reform. In their book *The Bleak Age* (Pelican Books, 1947) the same writers give an arresting account of conditions in the towns in the thirties and forties of the last century. A reading of it will give colour to the study of local government and town planning, because it shows the needs that called the modern machinery into existence.

It is true, of course, that industrialisation increased wealth, and that without private enterprise there would have been no industrialisation. The points are well made in *The Long Debate on Poverty*, edited by Arthur Seldon (1972). But the fact remains that our Victorian ancestors did far too little to mitigate the inequalities of the system. Those who think that Dickens exaggerated the social evils of his time should read the appalling evidence related in *A People's Conscience* by Strathearn Gordon and T. G. B. Cocks (1952). E. S. Turner, *Roads to Ruin* (Pelican Books, 1966) is an entertaining history of the lamentations that greeted attempts to pass obvious reforms.

Lawyers and the Courts, by Brian Abel-Smith and Robert Stevens (1967), covers the engrossing history of the legal profession to the year 1965, omitting none of our blemishes and indeed giving a general picture of selfishness, chicanery and corruption. This and its companion volume, *In Search of Justice* (1968), should take away any remnants of professional self-esteem left after reading the Hammonds. But the last work should not be read without the counterblast from E. J. Cohn in his review in (1969) 32 M.L.R. 336.

THE CONSTITUTION

Every lawyer will take delight in Sir Alan Herbert's *The Ayes Have It* (1937)—an account of the passage of the Matrimonial Causes Act—and *The Point of Parliament* (1946). If you feel that your knowledge of the working of government is deficient, read S. A. de Smith's vastly informative book, *Constitutional and Administrative Law* (1971), which is available in paperback.

Sir Geoffrey Vickers's *The Art of Judgment* (University Paperbacks) is a classic on policy-making not only in government but in industry.

JURISPRUDENCE, LOGIC, PHILOSOPHY AND ECONOMICS

Selection becomes more difficult when one turns to the theoretical treatment of the law. Much has been written on this, but not of a character to appeal to the general reader. A simple and readable account of juridical thinking is Lon L. Fuller's *Anatomy of the Law* (Pelican). Judge Jerome Frank's *Law and the Modern Mind* (reprinted 1951) is a pungent and provocative book, with which may be coupled Thurman Arnold's *The Folklore of Capitalism* (1937). A classic by a great American judge is Cardozo's *Nature of the Judicial Process* (1921).[20] All four of these books are American. Sir Carleton Allen's *Law in the Making* and Julius Stone's *Legal System and Lawyers' Reasonings* are heavier going, but every lawyer should read them.

Since much of a lawyer's work involves argument it is important to be able to detect and reveal a fallacy. R. H. Thouless's *Straight and Crooked Thinking* (1930) is the best popular exposition of practical logic. A cheap edition is published by Pan Books. Chapter 9 of E. R. Emmet's *The Use of Reason* (1960) is also helpful.

People are slowly becoming aware of the effect of language upon thought, and Stuart Chase's *The Tyranny of Words* (1938) is a racy primer of the subject. It has a chapter on law, but the possible applications that suggest themselves go much beyond that chapter. Readers who feel inclined may proceed from Chase to the strong meat of Ogden and Richards's *The Meaning of Meaning*, one of the most influential books of our time.

If anyone wants an acquaintance with Hegel, Marx, the utilitarians, and other political theorists, he cannot do better than start with Professor K. B. Smellie's *Reason in Politics* (1939), a readable account from a modern point of view. The liveliest history of philosophy for the general reader is Will Durant's *Outlines of Philosophy* (available as a paperback), after perusing which the student will be ready for Bertrand Russell's *History of Western Philosophy* (1946).

---

[20] Now available in a collected edition including other works of the author: *Selected Writings of Benjamin Nathan Cardozo*, ed. Margaret E. Hall (New York, 1947).

Antony Flew in his *An Introduction to Western Philosophy* (1971) combines extracts from the classical philosophers with his own comments on the issues.

Nineteenth-century Liberalism and economic *laissez-faire* have moulded the outlook of lawyers more than they themselves realise. In their application to constitutional law the classic is, of course, Dicey's *Law of the Constitution* (10th ed. by E. C. S. Wade, 1961); on the wider aspects there is the same writer's *Law and Opinion in England during the Nineteenth Century* (reissued as a paperback in 1962). A continuation volume, *Law and Opinion in England in the 20th Century*, was produced by a group effort under the editorship of Morris Ginsberg in 1959. It has become the fashion to decry Dicey's Rule of Law as well as Adam Smith's economics: before finally subscribing to the current opinion the student should read Professor Hayek's defence of these doctrines in his book *The Constitution of Liberty* (1960). This is an attack upon Socialism, written by a distinguished economist but employing chiefly political arguments which all can understand, whether they agree with them or not. Lord Robbins's powerful dissent from Hayek can be read in his *Politics and Economics* (1963). We must not leave the philosophy of Liberalism without mentioning J. S. Mill's famous essay " On Liberty." [21] This is not only a classic but one that can still be read with keen enjoyment. H. L. A. Hart's *Law, Liberty and Morality* is in the same tradition.

On economic theory in general a good elementary exposition is by G. L. S. Shackle, *Economics for Pleasure*, a Cambridge paperback. The pretty successful modern mixture of individual enterprise and governmental direction and planning is excellently studied in Andrew Shonfield's *Modern Capitalism*, an Oxford paperback.

If you are going to practise at the Bar or as a solicitor you must be able to understand a balance-sheet. *How to Read a Balance Sheet* (I.L.O., Geneva, 1966) is a programmed book; you learn by answering questions.

[21] Reprinted in Fontana Philosophy Classics (paperback) together with the same writer's " Utilitarianism " and " Essay on Bentham," ed. by Mary Warnock.

CRIMINOLOGY AND PENOLOGY

All those concerned with the administration of the criminal
law should make some effort to keep abreast of the work
done by criminologists and penologists.   Such knowledge
is needed not only by the judge or magistrate in the interests
of society but by the defending advocate in the interests of
his client.   When the accused has pleaded or has been
found guilty the question of punishment or treatment arises,
and with the width of choice now open it is most important
for the accused that his advocate should know the possibilities and be able to make proper representations on his
behalf.   Further, it may be said to be the professional duty
of every lawyer to educate himself in these topics in order
that he may help to spread enlightenment among the lay
community.

The best introduction is Nigel Walker's *Sentencing in
a Rational Society* (Pelican, 1972).   Detailed surveys of
sentencing possibilities are: J. D. McClean and J. C. Wood,
Criminal Justice and the Treatment of Offenders, and J. E.
Hall Williams, *The English Penal System in Transition*.
Good introductions to the modern attitude to crime are
D. J. West's *The Young Offender* (Pelican Books, 1967),
Howard Jones's *Crime in a Changing Society* (Pelican Books,
1965) and Sir Leo Page's *Justice of the Peace* (3rd ed., 1967).
A masterly exposure of the limitations of the present science
of criminology is Lady Wootton's *Social Science and Social
Pathology* (1959).   Hugh Klare's *Anatomy of Prison* (Pelican
Books, 1962) is a sober and readable statement of the prison
system.

INDEX

CRIMINAL
~~CIVIL~~ CASES → SUMMARY AND INDICTABLE
                    OFFENCES TRIED SUMMARILY
MAGISTRATES. C.
CROWN COURT.
                CRIMINAL
COURT of APPEAL (~~CIVIL~~ DIVISION)

        ↓

HOUSE OF LORDS.

INDICTABLE OFFENCES TRIED

ON INDICTABLE GROUNDS.

    CROWN COURT

COURT of Appeal (Criminal Div)

    H. of Lords